Notting Hill Editions is an independent British publisher. The company was founded by Tom Kremer (1930–2017), champion of innovation and the man responsible for popularising the Rubik's Cube.

After a successful business career in toy invention Tom decided, at the age of eighty, to fulfil his passion for literature. In a fast-moving digital world Tom's aim was to revive the art of the essay, and to create exceptionally beautiful books that would be lingered over and cherished.

Hailed as 'the shape of things to come', the family-run press brings to print the most surprising thinkers of past and present. In an era of information-overload, these collectible pocket-size books distil ideas that linger in the mind.

Andrew Jamieson is a psychotherapist based in Bath whose interests include psychotherapy's interconnection with philosophy, music and literature. He is the author of *Midlife: Humanity's Secret Weapon* (also published by Notting Hill Editions). Parallel to his psychotherapeutic career, Jamieson has promoted orchestral concerts throughout the UK for over forty years.

ON THE COUCH

Twenty Extraordinary Personalities, from Picasso to Putin

—

Andrew Jamieson

Notting Hill Editions

Published in 2026
by Notting Hill Editions Ltd
Mirefoot, Burneside, Kendal LA8 9AB

Cover design by Matthew Burne

Typeset by CB Editions, London
Printed and bound in the UK by Short Run Press Ltd

The publishers gratefully acknowledge the permission granted to reproduce
copyright material in this book. Every effort has been made to trace and
contact copyright holders and to obtain their permission for the use of copyright
material. The publisher apologises for any errors or omissions and would be
grateful if notified of any corrections that should be incorporated in future
reprints or editions of this book.

A CIP record for this book is available from the British Library.

ISBN 978-1-912559-81-7

nottinghilleditions.com

In memory of Rob Weston,
a visionary whose friendship I will always miss

Contents

Introduction

Western artistic culture is dominated by three essential constituent elements: story, melody and image. In our literature we are constantly drawn to the narrative power of a story. In music we are forever falling in love with melody. In painting, sculpture and photography our eyes are again and again seduced by the delight and thrill of an image. All three of these aesthetic domains can be blended together to create cinema, drama, dance and opera.

The centrality and dominance of the story is interwoven into the daily rituals of our lives. Ever since – as tiny children – we ended our day by being read to, narratives of every kind have been laced and intertwined with our own personal story, as it unfolds from week to week.

In recent years we have developed a ravenous appetite for the television mini-series, which our streaming services toss, so profitably, across the globe. *The Sopranos*, *Game of Thrones*, *Succession* and our own royal family as presented in *The Crown* are just four of the numerous family sagas which provide us with reassurance that our own families are not quite as contorted and dysfunctional as these afflicted dynasties. On a wet weekend, there are few activities that are more comforting than bingeing our way through a box set.

The streaming service mini-series is only the most recent

delivery system that indulges our cravings for story. Previous technologies supplied decades-long TV soap operas and a worldwide cinema, spawned by Hollywood, which filled picture house after picture house. Before that, for nearly 300 years the novel provided us with that most satisfying narrative that is both portable and somehow intensely personal, which we tuck away safely on a bookshelf, for a lifetime, like some precious treasure. And then there is theatre with its provenance ranging back two-and-a-half millennia when Euripides, Aeschylus and Sophocles created humanity's first recorded theatrical experience.

Personally I find the most compelling, the most all-embracing and complete story, is that of an entire human life, from cradle to grave, with all its complexities, paradoxes, effronteries, frailties and charms. Every one of us is living out of our own personal narrative, and it is these individual stories which are the bedrock, the content, the fascinating subject matter, which makes up the practice of psychotherapy.

This is a book containing an account of ten profound ideas from the first century of psychotherapy combined with the biographies of twenty remarkable human beings whose dramatic and intriguing lives were deeply impacted by one or more of these ideas. These exceptional individuals include one painter, one poet, one dancer, one philosopher, two scientists, two actors, three politicians, three novelists and six psychologists, including those twin peaks of our profession Freud and Jung. The reason that I have included psychologists is because their theories emerged from the challenges and experiences of their own fascinating psychobiographies.

Our psychotherapeutic enterprise has a pedigree of a little over 120 years, beginning in the very first weeks of 1900, when Freud published his founding text *The Interpretation of Dreams*. This groundbreaking work begins with an epigram from Virgil: 'If I cannot bend the Gods above, then I will move the infernal regions below', a poetic opening that is so prescient when considering the turmoil and trauma of the twentieth century that inaugurated the new discipline: something between an empirical science and a speculative philosophy, an apt positioning, given the complexity of the century that it foreshadowed.

Freud's debut was followed by wave upon wave of theories, conjectures and hypotheses as the new ideas sought a critical mass of philosophical and medical respectability. Psychotherapeutic theorists of every persuasion built elaborate models as they speculated about the nature of the psyche, patterns of infantile experience, strategies for adult adaption and, in some cases the purpose of our psychological development and of life itself. Freudians were followed by Jungians, who argued with Kleinians, as this intense debate whipped up a tsunami of different schools and creeds: the Kohutians, the Rogerians, the Winnicottians, the Gestalt practitioners, the Intersubjectivists, the Attachment Theorists, devotees of Cognitive Behaviour Therapy and many other groups and tribes, too numerous to mention here.

From this great cavalcade of ideas, concepts and propositions I have found that ten particular theories describe and explain behaviour patterns and personality styles which almost all my clients have presented. It is these significant and important ideas that seem to me to stand proud of the blizzard of conjecture that we as therapists are faced with. By and large, because of their pertinence, these ten big ideas have attracted a measure of consensus among all these competing theories and models and it is their application which is shared in the practice of most of the different schools of psychotherapy.

This is not an attempt to give an exhaustive, objective account of these theories. Rather it is a set of personal thoughts that arise, at this late hour, from a desire to re-examine and distil fifty years spent exploring psychological texts, undergoing the challenges and rewards of being a psychotherapeutic patient and training in this hybrid art as well as decades spent with numerous clients attempting to decipher and unravel the mysteries that lie deep in their psyches. So this book makes no pretence at scientific objectivity. It is a set of musings and reflections carved out of my own subjective views, coloured by my own particular preferences and prejudices and viewed through the skewed prism of my own psychobiography with all its woundings and distortions, clouding any hope of objective perception.

My editor and I, after much consideration, chose as our title a reference to what has been described as 'the most famous piece of furniture of the twentieth century': a well-upholstered couch, covered by a richly coloured Persian carpet, that resides at 20 Maresfield Gardens in north London, a shrine for so many of the visitors who make their way to what has become the Freud Museum. It was on this couch that Sigmund Freud would ask his patients to lie down and relax before relating to him their innermost thoughts, a process which seemed to relieve them of a range of perturbations and emotional disturbances that they were afflicted by.

In the early summer of 1938, this famous couch, with its even more famous owner, escaped from what had been their home in Vienna for almost forty years and made the perilous journey to London, thereby avoiding the fate that awaited four of Freud's siblings who were loaded onto trains bound for the Polish villages of Treblinka and Auschwitz a few years later.

So this iconic couch survives and has become a kind of talismanic emblem of the psychoanalytic movement, even though the vast majority of today's psychotherapeutic clients sit in an armchair facing their therapist.

Sigmund Freud's Theory of the Unconscious
(Pablo Picasso)

I n the earliest days of January 1900, in Vienna, a forty-three-year-old Sigmund Freud had the satisfaction of finally seeing in print the book that he would regard as his magnus opus, *The Interpretation of Dreams*, of which he wrote: 'Insight such as this falls to one's lot but once in a lifetime.' He felt certain that this was to be the founding work, the launchpad for his revolutionary theories, which in 1896 he had named 'psychoanalysis', and he was confident that this leviathan of a book would match the impact upon humanity that his great hero Charles Darwin had achieved with *On the Origin of Species* (1859). However, whereas Darwin had sold out all 1,250 copies of its first edition on its first day of publication, Freud had to bear the disappointment that in its first six years his supposed masterpiece only sold 351 copies.

A few months after the publication of *The Interpretation of Dreams* another revolutionary idea spluttered into existence. In this opening year of the new century the German physicist Max Planck told his son that he had just made a discovery as important as the theories of Newton, which would change the way in which scientists and humanity viewed the world. These ideas were first expressed in a series of poorly attended lectures at Berlin University in the earliest months of the twentieth century. As Max Planck made the first tentative steps in the new physics, which would become quantum mechanics, he shared with his Viennese counterpart the bitter realisation that his innovation was barely noticed.

These unobtrusive opening salvoes that heralded the new century would, during the next thirty years, attract two groups of remarkably talented individuals: young men and women who would, in parallel endeavours, totally alter the way in which mankind not only viewed human behaviour, but also the physical world within which our species exists.

Quantum mechanics would penetrate the mysteries of the sub-atomic world and provide us with nuclear power, nuclear weapons, the entire computer industry, the internet, micro-chips, smart phones, laser technology, global positioning and satnav, fibre-optic communications, MRI scanners and the beginnings of artificial intelligence. So Max Planck turned out to be right when he spoke so optimistically to his son in 1900.

This is, of course, a book about psychoanalysis and not quantum mechanics, but I have mentioned this strange coincidence of Freud's and Planck's simultaneous yet unnoticed announcements because of a central feature shared by both theories. Both psychoanalysis and quantum mechanics are based upon suppositions which are barely empirically observable. Lying at the centre of Freud's model is the 'Unconscious', his description of a deeply embedded, invisible psychic system that, while having discernible consequences, has no physical empirical reality. This unobservable, hidden, latent core of what Freud called our 'mental topography' dictates how human beings behave, yet it is not directly observable. In matters of the unconscious we have to contest American academic Brené Brown's satirical statement 'if you cannot measure it, it does not exist.'

The quantum world is, like the unconscious, barely observable and is so unpredictable and mysterious that it appears to remain above and beyond the laws of nature laid down by the rules of Newtonian science. As Max Planck's great colleague Niels Bohr said of the quantum world: 'When it comes to atoms, language can be used only as in poetry, as the poet is not concerned with describing facts but rather with creating images.'

The two disciplines would develop alongside each other, occasionally fusing together, when certain of their leading advocates realised that beneath the outward visible appearance of both matter and mind lay hidden subliminal realities which although concealed and out of sight provided both the observer and the observed with their true fundamental structures. The most notable of these collaborations was the work done together between Carl Jung and Wolfgang Pauli, whose books, articles and correspondence described the similar patterns shared by the sub-atom world and the individual unconscious.

Psychoanalysis and quantum mechanics preceded a similar shift in the cultural zeitgeist. By 1907 Pablo Picasso had completed his opening image of 'Cubism' – *The Demoiselles d'Avignon* – that would change the art of painting forever. Following Picasso's lead, revolutionary experiments were made in rhythm and dissonance in the music of Igor Stravinsky, Arnold Schoenberg and Béla Bartók. In the wave of new literature led by James Joyce, Marcel Proust, T. S. Eliot and Virginia Woolf, the formalities of the novel and poetry were taken apart and reassembled in a fashion that attempted to delve beneath the surface of human drive and behaviour, using new techniques that at first bemused the literary public.

What Freud and Planck began in the opening months of 1900 still reverberates today and I believe they are linked together by a strange karmic twinship that may retrospectively be seen as a strand of natural selection which will hopefully result in humanity safely navigating our species through this current perilous century. There seems little doubt that evolution not only involved genetic adaptions, but also cultural modifications.

Unlike any other technological advancement, quantum mechanics has created a technology which has given mankind the means to destroy itself. It is quite clear that both nuclear weapons and the development of artificial intelligence – the two most menacing progeny of quantum mechanics – have the capacity to ignite an extinction event, bringing our delicate Anthropocene to a premature end, joining that third potential terminal threat of our own making, global warming.

Perhaps the development of psychoanalysis alongside quantum mechanics can provide us with sufficient collective self-examination and wisdom to allow us to avert this terminal outcome. It is not that psychoanalytic theory might alone succeed in transforming humanity: it is rather that these ten ideas contain seeds of psychological insight which, combined with other features of evolutionary natural selection, will help us safely find our way through this hazardous epoch we have now entered.

The final chapter of *The Interpretation of Dreams* could easily stand alone as a book in its own right and as a debut recital of the prime ingredients of Freud's psychoanalytic model. Unquestionably the 'star of the show' is the Unconscious. Freud introduces his principle lead with the following words: 'The Unconscious must be accepted as the general basis of all psychic life. The Unconscious is the larger circle which includes within itself the small circle of the conscious mind.' In a torrent of seminal books that followed *The Interpretation of Dreams* Freud introduces us to the 'star of the show's' supporting cast: 'the Oedipal complex', his theory of neurosis, the ego, super-ego and id, concepts of regression, wish fulfillment and infantile sexuality, the primacy of the sex drive and walk-on roles for the defences of denial, displacement, projection, repression and sublimation.

Although the unconscious had been implicitly and occasionally explicitly referred to by many previous writers, beginning with Plato, what gave Freud's theory such potent force was that he ascribed to it not only star-performer status but also the role of ringmaster, impresario and sorcerer: a kind of Prospero figure who whips up our interior conflicts and turmoil. As Prospero says: 'My high charms work. And these mine enemies, are all knit up in their distractions. They now are in my power.' Nobody before had ever warned us that we are all dominated and ruled by the dark domain of the unconscious with its cavernous dimensions and its inscrutable secrets.

For Freud and his confederates and indeed the developing lay audience that would, in the years to come, make their
weekly pilgrimage to their own personal therapist, Socrates'
maxim, 'The unexamined life is not worth living' (which
launched both Western philosophy, and, by implication, psychotherapy), took on an urgent and compelling imperative.
Indeed for the thousands of women and men who heeded
Freud's call the maxim needed only a slight adaption to 'the
unexamined unconscious is not worth living with'.

Needless to say, all Freud's colleagues and disciples
wanted to share the action in regards to the Unconscious's
scene-stealing performance. Of all the many adaptions,
extensions and cover versions of Freud's principal lead I find
Carl Jung's account the most comprehensive and persuasive.

Whilst working as a most promising and talented young
psychiatrist at the world famous Burgholzli Hospital, situated just outside Zürich, Jung developed an admiration for
the groundbreaking books that Sigmund Freud had produced since the publication of *The Interpretation of Dreams*
and he wrote to the great innovator, sending him a copy of
his own book on schizophrenia, then known as 'dementia
praecox'. The two men began an animated correspondence
and on 3 March 1907, they met in Vienna for the first time,
where they had their legendary thirteen-hour-long conversation. During this marathon exchange of views Jung felt certain he had found the father he had always longed for, while
Freud was completely seduced by the intelligence, charm,
eloquence and enthusiasm of his young colleague. Martin,
Freud's son, remembering that famous Sunday lunch later
wrote: 'Jung did most of the talking while father listened

with unconcealed delight.' For a week they had further meetings that exhilarated both men, followed by an exchange of
what can almost be described as love letters. Within months
Freud not only invited Jung to become his surrogate son but
also elevated the position to royal status when he frequently
referred to him as his 'Crown Prince'.

But this father-son infatuation remained a passionate
affair, never progressing to anything like a stable, permanent marriage or partnership. Within five years they had
an acrimonious falling-out and never spoke again in the
remaining twenty-seven years of Freud's life. Jung was
poorly equipped to remain Freud's disciple. These two
charismatic personalities were always destined to develop
in separate directions rather than become collaborators as
both men had a lifetime's habit of terminal altercations with
their colleagues, always preferring protégés and acolytes to
peers and partners.

Yet the impact on Jung on losing this father figure was
devastating. He fell into a severe psychotic breakdown
between 1913 and 1918 and emerged, at the age of forty-three,
chastened yet brimming with new ideas regarding his own
model of the human personality. In the years following what
he now described as 'his experiment with the unconscious',
he produced book after book on the individual and collective psyche and espoused the view that the developmental
arc of our psychological existence required the establishment of a benign and equable relationship between our
conscious life and our challenging, inscrutable unconscious
processes. Jung named this quest to harmonise the tensions
between our unconscious and conscious life 'individuation',

an unconscious potential in every human being that is all too rarely unearthed and then activated.

During his four-year 'experiment with the unconscious' Jung believed that he was bringing into the light of day a whole hidden realm of his psychic nature as it emerged in dreams, visions, reveries and in the pictures he painted and the diaries he kept, which allowed him direct contact with the mysteries of his own unconscious. Once revealed he found they could be examined and then integrated back into his conscious life subduing the tensions, oppositions and antagonisms which had overwhelmed him.

This process of self-examination and reintegration became his model of psychotherapeutic practice, whereby this febrile, potentially debilitating unconscious part of our nature can be defused. However this could not be achieved in a handful of years but once begun became a lifetime's task. It was this work that he felt lay at the centre of the psychotherapeutic experience, echoing the ancient Greek philosophers' insistence on self-examination and self-awareness.

The overarching premise of Jung's model of the human personality is the notion that we have two separate areas of psychological authority that mould the progress of our lives. The first of these two primary domains of our psyche is the ego: the wilful, driven, energetic centre of our conscious existence which dominates and steers us through the first half of our lives. The second of these centres of authority is the 'Self' (Jung always insists on a capital 'S') which is the commanding, overall organiser of our total personality that sits quietly in the unconscious, remaining out of conscious view during the first half of life and then appears in the second half, when we have matured and developed sufficiently in our middle years.

The Self provides a unifying integrity and with this becomes the ruling presence in the conscious psyche, displacing the ego, whose narcissistic tendencies can't sculpt and shape the aspiration for wisdom and maturity which only the Self is capable of achieving. Once the Self has emerged from the unconscious, the ego becomes its acolyte and this transition of authority in the conscious realm activates the process of individuation.

The febrile drives and narcissistic compulsions and ambitions of the ego, interrupted by spasms of anxiety and depression, are expressed consciously and are clearly visible to us and those around us. Yet those hidden features of our personality that fashion, mould and motivate our egos remain out of view in our unconscious. The ego includes that part of our nature that was bruised and battered by early infantile trauma and these abrasions remain in the unconscious, out of sight, carefully tucked away behind our defensive strategies which we have unconsciously devised to conceal those traumatic woundings that as children were simply too much for us to bear head on. These defences we unconsciously construct include denial, displacement, projection, repression and sublimation. Yet despite the partial effectiveness of these psychological fortifications these childhood lesions form clusters of anxiety, depression and reactive dysfunctional behaviour patterns which Jung called 'complexes' and Freud called 'neuroses'. These complexes and neuroses interfere with the smooth progress of our adult lives, causing damage and disruption to us and those we are closest to.

It is these complexes and neuroses that psychotherapy can explore, as the therapist and client try to understand their nature and origin.

Almost all my clients, at an early stage in our sessions, seem to have one central traumatic wound that stands proud of all other lesser emotional abrasions. This key moment of trauma in their childhood is their 'primary wound', which leaves them with a singular, overwhelming psychological laceration that continually intrudes into their lives, persistently causing anxiety and depression and preventing them from developing a sense of security and a feeling of wellbeing. This 'primary wound' can occur anytime from birth up to the age of ten or beyond.

One of my clients, at the age of three, had fallen out of a moving car due to his mother's negligence. As a result he never felt, in his adult life, that he could be looked after − that his needs would be met − which resulted in a string of marital breakdowns. And then there was the young man who had lived in West Yorkshire as a child. When he was eight his mother dropped him off at school and had then driven 200 miles to the Sussex coast and thrown herself off the cliff at Beachy Head. This dreadful primary wound of what we came to call 'maternal desertion' devastated his self-esteem, as he was convinced that he was to blame for her death.

The ego and its 'persona', the mask it wears to hide its vulnerability − the acceptable appearance of ourselves that we present to the world around us − has as its prime task the maintenance of the ship of our conscious personality, which it hopes to keep seaworthy and afloat. Yet as Donald

Winnicott says in his influential paper 'Fear of Breakdown' (1974), behind the carapace of the persona a wedge of insecurities has been built up by our childhood traumas which go beyond mere anxiety forming eruptions of emotional misery that he calls 'primitive agonies', which from time to time overwhelm our defences.

Jung is quite clear that these eruptions which break out of our neurotic complexes, these 'primitive agonies', these demons, can only be shed by engaging the 'Self', whose power and integrity lie in our unconscious, waiting to be activated. The 'Self' has the potency to release the very best of ourselves, which can nurture and develop a self-healing capability, a wisdom, a capacity for love and compassion and an ability to engage with life's rewards and benevolences. This is the essence of Jung's concept of individuation.

Our ego defences which hope to keep our 'primitive agonies' out of sight, embedded deep in our unconscious, are projected onto our external environments through a set of narcissistic drives. These drives provide us with an energy which empowers us to forge careers and find suitable partners with whom we can produce the next generation. This narcissistic obsession with ourselves, which spurs on our aspirations and ambitions, generally gets a bad name. But narcissism is the principle emotional engine of the first half of life, which provides us with the focus, the single-mindedness and energy that allows us to make headway in the competitive world we find ourselves in. The marshalling of all this narcissistic power is the prime task of the ego and yet if the Self's developmental programme is to be achieved successfully we must in our middle years shed our narcissism and move into a new emotional realm that the Self represents.

To enable us to live a fulfilling, rewarding second half of life we will need to encounter a transforming experience that results in our ego-oriented narcissism being laid to one side and finally shed. This kind of transformation can only be activated by an unusually challenging and salutary experience such as a midlife crisis, a lacerating bereavement or a grave illness. This harrowing experience should provoke a major reassessment of life's priorities which sees the ego's dominance wane in favour of a more authentic, more compassionate, more rewarding and less exhausting way of life to emerge. Perhaps a simpler description of maturity is merely the move from narcissism to empathy.

This optimal model of a human being's psychological transit through the handful of decades that the cosmos has given us is, for the most part, based upon Jung's vision of the psyche's progress as it appears in a well-lived life. He accepts much of Freud's prognosis – the Freudian model of the Unconscious, the impact of childhood trauma, the unconscious arrangement of our defences and the ego's role managing our conscious drives and neuroses. But Jung refuses to accept that this description of our personality is the final resting place of our psyche. Jung's great diversion from Freud's theories begins with the notion that if we are fortunate enough to encounter a sufficiently challenging experience in our middle years, we may become capable of entering a very different kind of life when the ego is no longer dominant and the Self becomes the presiding authority within our personality, even though it has remained out of view, hidden in the unconscious, during the first half of life.

However the power of the ego is not to be underestimated. Although its drive and energy has produced a number of brutal, political tyrants, it has also provided us with the inventive creativity and the innovative vitality of a number of artistic geniuses. One such extraordinary ego-driven individual was born in southern Spain in 1882.

If you were to devote an hour or two of your time considering the question 'Who was the greatest artistic genius of the nineteenth century?' I suspect you would formulate a list of perhaps a dozen or more worthy contenders. From music, Ludwig van Beethoven, Giuseppe Verdi, Richard Wagner or Pyotr Ilyich Tchaikovsky might be your front runners. From literature either Leo Tolstoy, Fyodor Dostoyevsky, Honoré de Balzac, George Eliot, Jane Austen, Charles Dickens or Victor Hugo could emerge pre-eminent. In painting Eugène Delacroix, J. M. W. Turner, Claude Monet or Paul Cézanne might win the day.

If you were to ask the same question of the twentieth century I firmly believe that one name would stand proud of all others in regard to his immense output, the universal impact of his cultural influence and the range of his fame and celebrity. This unique, exceptional personality was Pablo Picasso.

By some fluke of history several of the main candidates for this twentieth-century accolade met at the Ritz Hotel in Paris on 18 May 1922 at a dinner hosted by Sydney and Violet Schiff after the world premiere of Igor Stravinsky's latest ballet *Le Renard*, produced at the Garnier Opera by Serge Diaghilev, with sets designed by Picasso. Diaghilev, Stravinsky and Picasso were joined for dinner by two writers who lived locally – invited to the Ritz dinner by the Schiffs. It was to be the only time that those two titans of twentieth-century literature, James Joyce and Marcel Proust, were destined to meet.

I have often heard conductors, composers and other eminent musicians say that Stravinsky was the greatest composer of the twentieth century and there seems little doubt that Proust and Joyce are the two most influential and innovative writers of the twentieth century who both still have a profound influence on contemporary culture. But the body of work produced by Stravinsky, Joyce and Proust would, I suggest, appear meagre when compared to the protean range of Picasso's work.

Critics and commentators specialising in Picasso don't readily agree on the number of works that he produced. The range of these estimations extend from 30,000 to 60,000 drawings, etching, paintings, ceramics and sculptures. And perhaps the only twentieth-century works of arts that join the pantheon of Western art's greatest masterpieces, alongside Leonardo's *Mona Lisa*, Michelangelo's Sistine Chapel and Rembrandt's *Night Watch*, are Picasso's *Guernica* and *Les Desmoiselles d'Avignon*.

The status and prestige of *Guernica* received a strangely resonating tribute on 5 February 2003. On that particular morning the US Secretary of State Colin Powell arrived at the Security Council chamber at the UN headquarters to give a speech announcing the American case for launching a bombing campaign and invasion against Iraq. The Security Council had for many years been decorated with a huge tapestry reproduction of *Guernica*, Picasso's commemoration of the first ever aerial bombing of civilians, during the Spanish Civil War, by the German Luftwaffe, when a third of the Basque town's population was killed or wounded. Because Colin Powell's announcement would undoubtedly lead to a similar loss of Iraqi life, the American government put pressure on UN officials to cover the tapestry with an expansive blue curtain, erasing the shaming impact of Picasso's world-famous anti-war mural. Such was the sheer power of the great painting that to announce an aerial bombardment of civilian cities in Iraq in front of *Guernica* was unthinkable, even for the military hawks of the Bush administration.

How did the only son of an unsuccessful and impoverished Andalusian artist become this dominating presence in the history of Western culture? What was the emotional environment in Pablo Picasso's early life that forged this extraordinary personality?

In the summer of 1928 Ernest Jones, Freud's colleague and biographer, visited the seventy-two-year-old founder of psychoanalysis, when he was on vacation in lower Austria. To Jones's delight Freud's mother, Amalie, aged ninety-three, had also joined the holiday party. To observe the adoration with which Amalie viewed her son, constantly referring to him as 'My Golden Sigi', despite his venerable age, provided the biographer with a most illuminating spectacle of maternal devotion. Her golden boy's worldwide success came as no surprise to this old woman, who basked in the fame and pre-eminence of her oldest child. No wonder Freud had written: 'a man who has been the indisputable favourite of his mother keeps for life the feelings of the conqueror, that confidence of success that often results in real success'.

This hero-worshipping maternal idealisation that Freud described and which Ernest Jones witnessed, was a galvanising, high-octane blessing that was also bestowed by Dona María Ruiz Blasco on her beloved son Pablo.

In the machismo world of Andalusia the arrival of the first son and heir was an event of the utmost importance and prior to Picasso's birth, Dona María's three sisters and her husband's numerous siblings had between them not produced a single son, a terrible generational deficiency for this extended family from Málaga. As Picasso's biographer John Richardson recounts, throughout her first pregnancy she spent many hours in her local church, praying for the longed-for son. When on 25 October 1881 little Pablo was born it was as if a Messiah had been gifted to the overjoyed María.

María's adoration of her son was further amplified by the presence of his maternal grandmother Inéz and his aunts Aurelia, Eladia and Eliodora. When the four women lost their only financial asset, a sizeable vineyard, which had succumbed to a fatal dose of phylloxera, they came to live in Dona María's home, just when Pablo's father, Don José, was struggling with his own career.

Don José was a painter and art teacher who displayed very little artistic talent and fared little better as a teacher. With his paintings unable to attract any customers and his meagre art school salary overwhelmed by his inflated household, Don José managed to secure a modest position as an assistant curator at Málaga's Municipal Museum. Despite this additional income, the Blasco family were woefully short of financial assests.

I have noticed among my clients how the combination of a loving, adoring mother and a failing father who disappoints the mother can create a vaulting ambition in an idealised son. As Picasso's biographer John Richardson contends, Pablo's response to his father's failure 'was embodied in a determination to exorcise the stigma of parental failure by a triumphant display of his own gifts'. With his mother, grandmother and aunts cheering him on each day to compensate for Don José's inadequacies, little Pablo's certainty of his own exceptional talent was never in doubt.

Dona María always insisted that her darling son started drawing before he could speak and that his first word was 'pig', the childhood word for pencil in Spanish. In an interview he gave to Hélène Parmelin in 1966 the elderly Picasso recalled his earliest work: 'I have never done children's drawings. Never. Even when I was very small. I remember one of my first drawings. I was perhaps six or even less. In my father's house there was a statue of Hercules which I drew. But it wasn't a child's drawing. It was a real adult drawing.'

At the age of four he started cutting up coloured paper, creating animals, plants and other magical creatures that delighted not only his mother and aunts but also his cousins Concha and María. The showman, the performer, was emerging at an early age. Picasso told Françoise Gilot, his partner between 1945 and 1953, 'when I was a child my mother said to me: "If you become a soldier you'll be a General. If you become a monk you'll end up as the Pope." Instead I became a painter and wound up as Picasso.'

This confidence that Freud described as 'the feelings of the conqueror', that a son idealised by his mother will feel, is therefore amplified considerably if alongside the adoring mother stands a failing, inadequate father. Indeed Freud's own father never succeeded in his chosen profession as a wool merchant and during his early childhood the impecunious family lived in a single room in a dilapidated house in Freiburg. To escape this provincial poverty the family moved to Vienna when little Sigmund was four. Freud wrote of this period, as his father's career in the Austrian capital continued to stall: 'Then came the long hard years. I think nothing about them was worth remembering.' One is left to wonder whether the originator of the Oedipus complex formulated his patricidal theory as a consequence of an unconscious hatred towards his father, who was unable to provide his beloved mother with the basic essentials of life.

The young Pablo found himself in a very similar situation to the founder of psychoanalysis. As John Richardson says 'Pablo's love for his father inevitably had a patricidal tinge to it' and this Oedipal element embedded in the conscious of the young Pablo was symbolically acted out when in 1901 at the age of twenty he discarded his father's family name. Until 1901 he had always signed his paintings 'P. Ruiz'. From the autumn of 1901 he simply signed his paintings and drawings with the flourish Picasso, his mother's maiden name, as if he had a prophetic understanding of the future iconic status of this one word.

Carl Jung, no doubt remembering the professional and

personal failings of his father wrote: 'I feel very strongly that I am under the influence of things and questions which were left incomplete and unanswered by my parents.' Jung's father, a priest who had lost his faith, was deeply depressed by his sense of being professionally impotent and ineffectual. This reminds me of a client of mine, who in his early thirties had achieved great success as a highly paid young barrister. This achievement had been fuelled by the compensatory need to soothe his mother's marital disappointment due to his father's inability to hold down a job, while the family were left to survive on her meagre teacher's salary.

In 1890, when Picasso was nine, the local economy in Málaga suffered a major downturn and the municipal museum where Don José worked was closed. As none of his pictures were selling and his income from teaching was insufficient to support his family, this redundancy forced Don José to look for employment beyond his beloved hometown. Eventually in 1891 he accepted a position at an art college in A Coruña, on the northwest Atlantic coast of Spain. This exile from the Mediterranean felt like yet another defeat for Don José, as it meant uprooting his family from their close proximity to much-needed friends and relatives and from the familiar and agreeable surroundings that they were used to.

The sojourn to A Coruña lasted just over four difficult and disagreeable years, but as far as Pablo was concerned the move was memorable for two particularly significant events: in 1894 an epidemic of diphtheria broke out in A Coruña and immediately Pablo's seven-year-old sister Conchita caught the dreaded disease. The twelve-year-old Picasso decided to make a pact with God, that if the deity saved his sister he would give up painting forever. There was to be no divine intervention and Conchita died. Jacqueline Roque, Picasso's widow, told John Richardson about this secret vow and how Conchita's death and his powerlessness to intervene instilled in him a permanent terror of illness, particularly in the women closest to him. Yet perhaps the young Pablo had had another thought – he had given God a choice either to save Conchita or to turn him into an exceptional artist, and God had chosen the latter, confirming the teenager's conviction that he was destined for great things.

Inevitably the loss of their beloved daughter cast Dona María and Don José into a pit of misery and grief. Don José's low self-esteem took a further nosedive, as he convinced himself that his daughter's death was entirely due to his insistence that his family should move to this accused city of A Coruña. Broken by bereavement and depression Don José asked his son to help him finish off a painting of some pigeons, a favourite subject of his. When Don José returned home that evening his young son had completed his father's picture with a vibrant flourish that enlivened the pedestrian canvas with an exuberance that was quite beyond Don José. Amazed by his son's mastery he immediately announced that he would never paint again. In an Oedipal gesture of paternal submission he gave his son all his brushes, paints and palette. This critical event took place in early 1895 and in the following weeks Picasso completed a series of phenomenal paintings for a boy of fourteen: *The Portrait of Don José, The Girl with Bare Feet* and *The Beggar in a Cap*.

*

The distinguished Austro-American psychiatrist and therapeutic theorist Heinz Kohut wrote extensively about his concept of 'the defence of grandiosity', a necessary phase of infantile psychological development that is taught widely in therapeutic training organisations. It is a phase of development that is normally short-lived but sometimes, as in Picasso's case, can become a central feature in the psyche for an entire life, a powerful aspect of the ego that never relents, that has a static permanence which never allows the individual to shed the voracious ego, never enabling the personality concerned to gain the solace, serenity and repose which can be found in the Self once the ego has lost its grip and has accepted its subordinate role to the authority of the Self.

If the infant, from birth onwards, senses the love, care and attention of its mother, father and other family members and the child enjoys the reciprocated oxytocin flow with all its blissful feelings with its mother, the sense of living in a benign, benevolent and predictable world will be secure. This is what Kohut calls 'the baby's original bliss', a primal stable connection with the parents. Yet inevitably this idealisation will falter when the child experiences a traumatic feeling of disillusionment as each parent is distracted away from the infant by other unavoidable obligations. Every parental shortcoming, as they accumulate, leads the child to make yet another attempt to retrieve the lost parental ideal. This inevitably leads to repeated disappointment and Kohut suggests that the child reverts to a different compensatory strategy by relocating the idealisation into what Kohut calls 'the grandiose self'. In the same fashion, as the infant overvalued the parent, he or she now overvalues themselves, creating a grandiose fantasy, in regard to their talents and capacities.

A good example of this 'grandiose defence' was when Boris Johnson, at the age of three, famously announced to his mother and other family members that one day he would become 'King of the World'. This grandiosity was triggered by the fact that his mother was deeply depressed and regularly hospitalised and his father was constantly absent. As his mother Charlotte subsequently said: 'his being "world king" was a wish to make himself unhurtable, invincible, somehow safe from pain'. No wonder Boris Johnson was so drawn to the personality of Winston Churchill, who – like him – was continually ignored by his mother and father, and like many politicians, had gargantuan political ambitions.

Kohut maintains that in order for the grandiose self to be sustained, it must be continually nourished by its successful attempts to seek witnesses, who confirm the reality of its grandeur and perfection. In other words, the child becomes an incorrigible and persistent attention-seeker desperate to find any opportunity to have its fragile invincibility confirmed by those around them.

Kohut also suggests the grandiose self should ideally be just an early developmental phase which needs to be passed through successfully and then shed. This is normally achieved when the child's grandiosity and exhibitionism is accepted and enjoyed by the parents. When these displays of expansiveness and powerfulness are responded to by the parents in a positive manner, the child will receive sufficient gratification and begin to shed their grandiose fantasies and replace them with more realistic expectations that appear more attractive to the parents. Yet where the grandiose self receives no such parental acceptance, the child has no alternative but to turn up the volume even further in its desperate attempts to achieve the attention it craves.

The sheer delight with which the female household greeted Pablo's birth in October 1881 and the pride with which Don José responded to his son's arrival would have provided the tiny Pablo with a permanent feeling of what Kohut calls 'the baby's original bliss'. His mother's powerful oxytocin flow was clearly in full spate and was amplified by his doting grandmother and his three enchanted aunts who lived alongside his besotted parents. Two further paternal aunts and a number of female cousins who lived in the neighbourhood added to the general idealisation of the infant. The entire extended family was bereft of young males, so Pablo stood alone in this large family of women, who all viewed him as the clan's only future male torchbearer. No wonder throughout his adult life Picasso had a ravenous, unappeasable need for the perpetual presence, love and attention of doting women who had to be permanently available not only from day to day but from hour to hour. This gluttonous greed for female attention remained throughout his adult life a key chauvinistic feature of Picasso's personality which would all too often morph into a spasm of acute misogyny if he didn't get what he wanted.

This near-worship of Pablo throughout his childhood remained a kind of redemptive compensation for the constant waves of misfortune that the depressed, feckless Don José seemed to attract. The financial consequences of the loss of the family vineyards coincided with Pablo's birth. This financial disaster was made worse as Don José was unable to sell his execrable paintings and the large household could barely get by on the pittance he received from his teaching. Dona María's disappointment in her husband's incompetence when it came to providing for the family's basic needs was clear to all, which only exacerbated Don José's depression, particularly as his mother-in-law's and sisters-in-law's disapproval would have been equally disempowering. This despondent mood in the Ruiz household would have been picked up by their growing son and heir.

Little Pablo's fragile personality became apparent when he went to school for the first time just after his fifth birthday. Outside the secure comfort zone provided by all the doting women of the Ruiz clan the five-year-old couldn't cope. The local municipal school was bleak, dank and cheerless. Little Pablo was completely unused to the strict discipline and hated the long tedious lessons. Normally when bored he would just pick up his pencil and draw but now even the simple pleasure of drawing was forbidden. Each morning the furious little boy would have an apoplectic tantrum and have to be dragged by his father to this dreadful place where he was forced to spend his days. The pampered child was used to getting his way and this horrible new world outside his cosy home was both intolerable and unacceptable. At home he was rightfully the centre of attention, adored by everyone. But in this grim school he was thoroughly disliked and when he wasn't making a fuss, he was just ignored.

The cunning child resorted to the one strategy that might work. He fell ill. Inflammation of the kidneys was diagnosed and it was suggested that Pablo would benefit from a change of school, away from the damp, fetid surroundings of the municipal establishment. The more salubrious College of San Rafael was chosen, but again the tantrums, the rage, the tears would become a feature of each morning. And yet Don José and Dona María would persist and somehow get their recalcitrant son to school.

Pablo's world had been turned upside down. His traitorous parents had now been revealed for what they were – cruel, callous and hateful. All that idealised love and expectation he had heaped on them had been misplaced. His blissful world was wrecked, his parents unreliable. And as Heinz Kohut suggests, the small child, having overvalued the parents, has no option but to transfer all his grandiosity onto himself. In Boris Johnson's case he would become world king; in Picasso's case he would succeed where his hopeless, inept father had failed. He would show them. He would become the greatest painter in Spain, or perhaps even the greatest artist the world had known.

If you had plans to become the greatest painter in the world in the early 1900s there was only one place to be: Paris. After several short visits Picasso settled permanently in the undisputed art capital of the world in the spring of 1904 when he was twenty-two.

In the preceding thirty years Paris had seen the birth, triumph and full maturity of Impressionism, but now – in 1904 – Camille Pissarro, Alfred Sisley, Gustave Caillebotte and Berthe Morisot were all dead, while Edgar Degas, Claude Monet and Pierre-Auguste Renoir were old men who no longer lived in Paris. Of the post-Impressionists few seemed to have made it into old age. Vincent Van Gogh, Paul Gauguin, Georges Seurat and Henri de Toulouse-Lautrec had all died, while Pierre Bonnard and Édouard Vuillard, now entering middle age, seemed to represent a conservative generation which no longer stood at the cutting edge of contemporary art. And Paul Cézanne, now a recluse in Provence, had only a year or two to live.

Despite the passing of so many great names, Paris remained a febrile cauldron of creativity, attracting all the young men who hoped to become the natural inheritors of Impressionism and post-Impressionism. But who would fill the vacuum left by the giants of these two waning movements? The Parisienne zeitgeist was clearly anticipating a new direction, a radical departure away from the art of the previous thirty years.

Picasso, convinced of his genius, with his grandiosity in rampant spate, arrived in the French capital just at the right time, sensing that European artistic culture required some kind of detonation, an eruption of innovation and invention worthy of the new century. During an earlier visit Picasso had managed to secure an exhibition at Ambroise Vollard's gallery and had produced sixty-four paintings that he hoped would secure his reputation and make him some money. But the critics had complained about the derivative, predictable quality of the work, clearly influenced by a range of other notable painters. Now in 1904, returning to live permanently in Paris, he was determined to establish his own original style and to achieve the radical, groundbreaking impact he was sure he was capable of.

He found the cheapest of studios, where he could paint

and sleep, at the Bateau-Lavoir, an ancient, dilapidated defunct piano factory in the roughest part of Montmartre. It was there he met Fernande Olivier, an artist's model, the first great love of his life. As would be the case throughout his life, on the arrival of a new wife or mistress, Picasso would undergo an almost immediate gear-change in his painting style. His infatuation with Fernande was no exception, as he moved from the depressed, anguished paintings of the Blue Period to the more exuberant, lively pictures of the Rose Period, with its harlequins and circus families.

As Picasso's reputation began to gain some kind of purchase among the members of the young Parisienne avant-garde, he also became aware that the leading artist of this group was a bespectacled, well-dressed, professorial looking individual named Henri Matisse, who shocked the Paris art world with his unconventional, florid canvasses at the so-called 'Favre Exhibition' at Vollard's in 1904. Vollard, who had exhibited both Matisse and Picasso, supplied paintings to the American collectors, brother and sister Leo and Gertrude Stein, and on becoming reacquainted with Picasso's paintings Leo became increasingly aware that these two young men were the most important artists of the new generation. As if to stoke up their rivalry he ensured that they both realised their competitive affinity and in March 1906 Leo Stein introduced Picasso to Matisse, activating a lifetime's rivalry.

A few days after their first meeting Matisse became the centre of cultural attention, when at the Salon des Indépendents his *Le bonheur de vivre* was exhibited which had an incendiary impact on those who saw it. The painting offended and incensed nineteenth-century decorum turning Matisse into the first radical of the twentieth century. For Picasso this canvas changed everything. This explosion of colour, evoking a kind of arcadian licentious bacchanalia, was something quite new – a startling, irreverent, crude caricature of the sources it drew upon. Art critics have seen strands of Giorgiane, Nicolas Poussin, Jean-Antoine Watteau, Jean Auguste Dominique Ingres and Paul Gauguin blended together in a synthesis of refulgent colour which irradiated a perverse yet compelling spatial originality.

If Picasso was to become the leader of the New Art, the principal artistic genius of his generation, then it was clear that this artist Henri Matisse and this painting *Le bonheur de vivre* stood in his way. He knew that his paintings were outdated by this blast that Matisse had delivered and that he had to respond with something even more shocking, something the Paris audience would find even more disturbing and unacceptable. Picasso's grandiosity was fired up by Matisse's masterpiece and he now retired to his studio and started to sketch endlessly. In the next few months he produced over 400 drawings, as ideas for a great breakthrough painting began to coalesce and take shape.

As if to prepare himself for what lay ahead, in May 1906 he and Fernande set off for a holiday. They travelled to Barcelona where Picasso introduced Fernande to his Spanish friends before travelling to Gosol, a remote village in the Pyrenees, just north of Andorra, where they had been lent a small house. It was just what Picasso needed. He was back in Spain and the glorious mountain landscape filled him with an elation that overflowed into his love for Fernande, whom he painted again and again, as if in celebration of her beauty. This romantic idyll with his beloved continued throughout June and July until, at the beginning of August, an outbreak of typhoid fever reached Gosol. Because of the death of his sister, disease of any kind terrified Picasso and within two days they were on their way back to Paris.

Back at the Bateau-Lavoir Picasso quickly lost interest in Fernande as he launched himself into further studies and drawings for the great work that he now described as his 'brothel painting'. In Gosol Fernande was Picasso's 'eternal beloved' but eternity turned out to be short-lived as he now found her an irritating, unwanted distraction, as he only had time for preparations for the painting that he had such ambitions for. He persuaded Leo Stein to pay for a second studio in the basement of Bateau-Lavoir, where he could paint throughout the night, while Fernande was literally locked away on the floor above.

In Gosol he had found himself drawn to the primitive art of the remote mountain region and that autumn he visited the Primitive Art Department of the Louvre and the Ethnographic Museum at the Trocadéro that was filled with primal African art, which seemed to influence yet more of his studies and some significant preparatory paintings. In the spring in his basement lair he had an enormous canvas stretched onto a reinforced frame. Throughout that spring and summer he devoted all his time to his brothel painting, his only distraction being a furious Fernande, who warned him their relationship was close to collapse, so jealous was she becoming of the five female figures who were beginning to appear on the huge canvas. It became a lifetime's habit of

Picasso's: the more intensely engaged he became on a canvas, the more he hated the woman he had so recently adored. And so in the summer of 1907 it was as if he used Fernande's fury to fuel his inspiration, as the expression on each of the faces of the five emerging women were filled with hostility and venom, displaying for the first time something that Picasso found frightening about women.

By August 1907 the painting that became known as *Les Demoiselles d'Avignon* was completed. He now introduced his friends to his brothel painting. No one seemed to understand. Georges Braque said: 'it was like drinking petrol in order to spit fire.' Leo Stein roared with laughter. Fernande was so offended she remained silent and Matisse was insulted as he saw the canvas as an attempt to ridicule the modern movement of which he was the leader.

Picasso said nothing, feeling he neither had to defend nor explain his painting. He knew exactly what he had accomplished. He knew he had surpassed even Matisse's opening salvo of this new phase of European art. He had achieved the detonation, the explosive beginning of the New Art of the century.

It wasn't until years later that he spoke publicly about 'Les Demoiselles', in an interview with the then French Minister of Culture, André Malraux. Picasso, remembering his visit to the Ethnographic Museum, said:

> I was all alone in that awful museum, with its masks, dolls made by redskins and dusty manikins. *Les Demoiselles d'Avignon* came to me on that very day ... The masks weren't like any other pieces of sculpture. They were magic things.

> They were against everything – against unknown, threatening spirits. I too believe everything is unknown, that everything is an enemy! Everything!

This painting now sits enthroned in its pomp in New York, the crown jewel in the Museum of Modern Art. It is undoubtedly the most revered painting in North America and one of the most highly regarded images in a thousand years of Western art. It is so astonishingly compelling, so seductive in its sexualised intimidation that it has this power over us because it is a deluge of unconscious feelings and drives that we all sense. We are either drawn towards it or repelled by it as it inflames our unconscious fears and longings and stirs up ambivalence about our sexuality. It ignites the subversive nature of our unconscious which resonates not only with his painting but also with remarks that he is 'against everything'. In our unconscious lies so much hatred, anger, guilt, regret, ambition, sexual tension, jealousy, competitiveness, envy and many other unacceptable emotions that sit behind our mask of collective compliance. *Les Demoiselles* is not compliant: it is fiercely, frighteningly truthful, feral, primal, predatory, challengingly authentic. No wonder we are drawn to it. No wonder it changed the direction of Western culture. The sheer power of Picasso's ego frightens us, but we are seduced by its magnetism.

In 1907, Sigmund Freud was also causing consternation because of his overt, explicit descriptions of human sexuality. In 1905 he had written and published his *Three Essays on the Theory of Sexuality*. Initially the book had only been read by Freud's colleagues and admirers, but by 1907 these essays had incensed and shocked a much wider readership. The second of these three essays, concerning childhood sexuality, seemed especially perverted to his angry audience.

Picasso had an almost clairvoyant sense of the next cultural development. Not only was his brothel painting in step with Freud's proclamations, it was also the first great work of 'Modernism', years ahead of the other modernist masterpieces created by his fellow guests at the Schiff dinner of May 1922. Only Freud kept pace with Picasso, whose brazen erotic painting was surely a visual representation of Freud's sexual theories. In Picasso's aggressive portrayal of female sexuality he had challenged and redefined the entire Western tradition of the female nude.

But at the same time in his brothel painting Picasso was giving a pictorial rendition of yet another great theory of the psychoanalytic century – that love and hate exist side by side in the human psyche and that this tension between this fluctuating love and hate is also felt by the infant and child in the earliest feelings they have for their parents.

Freud had pointed to this tension in his Oedipus complex, a patricidal feeling that Picasso felt towards his father. One wonders whether the twenty-six-year-old young man, as he painted *Les Demoiselles d'Avignon*, felt some sense of gratification as he compared his great canvas with his father's banal pigeon paintings. A decade or two later Melanie Klein presented humanity with a picture of an overwhelming rapacious hatred which children felt towards their parents whom they also loved, creating within them, embedded in their unconscious, an agonising ambivalence. Melanie Klein called this dislocating ambivalence, this tension between love and hate, which lurks in our unconscious, 'the depressive position'.

We can't leave this assessment of Picasso's unconscious without examining how this alternating love and hate plagued all Picasso's relationships with women. Fernande was its first victim, but Olga Khokhlova, Eva Gouel, Marie-Thérèse Walter, Dora Maar, Françoise Gilot and Jacqueline Roque would all suffer under the wrath of Picasso's complex.

In her memoir, published in 1964, entitled *Life with Picasso*, which so offended her ex-partner, Françoise Gilot described how all his wives and partners would experience the shift from 'the plinth to the doormat' as his misogyny crescendoed. As John Richardson writes: 'As an artist and an Andalusian, he felt entitled to have women cater to his deepest psychic needs as well as his childish caprices. To demonstrate this point, as an adult, the great man would time and again turn back into a fractious child and oblige his wife or mistress to indulge his infantile rituals and traumas.'

What John Richardson is rightly suggesting is that emotionally Picasso never grew up, always treating his women with a contemptuous hostility, always seeing them through the same psychological lens through which he had once viewed the female cohort of his mother, his numerous aunts, his grandmothers and his sisters. As the only son of an extended family of women, he had enjoyed a lavish degree of attention and adoration, that he viewed always as his right, a sense of entitlement amplified by the power of his ego, which was suffused by a great girdle of ever-expanding grandiosity and hyperbolic ambition.

Inevitably there was a great Shadow that all this empowered entitlement resulted in. He insisted that in all future female attachments the new partner would attend and serve all his needs and tolerate his infantile chauvinistic tantrums and displays of hostility. And if all his needs weren't met, and the hatred and rage wasn't tolerated, the partner would then be discarded and quickly replaced by an immediate successor who was instantly put on her initial plinth of adoration. But how can this oscillation from idealisation to hatred be psychologically explained?

Melanie Klein contends that a baby initially does not see its mother or indeed anyone else as a person but rather as a shape or 'object'. The mother is not perceived as an individual human being, with needs and other obligations of her own. From the infant's first days the only thing that counts is the life-giving breast, but quickly the baby views the breast as either 'good' or 'bad'. The 'good breast' is always present and available, providing essential sustenance, love and warmth, while the 'bad breast' is absent and hunger and discomfort are anticipated as the expected outcome. As Klein says: 'the first internalised good object acts as a focal point in the ego', while the 'bad breast' is by its absence causing distress, hunger and a kind of persecutory aggressiveness that terrifies the baby. This creates in the baby what Jacqueline Rose calls 'a black hole of negative emotion'.

To staunch these harrowing feelings that the good and the bad exist in the same object, the baby deploys a defence that Klein calls 'splitting' where the infant separates the good and the bad. If the baby does not succeed in this split-ting process it will be swamped by feelings of persecutory anxieties, laying the foundations of mental illness in later life. This 'splitting' is all too often taken into adult life and becomes the psychological strategy of many individuals throughout the entirety of their existence. Melanie Klein contends that if the individual is to mature fully she or he must give up the strategy of 'splitting' and accept the harsh reality that we will inevitably feel both hatred and rage towards those people we love. This is the aforementioned depression position that accepts and locates both these extreme emotions of love and hate in the same individual, causing within us great ambivalence and as a consequence psychological discomfort. At some point in their therapy I will impress upon the client that at varying times their chil-dren, partner or parents will both love and hate them and that hatred is a mobile emotion that comes and goes and must be tolerated as a reality. Conversely, they must accept that they will from time to time hate much-loved family members.

This inability of Picasso's to tolerate this ambivalence of both love and hate in the same person resulted in him using this infantile splitting throughout his life. The nega-tive feelings he obviously felt towards his mother and all his aunts, grandmothers and sisters is clear from the enraged hateful fury he expressed towards them as a small boy when he was sent to school. In late adolescence, unable to cope with the mixed emotions he felt particularly towards his mother, he moved to France and only very occasionally returned to Spain to visit her. When she died in January

1939, he refused to leave Paris and travel to Spain to attend her funeral.

Most long and successful marriages must tolerate these oscillating feelings of love and hate, but this wasn't something Picasso could manage. Between the age of twenty-three and ninety-one he had seven partners whom he loved and then hated. He would love and live with a woman for a period but as his irritation and growing loathing escalated, rather than tolerating this emotional ambivalence he would simply 'split', discarding the offending partner and move onto the next 'love object' almost immediately. He could never manage a long-term secure attachment as he was unable to tolerate the whole range of emotions that a mature, long relationship will stir up. For Melanie Klein, Picasso never managed to reach the maturity of 'the depressive position'.

As we have seen, Jung's model of the psyche contends that we all have an opportunity in our middle years to escape the tyranny of the ego and if we succeed in transferring the ego's dominance to the authority of the Self, with its wisdom and integrity, we have a good chance of shedding our neuroses and complexes. If this transition from ego to Self is not achieved, the ego will plague our old age and our fear of death will become an unwanted and persistent intruder in our later years.

Heinz Kohut agrees with Jung's vision of the maturity of individuation and refers to it as 'the achievement of wisdom', which includes humour, empathy, integrity and what he calls 'the acceptance of life's transience'. This acceptance of our mortality is, for Kohut, one of the most important achievements of our maturity. In Jungian terms it is the ultimate accomplishment of the Individuated Self, a state of inner repose the ego alone could never acquire.

This equanimity in old age, when faced with our close proximity to death, the psychotherapeutic theorist Erik Erikson called 'Gero transcendence' of which he wrote: 'It is the acceptance of one's one and only life cycle as something that had to be and that, by necessity, permitted no substitutions . . . In such final consolidation death loses its sting.' In such a composed state of being Erikson suggests that the past holds no regrets and the future no fears.

Picasso never succeeded in replacing the ego with the Self and was plagued in his last years by the terror of extinction and his ageing body's physical entropy. His ego had an extraordinary, formidable energy. Through its power he became one of the greatest creative geniuses in humankind's history. If ever there was an artist who allowed his nose to be led by his unconscious it was Picasso. Indeed his immense artistic output is an unconscious exploration and expression of his ego with all its fault lines and feral topography. His complexes and neuroses, his loves and hatreds, his patricidal and matricidal rage, his atavistic sexuality and his gargantuan grandiosity are all there to be seen in the tens of thousands of paintings, sculptures and ceramics which he produced. He could never hold back – virtually every day was filled with a promethean fury. And this was the only defence he had as he battled with his dread of death. In his final years he withdrew to the seclusion of his last home, where he fell into a kind of creative incontinence, void of wisdom, void of equanimity, void of love and affection for his many children and grandchildren, all of whom were now banished from his presence.

Presiding over this lonely purgatory stood his young wife Jacqueline, who somehow endured his dark, saturnine moods and became the doorkeeper and finally his jailer, who kept all friends and family away from the forlorn colossus of twentieth-century art. Rather appropriately Picasso called Jacqueline 'mummy'.

This rampant, senescent ego was on full display at his last exhibition before he died, held in Avignon in 1972, in the Palace of the Popes, when Picasso was ninety-one. His old friend and neighbour, the novelist Patrick O'Brian, a loyal admirer of Picasso, wrote of these later paintings: 'All were marked by furious haste, coarse slashing brushstrokes, the paint flung onto the canvas, a deliberate denial of all technique . . . They made me feel uneasy for the painter, for although it was absurd to look for the serenity of Matisse in Picasso, this half-seen string had a nightmarish quality.' Of the drawings in the 1972 exhibition he said: 'Row after row they stretched away, a continual reiteration of themes stated long ago on variations of loveless sex . . . now the icy brothel squalor invaded everything and everywhere there was a continual nagging insistence upon women's hairy genitalia. The drawings struck me as frigid, sterile and obsessive.'

These works of art were the fruits of Picasso's old age and in this final blast from his terrified ego, he strove to deny his inevitable end which stood only months away. He had once proclaimed 'I don't develop. I am.' What a true statement of his condition. He was nothing more than his ego, which was immense, dominating, spectacular in its imagination and vision, predatory in its carnal, febrile acquisitions. Yet Picasso never reached his Self, with its consoling sense of composure, equanimity and wisdom and as a consequence he died a lonely, frightened old man, bereft of love and of the intimacy he was unable to share with his many children and grandchildren.

If we compare the resigned poignancy and valedictory repose of Rembrandt's last self-portraits with Picasso's final self-portrait of 1972, the anguished, nightmarish skull which appears before us is testament of a man who never got near the serenity and consolation that the Self can provide, so redolent in the Dutch painter's final masterpieces. Picasso remained, until his death, a prisoner of his terrified, blazing, gargantuan unconscious.

Carl Jung's Concept of Individuation
(Nelson Mandela)

I have always regarded Jung's theory of 'individuation' as his most inspiring idea. This notion that the purpose of our lives is to develop our emotional, psychological and creative potential as much as possible has a long provenance, going all the way back to Socrates's concept of the well-lived life which via Plato became the central idea of Aristotle's Ethics in his formulation of 'Eudaimonia'. In his *Nicomachean Ethics* Aristotle asks what is the highest good – what is happiness? He maintains that the psyche or human spirit is drawn to the quality 'aretai', which means 'excellence' or 'virtue' and this desire or aspiration, innate within us all, is one of the qualities of our nature that separates us from other animals. This compulsion or urge may get diverted or stifled by other baser emotions in our character, but it remains latent in us all, as it hopes to eventually activate features of our potential that reveal the higher qualities of our nature. It is this actualisation of the fullness of our faculties which allows our life to flourish as this spirit of eudaimonia brings out the best in us. As Aristotle says the pursuit of 'eudaimonia' is a lifetime's task, which takes us right up to our death

While our quest for eudaimonia can be conducted through the solitary practice of contemplative experience such as meditation, prayer, yoga, mindfulness or tai chi, Aristotle believes it can also be gained through the art of friendship and intimate discussion. If you find a friend who shares your view of virtue and eudaimonia the interaction, affection and shared aspiration can assist this process of 'theoria'. This kind of reciprocated, empathetic bond with another can be experienced in the very particular type of friendship that psychotherapy can provide.

Carl Jung was certainly familiar with Aristotelian ethics and there are frequent references to Aristotle in his collected works. I am sure Jung developed his concert of individuation taking as his starting point Aristotle's idea of 'eudaimonia'. Yet he wants us to reveal and acknowledge the full range of our nature – every aspect of the conglomeration of features which make up the totality of our personality, both good and bad, both positive and negative, both admirable and contemptible, both generous and mean-spirited. If the unexamined life is not worth living, we must become aware and familiar with every characteristic that makes up the range and full expanse of our unique individuality.

Aristotle and his fellow Greek sages had no knowledge or understanding of the unconscious: Freud changed everything with his investigation of this hidden realm of our psyches. In Freud's wake, Jung came to know, through his own personal experience, all about the repressed and sublimated aspects of our unconscious, qualities that are unacceptable to us and those around us and the society within which we live. These saturnine elements of our unconscious include levels of anger and hatred we never express, matricidal and patricidal feelings of rage towards our parents, combustible accumulations of complexes and neuroses, unpredictable sexual feelings and effusions of grandiosity, full of narcissistic hubris. These and many other reprehensible traits sit in a tense and uneasy coalescence with the finer, more acceptable elements of our personality.

This is the difference between eudaimonia and individuation. Eudaimonia is an account of our virtuous, principled, reputable qualities, referred to by Abraham Lincoln as 'the angels of our better nature'. Individuation is the slowly accumulated self-knowledge that also reveals all the baser, shameful, feral, distasteful aspects of our true identity, which we prefer to lock up, out of sight, even from ourselves, deep in the unconscious.

Freud and Jung let it be known that all this unconscious effluence made itself felt through our neuroses, in spasms of anxiety, depression and physical pathology. The innate aspiration and drive for individuation left within us a latent impulse to reach down into our psyche and reveal these vilified tendencies *not* in a vein of shame and guilt but rather in a spirit of acceptance, guided by the understanding that these elements of our Shadow are the consequence of our early wounds and traumas. This awareness needs a generous redemptive act of self-compassion which embraces and comforts our afflictions which long to be listened to and integrated into the whole aspect of our conscious being. But as Aristotle said, this is a lifetime's work which will take up much time, energy and attention in the second half of our lives. While Jung called this 'individuation' there are many other terms and metaphors used by other psychotherapeutic theories to describe this process.

Abraham Maslow's idea of self-actualisation maintains that once our physiological needs, our safety and security, and our sense of belonging to a family and community are met, we can develop our self-esteem and then have the opportunity to achieve the fulfilment of our true potential. This will be articulated through spontaneity, creativity and an abundance of personal integrity which produces a sense of competence and measured individual authority.

Heinz Kohut's concept of wisdom includes its emphasis on humour, an ability to express seriousness with a lightness of touch and the capacity to accept the inevitable imperfection inherent in human nature. Kohut is suspicious of unflinching serenity and suggests wisdom requires a critical assessment of ourselves, balanced with compassion and acceptance, that lead to a modesty that avoids inflation or conceit. He sees empathy as the key ingredient of wisdom, stating that maturity is mainly achieved when the narcissism, necessary in the first half of our lives, is transformed into empathy towards others. And finally Kohut's wisdom includes the acceptance of life's transience and the proximity of our mortality.

Carl Rogers, one of the founders of humanistic psychotherapy, had an idea about the 'organismic self' which can be realised through the establishment of 'the good life', which he sees as a development away from 'the pole of defensiveness towards the pole of openness to experience'. As 'the organismic self' emerges the individual can listen more attentively to him or herself and is more accepting of feelings of fear and discouragement, which are opposed by 'feelings of courage, tenderness and awe'. This process encourages the ability to live in the present moment, spending less time concerned with past regrets or anxiety about the future.

These are just four of the many psychotherapeutic models of maturity and wisdom that lie within the grasp of every individual, which echo Aristotle's idea of eudaimonia and Jung's concept of individuation.

Notions of wisdom, of course, abound in pre-industrialised tribal cultures, prior to the infringement of colonial and missionary attempts to establish Christianity by displacing these ancient codes of tribal morality. For instance the Bantu tribes of Southern Africa – the Shona, the Zulus, the Xhosa and the Batswana – have the concept of 'Ubuntu', a quality of compassionate responsibility and care for others, which Archbishop Desmond Tutu spoke of in 1986 when he said that 'Ubuntu' refers 'to gentleness, to compassion, to hospitality, to openness to others, to vulnerability, to be available to others and to know that you are bound up with them in the bundle of life'.

The full expression of this eudaimonia, this individuation, this 'Ubuntu' is a rare achievement. Yet on occasions an individual appears at a crucial moment of history, who has these inevitable qualities to match the challenge of his or her time. When Archbishop Tutu defined the quality of 'Ubuntu' in 1986 he surely had in mind his friend Nelson Mandela who would shortly be released from his twenty-seven-year-long prison sentence.

The psychotherapeutic description of our earliest weeks and months is a rather pessimistic account of our first experiences which have such an indelible impact on our future life.

If we combine together Melanie Klein's chronology of the anxious ambivalence, with which the baby regards the good and bad breast, Winnicott's model of the infant's experience of 'primitive agonies' and the febrile emotions of Freud's Oedipus complex, we might wonder how an infant ever turns into a well-balanced, high-functioning adult. If you throw into this mix the neurological imbalance between the terrified amygdala and the underdeveloped hippocampus that is supposed to appease the amygdala's dire forebodings, but which is only effective when the child reaches three, one becomes aware what an onerous task the mother is faced with. Whenever I encounter an adult under the age of forty who combines emotional poise, equanimity and an untroubled and optimistic response to their surroundings, then I know I am in the presence of someone who received the best possible maternal care in his or her early life.

One such lucky individual was Nelson Mandela, whose birth, infancy and childhood seems to have proceeded with the minimum of trauma, no doubt because he was blessed by the fact that he had four mothers. Nelson's father was Henry Mandela, a tribal chief of the Xhosa people, who followed the indigenous practice of polygamy and enjoyed the advantages of having four wives, the third of whom was Nosekeni Fanny who was Mandela's biological mother. The four mothers lived in their own respective kraals and although Nelson was very close to his birth mother, he would often stay with one of his other mothers who afforded the same measure of love, attachment and safety that Nosekeni provided him with. He later explained: 'I had four mothers who were all very supportive and regarded me as their son and not as their stepson or half-son, as you would say in the culture amongst whites. They were mothers in the proper sense of the word.'

Psychotherapeutic theorists, to my knowledge, have never given an account of this kind of polygamous mothering but clearly in Nelson's case it had the best possible impact, as throughout his life he maintained this calm composure, this poise, this equilibrium when faced with the very considerable challenges that his adult life would present him with.

Nelson's father Henry was the grandson of Ngubengcuka, the great King of the Tembu people, who lived in the Transkei with its imposing landscape, where Nelson was born in 1918, where he spent his idyllic childhood and where he eventually lived in his retirement. So Nelson was minor royalty and his father Henry became a kind of Prime Minister to the current Prince Regent Jongintaba.

When Nelson was nine, his father Henry died. Jongintaba, the Prince Regent, agreed to adopt his friend's young son and Nelson moved to his adopted father's home known as 'the Great Place of Mqhekezweni', a rudimentary palace where the royal family lived. It was here that Nelson would develop his regal bearing, his extended sense of responsibility for others and his all-pervasive sense of mission. It was these qualities which would in his adult life provide him with his charismatic presence and instil in his companions and followers the confidence that here was a man who might succeed in ending the iniquitous political and cultural abuse that a century of exploitative colonialism had caused. Nelson may have, as an infant and child, avoided the usual traumas and tensions, yet that benevolent, benign world of his childhood would throughout most of his adulthood be replaced by the cruel, despotic environment that brutalised the entire indigenous population who lived in South Africa.

The fact that Nelson became this pivotal figure in the transformation of South Africa from a vicious, racist dictatorship to a thriving democracy without recourse to an apocalyptic civil war or prolonged racial violence is a testament to the near-perfect parenting provided by four mothers and two fathers. However, I don't think he could have accomplished his feat of masterful political leadership purely as a result of a perfectly calibrated childhood: this childhood merely laid a firm foundation upon which his personality was further shaped and tempered by decades of traumatic adult experience that eventually produced a truly individuated leader who became the father of his nation.

A vital element of Nelson's education was observing his adoptive father's rule as regent and putative king of the Tembu people. Commenting on Jongintaba's benign governance, Mandela wrote in his 'jail memoir':

> One of the marks of a great chief is the ability to keep together all sections of his people, the traditionalists and reformers, conservatives and liberals despite the sharp differences of opinion . . . The Regent was able to carry the whole community because the court was representative of all shades of opinion.

Jongintaba quickly became aware of his adopted son's unusual qualities and insisted that Nelson be given the best available education. In 1934, at the age of sixteen, he was sent to the highly regarded Clarkebury Methodist school, the largest educational establishment in Tembuland, known for its unusual racial diversity, where merit and intelligence were regarded as much more important than colour or ethnicity. Two years later he went to a similar Methodist school at Healdtown that prepared him for the only south African native college of Fort Hare, founded in 1916, a pioneering institution of higher education for Black people, where he was treated as a young prince of royal lineage.

In April 1941, aged twenty-three, Nelson thought he had finished his education and finally left his home in the Transkei for Johannesburg, known as the 'City of Gold', where the Second World War had created a boom economy resulting in many employment opportunities for young Africans. It was in Johannesburg that Nelson would first experience the full impact of the government's insidious racial segregation laws. He already knew how the white leadership had plundered African land ownership, using the hated Native Land Acts, that simply confiscated African-owned land and sold it cheaply to new white owners. This cruel injustice was followed by the 1936 Segregation Bill, which laid the grounds for the much-hated 'Apartheid' laws which literally means 'separatedness'.

Mandela's first job was as a goldmine policeman and after three months he was given a clerical job by the mining company. It was at this time that he met his lifelong friend Walter Sisulu, a young African estate agent, who was immediately impressed by Mandela's commanding presence, commenting that 'when he came into my office, I marked him at once as a man of great qualities, who was destined to play an important part'. Walter Sisulu very soon introduced Nelson to his friend Lazar Sidelsky, a prominent lawyer who worked for both Black and white clients. Sidelsky recognised Mandela's potential too and employed the imposing young man as an articled clerk. Mandela later described Sidelsky as 'the first white man who treated me as a human being . . . the man who trained me to serve our country'. Before long it was agreed that Nelson should train to become a qualified lawyer and in the spring of 1943 he became a student at the University of Witwatersrand, which had a policy of enrolling a few Black students each year.

It was while at Witwatersrand that Mandela first became political and before the end of the year, he had joined the African National Congress, his political home for the rest of his life. By April 1944 the ANC launched their Youth League with Sisulu and Mandela on the executive committee, in the company of a new friend Oliver Tambo, who would become one of Mandela's closest companions in the years to come. Soon Mandela was selected to become Secretary of the ANC Youth League. So effectively did he succeed in this position that before the end of the decade he was elected on to the ANC's National Executive Committee.

In 1951 Walter Sisulu and Mandela began to discuss and then formulate a strategy of passive resistance and civil disobedience which they hoped the ANC would commit to. This they felt confident would place the National Government under sufficient pressure to force them to repeal six of their most oppressive racial laws. If the government refused, a 'Defiance Campaign' would be launched. By May 1952 the ANC executive adopted the motion that a campaign of passive resistance against the Government would begin in late June. It was at this time that Mandela began to tell friends that he would become the first Black president of South Africa and he would now regularly address large crowds of up to 10,000 supporters. Indeed, by the end of the year, Mandela had his first experience of prison when the security services arrested and jailed 8,000 protestors for marching into whites-only railway stations and for ignoring the racist curfews.

Although the Defiance Campaign gave the ANC members and indeed Africans generally a new sense of confidence, it also gave the white government an excuse to pass much harsher racial laws and soon after he was released from his first brief jail sentence Mandela was arrested again for being a leader of the Campaign. Fortunately the case was heard by one of the few humane and fair-minded white judges, who – because of the stringency of the new laws – found Mandela guilty but imposed a sentence of nine months in prison, suspended for two years.

During this busy year of 1952 Mandela and Oliver Tambo founded the first African law firm in the country and were quickly swamped with work when they became the ANC's official lawyers. Mandela became known for his commanding court appearances, which were full of fiery rhetoric. However, in the spring of 1953, he lost all his formal positions with the ANC when the government won a case banning him from making speeches and he was subject to new restrictions which required him to remain in Johannesburg.

In the mid-1950s an even more ruthless figure appeared in the government ranks. Hendrik Verwoerd was appointed

Minister of Native Affairs and then later in 1958 he became Prime Minister. He originated the policy of 'Grand Apartheid' and began his range of draconian policies by nationalising the network of Methodist and Anglican schools which had benefitted so many Africans, including Mandela himself. Across the education system strict segregation was imposed, ending educational opportunities for the African majority. Soon this policy of segregation was extended to the universities, which were also nationalised. Dr Verwoerd underlined these aggressive measures by saying 'There is no place for the Bantu in the white community above the level of certain forms of labour. Racial relations cannot improve if the wrong type of education is given to natives, thereby creating a frustrated people'. 'Grand Apartheid' now swamped the whole educational system. Mandela was clear that Verwoerd was an African Hitler, declaring that 'Fascism has become a living reality in our country and its defeat has become the principal task of the entire people of South Africa.'

By December 1956 the Government unleashed a new attack on the ANC leadership when Mandela and 155 others were arrested on a charge of 'High Treason'. The accused were immediately imprisoned, although Mandela was released on bail after a few weeks. The 'Treason Trial' would drag on for four years when the judges finally decided on a verdict of 'not guilty', ruling that there was insufficient evidence to convict Mandela. Despite the fact he won this labyrinthine case, the amount of time and effort he spent defending himself left him little time to pursue his political battle against the Verwoerd government.

Throughout the trial, because of its sluggish pace,

Mandela found himself living in a kind of limbo. His first marriage to Evelyn Ntoko Mase, mother of his two children, collapsed early on in the trial, partly because she hadn't the slightest interest in politics and partly because of his long absences when she suspected that he was conducting a succession of extra-marital affairs. Shortly after Evelyn left Mandela, he began a relationship with Winnie Madikizela, a fellow political activist who became his second wife when they married in June 1958.

Time and again the trial was adjourned and then resumed and then adjourned again, making his law practice hard to sustain. To make matters more complicated the authorities shifted the trial from Johannesburg to Pretoria where ANC support was weak and where the white population had a particular loathing for Mandela and his fellow defendants. And yet his optimism remained high as he watched the hated government of Dr Verwoerd constantly stiffen the draconian apartheid laws. He described their harsh policies as 'The last desperate gamble of a hated and doomed fascist autocracy, which fortunately is soon due to make its exit from the stage of history.'

Mandela's words seemed to be prophetic. In March 1960 the ANC started organising anti-pass law demonstrations, when all the men left their 'dompas' (the name used by the Black population to describe the much-hated racial passports they were required to carry) at home. Their strategy was that if hundreds admitted to this crime and surrendered themselves to the authorities, they would overwhelm the network of police stations and prisons.

Support for this civil disobedience was greatest in the

Black townships of Cape Town and in the Transvaal, where over 10,000 protestors circled the police station in Sharpeville. The nervous local police force opened fire, killing sixty-seven people and wounding many others.

This disastrous event for the Verwoerd Government sent shock waves around the world and while the level of Black political opposition began to increase exponentially. Mandela persuaded the ANC leadership to burn their dompas in public and this was followed by a nationwide national strike. The white government seemed to be faltering when the national Commissioner of Police announced that the law requiring the carrying of dompas passbooks was to be suspended. But then a jittery Dr Verwoerd reacted sharply and had Mandela arrested and imprisoned without trial and then declared the ANC to be an illegal organisation. This was followed by a new policy of torture and surveillance being adopted by the security services: Sharpeville and its aftermath had proved to be a false dawn.

Mandela was released from prison after five months, but by the end of 1960 his life was in disarray. His law practice had collapsed and his partner, Oliver Tambo, was living in exile in Ghana. He was financially ruined and the ANC was now a banned organisation. His marriage to Winnie followed a similar trajectory to that of his first marriage. As she brought up their two young children singlehandedly, Winnie wrote of this period: 'I rarely sat down with him as a husband. The honest truth is that I didn't know him at all.'

Once the Treason Trial finally ended in March 1961, with Mandela's acquittal, he began to tour the country disguised as a chauffeur, organising a new network of ANC secret cells which resulted in Mandela becoming known as the 'Black Pimpernel'. He was laying down plans for a three-day national strike to coincide with 31 May 1961, the day that South Africa was due to become a Republic. His rather theatrical 'Black Pimpernel' strategy, with the security services in hot pursuit, inevitably increased both his national and international celebrity, as he became a kind of legendary Robin Hood figure. The Johannesburg Star described him as 'the official spokesperson of the Native People' and he gave a much-heralded interview in the South African *Sunday Times*. The British ITN televised a profile of him and there were approving articles about him in the *Financial Times* and the *Observer*.

Although the 'Republic Day' strikes made a considerable impact, both Mandela and many of the ANC leadership were beginning to realise that non-violent strikes, boycotts and protests would never, on their own, see the collapse of apartheid and the Verwoerd government. A month after the Republic Day action, Mandela submitted a proposal to the ANC National Committee abandoning non-violence for a much more militant programme of insurrection and military action, commenting 'The attacks of the wild beast cannot be averted with only bare hands'. The ANC confirmed the proposal and it was agreed that Mandela should create a military wing of the ANC called 'the Spear of the Nation' (Umkhonto we Sizwe), subsequently known as the MK, of which he was appointed Commander-in-Chief. From now on Mandela became a fugitive professional revolutionary. He ended a press statement announcing his new military role as leader of 'the Spear of the Nation' saying: 'I had to separate myself from my dear wife and children, from my mother and sisters, to live as an outlaw in my own land.'

He moved into the home of his white journalist friend Wolfie Kodesh who lived in Yeoville, a white suburb where the police were unlikely to look for a Black fugitive. Unable to leave his new home Mandela filled his empty days with a furious programme of reading, focusing his attention on accounts of the great revolutionary struggles led by Mao Tse-Tung in China, Ben Bella in Algeria and – most inspiringly of all – Castro and Che Guevara's rebellion in Cuba. As police attempts to catch Mandela were intensified, he was moved to the home of an admiring, sympathetic doctor in the affluent white Johannesburg suburb of Norwood and accommodated in the servants' quarters, where he took up the role of one of the doctor's gardeners.

Mandela realised that he and the ANC lacked any military expertise, having little experience of explosives, armaments and the basic tactics of guerrilla military activity, so he forged a partnership with his communist friend Joe Slovo and with the help of a number of military experts from the South African communist party began to train 'the Spear of Nation's' growing underground army. Mandela now moved to an isolated farmhouse near Rivonia from where, disguised as a mechanic, nightwatchman or priest, he would travel to meet ANC leaders to discuss the imminent commencement of military action. But as his friend Dennis Goldberg said: 'There's a downside to being the romantic leader. It makes you take more and more risks, because you must maintain the publicity.' Indeed all this overt publicity made the South African government realise they were sitting on top of a volcano that was about to erupt. It seemed the 'Black Pimpernel' had made the transition from politician to effective military leader when, just before Christmas, the MK struck with multiple explosions in most of South Africa's major cities, with government offices and electric power facilities being the primary targets.

The ANC leadership realised that if their military insurrection was to succeed, they would need a reliable arms supply and further training for their MK detachments, so Mandela decided to travel to Ethiopia to give a speech and meet the delegates at the pan-African summit that was due to take place in early 1962. His travel itinerary would also give him an opportunity to visit a number of African countries that had won independence during the previous decade. Exiting South Africa across the unguarded border with Bechuanaland, Mandela travelled to Dar-es-Salaam in Tanzania, which had only just gained its independence from Britain the previous month. He particularly enjoyed meeting the country's new President Julius Nyerere whom he admired greatly. He then travelled to Ghana, another recently liberated country, before flying on to Addis Ababa, capital of Ethiopia, where he met an old hero of his, Emperor Haile Selassie. At the conference he gave a powerful speech where he described his leadership of the insurgency as 'the most inspiring period of my life. Everywhere I have been inspired by the warm affection and the amount of confidence I have found among the African masses.' Many of the British and American newspapers reported the speech, but it wasn't mentioned in the South African press.

After the conference he travelled to Egypt and then

Algeria, which had recently won its eight-year war with France, during which over half a million Algerians had died, a sombre premonition of the bloodbath that could so easily overwhelm South Africa. Then he travelled for the first time to London, where he met a number of leading British politicians, and back to Ethiopia, where he undertook a six-month course in guerilla-warfare training. He eventually returned to South Africa just after the government had passed a draconian sabotage act that made the death penalty a possible sentence for all those committing any form of insurrectional violence. Returning to the farm in Liliesleaf in Rivonia he had a brief reunion with Winnie and the children. A few days later in early August 1962, disguised as a chauffeur, he was driving to attend an ANC meeting in Johannesburg and on the way, near Pietermavity, three police cars tracked him down, forced him off the road and arrested him. He spent that night locked up in a prison cell at the back of the Pietermavity police station. He would remain in jail for the next twenty-seven years.

In 1940 W. H. Auden observed with some considerable insight that 'The so-called traumatic experience is not an accident, but the opportunity for which the child has been patiently waiting – in order to find a necessity and direction for its existence, in order that its life may become a serious matter.'

As we have seen, it is unusual for an individual to progress from the birth experience, through early infancy and later childhood without encountering some kind of trauma. And yet the emotional dysfunctionality that comes with each particular trauma, expressed through those constellations of neuroses with which all of us are endowed, does have 'a gift in the wound'. I ask all my clients to look for this significant benefit, this advantage, this resource that lies embedded and out of sight within the wound. For instance, the child who has been poorly parented often develops a considerable natural charm which they deploy in their attempts to recruit surrogate parents to compensate for the neglect they experienced at the hand of their natural parents. This natural charm is then taken into adulthood and becomes an appreciable asset. A most obvious conscious example of this gift in the wound is where a toxic marriage which has caused great pain and discomfort has as its primary consequence the birth of one or more beloved children. Each of my clients who has been through such a marital ordeal always feels that the torment was worth enduring because of the existence of the much-loved child or children. It is, I believe, our task as therapists to help the client reveal this paradox: that within the pain and discomfort of the trauma there is to be found this prize or reward of considerable value.

This 'gift in the wound' is what Auden is suggesting – that unconsciously the child is drawn to the trauma because it provides the provenance and origin of much of the child's talent, flair, drive, ambition and competence.

This is one of the primal features of individuation: that the childhood trauma, the adolescence upheaval, the midlife misery has a potential transformational energy which can mould and sculpt the higher, better aspects of our nature. Jung talked of his own midlife ordeal like being flayed on the 'anvil of crisis', a process which fashioned his wiser personality, that was no longer driven by the demands of his ego and was more in touch with the enlightened Self. Whenever the trauma is encountered it has within its compass the seeds of future transformation.

Bearing this paradox in mind – that trauma is the origin of self-development and maturity – although Mandela's early family life was very secure, the traumatic environment created by the vicious racism of apartheid undoubtedly shaped his personality, which then received a brutal increase of traumatic experience when he arrived in his bleak prison cell on Robben Island in June 1964 at the age of forty-six.

Mandela's home, for the first eighteen years of his incarceration, measured eight feet by seven, furnished with nothing more than a straw mat and three tattered blankets. He described his dank cell, freezing in winter, sweltering and airless in summer as 'unredeemably grim'. His contact with the outside world was reduced to one letter received every six months, while the provision of a radio or newspaper was strictly banned. He wrote of his life on the bleak outcrop of rock that was Robben Island: 'The prison is above all primitive, it operates to break the human spirit, to exploit human weakness, undermine human strength, destroy initiatives, individuality and negate intelligence.'

And of the treatment meted out by the prison guards he would write: 'You have no idea of the cruelty of man against man until you have been in a South African prison with white warders and Black prisoners.'

Yet despite these brutal, austere circumstances he seemed, as time went by, miraculously to prosper. His close friends with whom he was imprisoned could sense that his personality was somehow being tempered – both strengthened and deepened. His tendency towards arrogance and entitlement seemed to have ebbed away and he seemed at peace with himself. His proneness towards irritation and anger towards others subsided, replaced by powers of empathy and understanding that reinvigorated his personal authority, which appeared to influence and affect not only his fellow inmates, but also the white prison staff.

This stoical ebullience, this resilience to the harshness of his surroundings and circumstances, seems to have been the result of two aspects of his new life. Firstly, the unfamiliar periods of solitude he endured when he was locked in his cell gave him time for deep thought that only seemed to invigorate his certainty in regard to his life's mission. As time went on, he was developing the slow realisation that revenge and retribution would be a catastrophic response to all the injustices and abuse that he and his comrades and indeed fellow Africans across the nation had suffered at the hands of the white authorities. If the disastrous slaughter that had occurred when India and Algeria had gained their independence was to be avoided and if democracy and a Black government were to be achieved without recourse to a terrible civil war, forgiveness would have to be the ANC's response when they finally became the nation's government. It was as if a magnanimous forbearance, a humane benevolence was slowly fermenting within Mandela's evolving political strategy. This clemency emerged from his conviction that his imprisonment was only strengthening both his psychological and political wisdom, qualities that would be needed when that inevitable moment came and he was released from prison and was elevated to the position of South Africa's first Black President. It was almost as if he understood that his long prison sentence on Robben Island provided him with a period of further preparation for the inevitable destiny that lay before him; it was as if he realised that this period of seclusion and solitude provided him with the time and opportunity to explore and examine every aspect of his nature and personality.

The second aspect of his imprisonment that gave him great fortitude and encouragement was the fact that the South African authorities had foolishly incarcerated the ANC leadership convicted alongside Mandela in adjacent cells on Robben Island. To exacerbate their error, they had placed a considerable number of other political prisoners on that desolate island, inadvertently creating a kind of academy of revolutionary culture and scholarship. As Mandela wrote in his autobiography *Long Walk to Freedom*: 'The authorities' greatest mistake was to keep us together, for together our determination was reinforced. We supported each other and gained strength from each other. Whatever we know, whatever we learned we shared and by sharing we multiplied whatever courage we had individually.'

There were three particular old friends who lived alongside Mandela who he depended on for support and advice, the most trusted of whom was Walter Sisulu, who had always been his principal mentor. In his description of Sisulu, Mandela wrote of his 'clear vision and judgement, his accessibility and openness to new ideas, his simplicity and his love of nature'. Ahmed Kathrada, the only Indian among the seven ANC comrades who was convicted and imprisoned alongside

Mandela, was a man with tremendous empathy and inner calm, whose loyal admiration for his friend was unconditional. And then there was Goven Mbeki, the oldest and most cultured and educated of the inner circle, whose historical and political erudition was a resource of particular significance. Yet apart from old ANC comrades there were also numerous prisoners from other parties and persuasions to enliven the political debate and to forge political alliances with.

An important British politician who had met Mandela on his visit to London in 1962 was Dennis Healey, who now – in September 1970 – travelled to Robben Island to meet again the imprisoned African leader whom he admired so much. Healey was astounded at the change in Mandela's bearing and demeanour. His morale was so high, his appearance calm and composed, his dignity and bearing more certain than when they had met in 1962. Dennis Healey wrote of Mandela 'his moral authority, even over his warders, was immense'. The Labour politician returned to London with news of Mandela's charismatic presence, his patient forbearance and his compassionate humanity, even towards his white oppressors. Life on Robben Island appeared to be shaping a political leader of exceptional stature.

These qualities of leadership were put to good effect as Mandela found a way to confront the harsh prison regime of the hated prison governor, Colonel Piet Badenhorst, by way of strikes and other refusals to follow prison regulations which eventually resulted in three judges arriving from the Commission of Prisons. One of these judges was Michael Corbett, who – thirty years later – would be appointed the Nation's Chief Justice by the then President Mandela, and who – with his two colleagues – interviewed both Baden-horst and Mandela. The contrast between the two men was shocking: the prison governor exuding his brutal, inhumane approach to penal protocol, while Mandela displayed an extraordinary acceptance of the harsh treatment, as if he could somehow forgive the brutalities and sadism of the warders because of the toxic culture in which they had always lived. A few weeks after the Judges' visit, Badenhorst and his vicious warders were all relieved of their duties.

The new governor, Colonel Willie Willemse, introduced an unexpected laissez-faire attitude to prison protocol. Mandela, surprised by the new regime, commented: 'The inmates, not the authorities, seemed to be running the prison.' There were far fewer warders and as Kathrada wrote of the work details: 'We now just go to the quarry and do nothing.' It was as if the warders were almost intimidated by the prisoners. Governor Willemse seemed to understand that Mandela had much more authority than he had and asked him to impose some discipline on the work details. Mandela agreed and spoke to his fellow prisoners who resumed work, but in a more leisurely fashion than before. Willemse said of Mandela 'He had a special stature. He was experienced in the politics of change. I never felt he was waiting for revenge'. He also mentioned how Mandela's benign authority seemed to affect the way in which the warders treated and spoke to the prisoners.

As for Mandela's conditions, these now changed radically. He was allowed three letters and two visits a month, his threadbare mat was replaced with a proper bed, his diet improved and his days working in the lime quarry came to an end. As well as Dennis Healey, his visitors now included Helen Suzman, the only member of the Liberal Progressive Party in Parliament, visits from Red Cross representatives, Philip Zuger and Jacques Moreillon, the Delegate General for Africa and George Bizos, Mandela's lawyer who all gave interviews about Robben Island's star inmate. Because of all this publicity, the authorities had to maintain their famous prisoner's health and wellbeing. Indeed this star status was keenly felt by newly-arrived warders, who hoped to have contact with the great man, who now took an active interest in the lives and personal histories of the warders who tended to his needs. Mandela's power of forgiveness seemed to spread amongst his fellow prisoners. The young Fikile Bam, a great friend of Mandela's on Robben Island who became one of the most respective judges of the future South Africa, for instance, commented on the example of Mandela's model of tolerance which had such an infections impact on his fellow prisoners, saying: 'Prison completely cured me of self-pity and of being self-centred.'

The most significant consequence in this change in the prison's ethos was the development of opportunities for study. Mandela had told the Prison Commissioners 'Let the atmosphere of a university prevail', and what became known as 'the University of Robben Island' began to be established. Any prisoner who had a degree became a teacher. Somehow they combined a teaching schedule with work in the lime quarry. Lectures would be given while the prisoners were swinging a pick or shovelling lime. As Fikile Bam reported 'Little groups assembled in different places and you knew that there were classes in progress.' Mandela gave a course of lectures on political economy. He saw the prison becoming a kind of centre of Socratic learning where all the prisoners were encouraged to ask questions and join in a vigorous debate in regard to the subject under discussion. Some inmates were in fact illiterate so their reading and writing skills were immediately developed and soon their families were receiving unexpected letters. The warders too could join in and take advantage of these educational opportunities. As Governor Willemse said 'Many recruits to the prison service volunteered for Robben Island as it was a University for the warders too.' Sergeant du Toit, the warder who ran the Prisoners' Studies Department said of Mandela: 'He was very strict about people studying. He insisted on not only prisoners but also warders attending classes.'

The South African historian Tom Karis described this striking change in the penal reform engineered by Mandela as follows: 'a culture of comradeship, cooperation, learning and debate were coupled with political tolerance.' This transformed the culture of Robben Island, with Mandela's authority leading this mutual acceptance and forbearance between Black prisoners and white warders becoming a template for the peaceful transfer of power in South Africa twenty years later.

It was as if a miracle had occurred on Robben Island. Mandela had somehow conjured out of its harshness and brutality an extraordinary transformation as he fashioned and took part in this new mood of cooperation and unity between all those who lived on this barren island. The general expectation shared by almost everyone was that sooner or later the de facto leader of Robben Island would eventually become the President of a racially integrated democratic South Africa. The prison community had become a laboratory of racial diversity and co-operation which might perhaps provide a template in the years to come for a transition from white to Black government without recourse to recrimination, hatred and violence.

By late 1983 the Government in Pretoria could see that Mandela's position as effective master of Robben Island could not continue and he, Sisulu and Kathrada were transferred to Pollsmoor, a large prison for common-law prisoners an hour's drive north of Cape Town. Yet leaving Robben Island and his many friends and comrades didn't dampen Mandela's spirits. He wrote to Fatima Meer, an old childhood friend, in a mood of confidence: 'I feel fine and ten years younger than I am. The only difference is that I am not as active as I used to be on Robben Island. Yet morale is high and as I write this letter my body is literally boiling with optimism and hope.'

He had good reason to be optimistic. Although the ANC was still officially banned, its campaign of sabotage, while avoiding civilian targets, focused its attention on energy, infrastructure and military installations. The leadership under Oliver Tambo were proving most effective, operating from their headquarters in Zambia. But perhaps more significantly 'The Free Mandela Campaign' had now exerted a vociferous outcry internationally, as the ANC's legendary leader became a popular cause in most of the world's democracies.

So considerable had the pressure become on President Botha that he felt he had to respond and in January 1985 he announced in parliament his offer to release Mandela if he renounced violence unconditionally. The imprisoned ANC leader immediately wrote a speech, responding to Botha's offer by demanding that the South African government should relinquish violence themselves by dismantling apartheid and legalising the ANC before Mandela could accept his freedom. On the 10 February 1985, his first speech for over twenty years was read out by his daughter to a huge crowd in the Jabulani Stadium in Soweto, who reacted ecstatically.

The violence escalated and a month after Mandela's speech the police killed nineteen ANC protestors in Uitenhage. During the winter of 1985 the townships were becoming ungovernable and police forays into these centres of ANC activity became rare. Press reports confirmed that law and order had virtually broken down and the whole country was close to anarchy. Mandela's speech had lit a fuse paper, as television audiences around the world watched the battles on the edges of the townships. International investors and banks took fright and stopped investing in South Africa. Huge loans from American and European banks were recalled as their repayment became due, the South African rand collapsed and the central Bank could only prop up the failing national economy by paying Swiss and German banks' exorbitant interest rates.

Mandela's first speech in two decades had dramatically displayed the immense influence his moral authority had throughout the world. His words had brought the South African economy to its knees and Foreign Minister Pik Botha was forced to reassure foreign banks and global political leaders by saying 'today we have crossed the Rubicon and it will not be long before Mandela will be released and apartheid will be dismantled'. It was an extraordinary turn of events. International capital had joined forces with Mandela and political victory, without recourse to violence, now seemed an eventual certainty. From Pollsmoor Prison Ahmed Kathrada wrote: 'You must wonder what it is like to live with a "celebrity" like Uncle Nelson. Not a single day goes by without something about him in the papers or on the radio. He unfailingly makes a great impression upon people. No matter how affected or excited he may be about a particular incident or event he still manages to display a calm which is unbelievable.'

The South African economy in August 1986 received a further near-terminal blow when the US Senate voted by a large majority in favour of a ban on American companies investing in South Africa. A variety of export bans on American products, including oil, were also imposed. Within a few weeks this was followed by a similar set of restrictions agreed by all European Community members, which included all new investment until Mandela was released and the ban on the ANC was lifted. Few individuals have ever had such an impact on global political and economic policy. And yet President Botha still refused even to meet Mandela, let alone consider his release.

In the summer of 1988, the BBC organised a historic rock concert at Wembley Stadium to celebrate Mandela's seventieth birthday. The line-up included Harry Belafonte, Whitney Houston, Roberta Flack and Stevie Wonder. The concert, in front of a crowd of 80,000, was watched by a global television audience of over 200 million. As Kathrada said 'apart from the Birthday of Jesus Christ, no birthday has ever been as widely celebrated as Nelson's seventieth.'

In the opening few days of 1989 President Botha's intransigence came to an end when he suffered a stroke and was forced to stand down from the leadership of the National Party. The membership then voted for F. W. de Klerk, the education minister, to become the new party leader and acting president. Initially de Klerk moved forward cautiously, but when he won the General Election later that year he regarded his victory as a mandate for change. Immediately eight of the ANC leadership, including Sisulu and Kathrada, were released from their long prison sentences. He then withdrew many of the apartheid restrictions: beaches, parks, lavatories and restaurants were no longer segregated.

Before the end of 1989 the two men met. De Klerk was struck by Mandela's courtesy and magnanimity. He seemed to understand and empathise with the fears of the white minority and he promised that the ANC would do everything necessary to allay these fears, once the ban on the party was lifted. Clearly de Klerk was deeply impressed by the ANC leader and he told his brother that Mandela was 'a man with tremendous style and a politician to be reckoned with'.

On the 2 February 1990 de Klerk announced to parliament that the ban on the ANC would be lifted and Mandela would be released. On the 11 February, in front of a huge expectant worldwide television audience, Mandela walked out of Victor Verster Prison with his wife Winnie, having completed a sentence of twenty-seven years. The television pictures of this long-awaited occasion were some of the most iconic and moving images of the twentieth century.

How had this man from a small, obscure tribe located in the remote state of Transkei become perhaps the most revered and admired individual of his generation? As Mandela said on the occasion of his retirement from the Presidency in June 1999, after he had governed his country for five transformational yet peaceful years: 'One of the most difficult things is not to change society – but to change yourself.'

This Mandela achieved during his long imprisonment. And this personal transformation is one of the most striking examples of what Carl Jung called the process of individuation. Through the sheer hell of his early years of imprisonment Mandela changed himself into a human being of immense personal stature. One of the dangers of the individuation process is that it can result in what Jung called an 'inflation' – a self-congratulatory arrogance which can overtake an individual if he or she is seduced by a surfeit of admiration and idealisation. This never happened to Mandela. Throughout his presidency the primary comment of those who met him, who worked with him and those who knew him was that he was a man of great courtesy and humility, a trait of personality in stark contrast to the arrogant younger man who had arrived in Robben Island twenty-seven years earlier. The slow process of transformation that took place during his long incarceration resulted in the peaceful revolution in South Africa, and it also provided humanity as a whole with an inspirational example of one of history's most exceptional human beings.

If mankind is going to safely traverse across the decades of peril ahead, when we will be faced with a series of possible extinction events, it will be essential that this process of individuation produces a number of visionary individuals like Mandela, with sufficient emotional intelligence and moral authority to nurse our battered and bruised species through the hazardous years which lie ahead. Nelson Mandela provides us with a prototype, an inspiring example of the kind of exceptional individual we will need to overcome the challenges ahead.

It is crucial that men and women who emerge through the process of individuation and have become individuals of moral integrity, compassionate humility and strength of purpose, can be set against narcissistic, morally corrupt and venal personalities like Vladimir Putin and Donald Trump. The presence of individuated human beings amongst our political leadership therefore becomes essential if our species is to survive and prosper in the centuries to come. If the process of natural selection results in humanity remaining the dominant species on planet Earth, the concept of individuation fulfills a key evolutionary role in the continuation and improvement of homo sapiens' stewardship of our planet.

Perhaps this gathering critical mass amongst more and more ordinary men and women will build up the necessary collective wisdom which in the past has been the province of just a few outstanding individuals. Perhaps some essential evolutionary mechanism is spreading this aspiration towards individuation beyond just a few Olympian individuals and it is now to be found, because of the perils of our age, in a widespread zeitgeist, a developing collective consciousness that is galvanising more and more people towards a level of emotional intelligence and ethical concern that creates the necessary collective enlightenment which will rescue our species from its current descent.

Carl Jung and Viktor Frankl's Theories of Meaning
(Carl Jung, Josephine Baker, Viktor Frankl)

O f all Carl Jung's numerous books, by far the most popular and widely read is his autobiography *Memories, Dreams, Reflections: An Autobiography* (1961) which he wrote at the end of his life in his eighties. In the final pages of his book, he ponders on the meaning of both our individual lives and that of our species. As he makes his closing conclusions he writes 'I do not imagine that in my reflections on the meaning of man I have uttered a final truth', and yet he goes on to say 'Meaning makes a great many things endurable – perhaps everything.' And then in the last few lines he writes 'Life has meaning and meaninglessness. I cherish the anxious hope that meaning will preponderate and win the battle.'

These then are the concluding remarks of this sage, who seems to speak to our condition, as we nudge our way apprehensively through the early decades of the twenty-first century. This search for meaning and purpose seems to run through so much of Jung's life and work, which appears haunted by the questions – Why are we here? Does our existence have any meaning? Do the few fleeting years that we have been granted have any purpose? In the deluge of words Jung produced and in a lifetime rich in experience, he maintains as one of his central ideas that we, homo sapiens, are meaning-seeking creatures and if we don't find in our lives a sense of purpose, beyond just extending our gene pool, we will become incapable of leading a rewarding, fulfilling life. As he wrote in 1934: 'The same way that the body needs food the psyche needs to know the meaning of its existence.'

The fact that Jung grappled with these questions of meaning throughout his life is perhaps understandable given the fact that our incarnation, our very being, is the result of a wildly improbable cosmic fluke. That we, as individuals and as a species, exist at all on this planet of ours is so unlikely, so preposterously implausible, that how can such a state of affairs have any consequent meaning?

Just look at the unlikely cosmic process that has resulted in our existence. Two colliding hydrogen atoms, some 13 billion years ago, which we have come to call 'the Big Bang', spawned an infinity of stars. After a near-eternity of chemical change, these stars disintegrated in supernova explosions, resulting in a diaspora of star dust. 4.5 billion years later this stellar debris formed dust clouds that circled our own young star. This was followed by a process of accretion, whereby the accumulating stardust attracted by the sun's gravitational field, was slowly transformed into a set of spheres that became our solar system's planetary alignment. One of these planets positioned herself on an orbit of such optimal precision that a process of chemical evolution began, blessed by the energy of the sun and the revitalising presence of water. The original atoms from the supernova explosions, collected by the orbiting Earth over an extended measure of time, formed molecules. The molecules became bases, the bases became amino acids, the amino acids formed proteins and the proteins developed into cells. The cells eventually became simple animals, then developed into more sophisticated creatures and over eons of evolutionary time human beings were created.

This 13-billion-year process of evolution has resulted in us – humans – who, as far as we know, are the most complex, sophisticated entities in the universe. This immense cosmic improbability has given us a mere handful of decades to experience this miracle of consciousness. It was this unlikely, unfathomable state of affairs that Jung implicitly insisted we needed to honour. These extraordinary natural processes have resulted in this fleeting scrap of time that we have been bequeathed. It is in such privileged circumstances that we have to decide what our purpose is. As Jung said in the concluding words of his famous 1959 BBC television interview with John Freeman: 'Man cannot stand a meaningless life.'

As we have seen, this quest for life's meaning goes back 2,500 years, all the way to Socrates' maxim 'The unexamined life is not worth living', with its premise that self-examination, self-knowledge and self-realisation is the prime purpose of life. This philosophical consideration of the meaning of our existence then travels from Plato and Aristotle through many shades and diversions until it erupts, like some solar flare, into a zeitgeist of debate, in the Enlightenment of the eighteenth century. Denis Diderot, John Locke, David Hume, Montesquieu, Jean-Jacques Rousseau, Adam Smith, Immanuel Kant and many others all had their say. Then in the eighteenth century Jeremy Bentham and the Utilitarians came up with their 'greatest happiness principle'. This optimism was soon deconstructed by Nietzsche, who having claimed that 'God is dead' saw this consequent nihilism as an obstruction to be overcome by embarking on a search for purpose in a meaningless world. This call to arms was taken up by legions of Existentialists led by Martin Heidegger, Jean-Paul Sartre and Albert Camus. Their exploration into this fog of futility was accentuated by the cataclysms of the first half of the twentieth century with two world wars, the Holocaust, Hiroshima and the Gulag. These displays of human depravity influenced almost every art form of the day, from the harshness of atonality in music, to the seeming confusion of abstract art, to the emptiness of absurdist literature – all profoundly powerful in their response to the bleak historical events that they were surrounded by, as they posed the question as to whether the barbarities of the twentieth century engulfed us in a mire of futility. Alongside these philosophical debates the world's religions continued to provide us with fixed immutable instruction as to why we were here and how we should behave. But increasingly their dogmatic certainties seemed less and less attractive to their once committed followers, who now saw diminishing evidence in the world around them of a benign, supernatural divine presence.

Popular culture had its say as well, culminating in Monty Python's film *The Meaning of Life*, which suggested that the answer lay in being nice to people, reading good books and taking regular exercise. The final definitive answer was given in Douglas Adams' book *The Hitchhiker's Guide to the Galaxy*, where a giant super computer named Deep Thought – after wrestling with the problem for 7.5 million years –

resolved the whole labyrinthine dilemma by proclaiming that the meaning of life was the number '42'.

This surreal, satirical solution is instructive. It shows us that these questions of meaning and futility aren't solvable in any rational sense. No mathematical proof or set of empirical facts can provide us with an answer. Perhaps a sense of meaning or a sense of futility are simply two opposed moods that come and go, or perhaps meaning is just an emotional state that may fill days and weeks when our actions and feelings are purposeful and full of intent which then modulate into a kind of listless despondency, when the tasks and actions that fill our days lose their sense of purpose. As Jung says in the last few sentences of *Memories, Dreams, Reflections*: 'Life is – or has – meaning and meaninglessness'.

I see this perpetual pendulum swing in all my clients in my psychotherapeutic practice. For weeks they will be filled with a sense of forward momentum and fulfilment in their jobs and careers, then quite suddenly they enter a kind of doldrum of inertia and apathy and their profession appears pointless and monotonous. The same feelings of tiresome, dreary tedium can engulf a marriage or other significant relationship and this morose state of mind may deepen into a depression.

The work with the client then becomes a careful examination to see whether the feeling of futility and pointlessness is merely a passing mood, lurking within the psyche, that fixes itself upon the most prominent feature of the client's life, namely the marriage or profession. What has to be established is whether the negative state of mind is simply a projection of one of the client's complexes onto the job or relationship or whether there is a fundamental element in the career or marriage that is flawed and needs attending to.

Perhaps what we are trying to achieve with our clients is not the final vanquishing of futility within a mindset that wishes to eradicate these uncomfortable feelings of meaningless but rather to accept the pendulum swings between meaning and futility, understanding that this fluctuation represents a perpetual duality which we are destined to go on experiencing until our final years. Futility can then be seen as a returning emotion that we simply have to bear, while being comforted by the expectation that in its duality it will eventually be replaced by a return to that reassuring sense of purpose. Perhaps the aim of effective psychotherapy is to develop in our clients an acceptance of this endless pendulum swing from meaning to futility.

In Jung's life we can see these oscillations between an extreme sense of meaning and purpose and a feeling of pointless futility. For ten years between 1903–1913 Jung led a life of incessant, unremitting activity, pursuing a driven ambition both professionally and in his personal life. During this decade, at only twenty-nine, he became the deputy to director Eugen Bleuler at the renowned Burgholzli Mental Hospital; he became a lecturer and then one of the youngest professors of psychiatry at the University of Zürich; his papers and articles began to attract an international reputation and he became the confident and prime collaborator of Sigmund Freud. Around this time Jung also became President of the International Congress of Psychoanalysis, he and Freud lectured throughout North America and Europe and he also married Emma Rauschenbach, daughter of one of Switzerland's richest industrialists, and in a handful of years the couple had five children.

Then suddenly all came to a sudden halt in 1913, replaced by years of inertia, breakdown, depression and hopelessness. The thirty-eight-year old retired from every aspect of public life. All sense of direction, all his aspirations and ambitions, all his energy and vigour collapsed. He was filled with a sense of futility and emptiness. His life's meaning evaporated, pushing him close to suicide.

After four years in this wasteland of incoherent fragmentation, a very different man began to emerge, who in later life was to write of these experiences: 'The years when I was pursuing my inner images were the most important of my life – in them everything was decided. It all began then . . . it was the "prima materia" of my lifetime's work.' Jung found in his breakdown a sense of breakthrough, a slow revelation of what his life was really about. In these years of meaninglessness he discovered his true purpose.

And yet these pendulum swings between the polarities of his nature didn't finally end with this breakdown since he was to encounter similar swings from meaning to futility time and again in his mature years. Indeed he saw the tension of these polarities as a necessary feature of psychological development, the very sculpting process of individuation. He wrote in *Memories, Dreams, Reflections*:

Nothing so promotes the growth of consciousness as this inner confrontation of opposites . . . Just as all energy proceeds from opposition, so the psyche too possesses its inner

polarities, this being the indispensable prerequisite for its
aliveness.

The implication here is that we shouldn't over-identify
with the chaffing of our polar opposites but rather with the
creative energy that this tension of opposites can provide us
with. Jung's life frequently provides us with examples of how
periods of aimless dullness and debilitating fatigue when all
sense of purpose appears lost are in fact a preparation for
a vigorous move forward. I often tell my clients that doing
nothing is a very productive use of their time. For instance,
when Jung was sixty-five, he appeared to his friends and colleagues to be a spent force. He seemed to have aged dramatically, exhausted in mind and body, empty of his legendary
intellectual curiosity. The photos of this time show a gaunt,
stooped, prematurely aged figure. In 1940 he wrote to his
friend Mary Mellon that he was feeling like 'a heap of scrap
iron, rusty and deformed'. Yet this phase eventually passed
and he entered a period of renewed creative and meaningful
endeavour, in his seventies, when he was once again extraordinarily productive.

Jung's obsessive concern with the tension between
meaning and futility originated from a severe trauma that
he suffered in his earliest years. The marriage of his parents and the family they created barely functioned as a viable thriving unit. Paul and Emilie's brief courtship before
they married was notable for its lack of romance or even a
degree of enthusiasm or affection. Emilie was the daughter of a priest and therefore her parents considered that she
would be suited to become the wife of the twenty-seven-

year-old pastor who was in need of a spouse to help him run the country parish to which he had just been appointed. Almost immediately Emilie found her new life tedious and cheerless and her husband dull and unoriginal, a situation made worse by a succession of problematic pregnancies that resulted in three stillborn babies. All this corrosive misfortune soured the troubled marriage into which Carl Gustav was born.

Many of my clients have been born into similar dysfunctional marriages in which their mothers have been emotionally disappointed. In such cases the mother hopes that this regret will be eased and compensated by the emotional fulfilment that a newborn baby can sometimes provide. When the infant arrives, the mother expects to experience a wave of consoling emotional pleasure. Yet so often the mother is setting herself up for further disappointment when the gruelling exhaustion of early motherhood begins to take its toll. Through its exceptionally attuned, intuitive antenna the baby, as it grows through infancy, will begin to feel that its prime purpose in life is to provide the emotional meaning and fulfilment that their mother yearns for. This growing sense that the young child has some kind of duty to tend to their mother's emotional needs that are not provided in her marriage, can easily result in an unsettling apprehension that they are failing in this task, or worse still, that they have caused their mother's troubled state of mind.

In my own case I often wonder whether the reason I became a therapist and find the work so gratifying is that I failed in my first crucial duty as a little boy in my attempt to soothe and ease the emotional disappointment of my mother who, two years before I was born, married a naval officer who spent most of his time away at sea. When I asked what she remembered most about my birth she replied that it was my father's absence and the fact she had no one to share this momentous experience with. These early experiences of mine have led me to believe that many therapists felt in their childhood that their first crucial role was to comfort their emotionally disappointed mothers and that by way of compensation for failing to do this, they spend long gratifying careers attempting to heal their clients. In this sense, Carl Jung can perhaps be characterised as the ultimate psychotherapist who wished to redeem the world,

Most children in this situation have only one parent whom they feel emotionally responsible for. An only child, until he was nine, Jung also had to deal with his father's profound disillusion with life. From the age of two Carl shared a bedroom with his father, so toxic had the marriage become. Paul's response to Emilie's ever-deepening depression was to erupt into furious rages and soon the entire village was aware of their parson's turbulent, troubled marriage. The only answer was to send his wife off to spend long periods away in spas and rest homes. Paul's disenchantment with his marriage now infected his professional life, as slowly he began to lose his faith, continuing to preach to a diminishing, bored and uninspired congregation. He simply went through the motions in order to earn his salary, as his belief in God slipped away. In *Memories, Dreams, Reflections* Jung writes: 'There arose in me profound doubt about everything my father said. When I heard him preaching about grace he sounded stale and hollow . . . I wanted to help him but I did not know how . . . I was seized with the most vehement pity for my father. All at once I understood the tragedy of his life and profession.' Paul was to die a depressed old man, 'just a sack full of bones' as his son described him, appearing far older than his fifty-four years.

Jung was later to write: 'I feel very strongly that I am under the influence of things and questions left incomplete and unanswered by my parents and grandparents. It often seems as if there were an impersonal karma within a family, which is passed from parents to children.'

It was this 'karma' – these 'questions left incomplete and unanswered by my parents' – that Jung's life and work were driven by as both his parents suffered intensely from a lack of meaning and purpose in their lives. No wonder he became so obsessed with questions of meaning and purpose, fearful that he might fall victim to the futility of life, but to redeem his parents was not enough: he had to redeem himself and everyone around him. Indeed he needed to save the whole world from the scourge of futility.

Josephine Baker sang and pirouetted her way into the hearts of an adoring Paris public during two tantalising seasons of cabaret at the Théâtre des Champs-Élysées in 1925, followed by the Folies Bergère in 1926. The French writer Colette called the nineteen-year-old Josephine 'a most beautiful panther'. Ernest Hemingway described her as 'the most sensational woman anyone ever saw' and her many lovers included the artist Frida Kahlo, the novelist George Simenon and the architect Le Corbusier. Her sensational erotic dancing style was honed and polished by George Balanchine and Picasso pursued her, desperate to paint her portrait, describing her as 'The Nefertiti of Now'. The barely literate waif from the American Midwest became a regular visitor to the exclusive 'Le Boeuf sur le Toit' where she consorted with the likes of Charlie Chaplin, the Prince of Wales, the Aga Khan, Chanel, Jean Cocteau and Scott Fitzgerald. As the distinguished Jungian scholar James Hillman wrote: 'The motions of her frenzied, dancing body gave all of Paris a hard-on.' Yet Josephine Baker insisted 'I wasn't really naked. I simply didn't have any clothes on.'

Despite all this erotic provocation, Baker was inducted into Paris's Panthéon alongside Voltaire, Jean-Jacques Rousseau, Victor Hugo, Marie Curie and Simone Weil. In November 2021, in a speech honouring her, President Macron said: 'Stereotypes are taken on by Josephine Baker, then she shakes them up, digs at them, turns them into a sublime burlesque in a spirit of enlightenment, ridiculing colonial prejudices to the music of Sidney Bechet.' Her extraordinary biography, full of transformatory changes, illustrates how an empowering sense of purpose can overcome periods of debilitating misfortune and invigorate a life, which is sustained by an over-arching feeling of meaning.

But what exactly happened to this Black American, Josephine Baker, that resulted in her receiving the greatest honour the French state can bestow on one of its citizens?

She was born in June 1906 in St Louis, Missouri. Her mother, Carrie McDonald, was the daughter of an ex-slave and was twenty-one when Josephine was born. Her father, Eddie Carson, spent most of his time in the local bars and poolhalls, earning a tiny pittance as a dance teacher in the neighbourhood dance hall. The unmarried couple lived with Carrie's mother, known to everyone as Grandmother Elvira, who always adored Josephine. Carrie and Eddie developed a dance routine that they performed to small audiences which earned them some extra money, but when Josephine's brother Richard was born, Eddie found his growing family responsibilities interfered with his free-spirited nature and he disappeared to pursue his career as a drummer. Josephine never forgave Eddie for this desertion and her family's consequent plunge into extreme poverty. Two years later Carrie married Arthur Martin, an unskilled labourer, who was in and out of work, according to the vagaries of the local economy. Two further sisters, Margaret and Willie Mae, were born and the family's woefully stretched finances resulted in regular evictions from the squalid apartments in which they lived. As a result, Josephine lived much of the time with Grandmother Elvira.

How did the near destitute, poverty-stricken child become, within a dozen years, the toast of the Folies Bergère in Paris and then move onto a life of such success that she eventually joined the most illustrious names of French history in the nation's Panthéon?

I remember a probation officer talking about prison recidivism on the radio, over thirty years ago. She said that an essential experience which every human being needs as they grow through childhood and adolescence, if they are to develop into a secure adult, is that at least one person thinks they are simply wonderful and adores them unconditionally. During early sessions with a new client I always raise this theory, as all too few individuals encounter this experience in their childhood. If they have had a person who adores them, who is a regular presence in their early years, the therapeutic work will invariably progress smoothly. If this experience of unconditional love has been absent, I know how important my level of what therapists call 'unconditional positive regard' will be. As the eminent Hungarian psychotherapist, Sándor Ferenczi, who became one of Freud's closest collaborators, wrote:

> In the end one becomes convinced that patients are right in demanding from us a genuine interest, a real desire to help and an all-conquering love, which alone makes life seem worth living and which constitutes a counterweight to their traumatic past . . . furthermore, no analysis can succeed if we do not succeed in really loving the patient.

This will be a highly controversial view for many therapists but it has certainly influenced me in regards to my feelings for my clients.

However Josephine didn't have to wait to find this response from some future therapist as this unconditional love was available in spades when she was in the company of her devoted grandmother, who would always provide her with the food she liked most, who would read her the bedtime stories she loved to hear, who would always be close by to give her the hug and cuddle that comforted her when the challenge of life just seemed too much. All this ever-available affection and devotion gave her a feeling of not only security but also the sense that the world was a benevolent, benign place, despite all its pitfalls.

This general sense of wellbeing was then expanded and amplified by her mother's resilience, courage and zest for life. Although Carrie would often be cruel to Josephine, no doubt because of the immense pressures of bringing up four children in such straitened circumstances, she undoubtedly loved her eldest daughter. But almost more important was her fortitude and her ability to meet life's hazards head on, qualities she passed onto her daughter, who throughout her adolescence and adulthood displayed an obstinacy, a tenaciousness and self-reliance that she inherited from her mother. Even in a city like St Louis, renowned for its extreme racism, these personal strengths fuelled an outlook that gave her a determination to live her life beyond the restrictions and limitations of this harshly segregated society in which she had been brought up.

Thanks to her grandmother's love and devotion and her mother's resilience and tenacity she saw herself as exceptional, as superior to all those who surrounded her in St Louis, both Black and white. The pursuit of this excellence, this high value she placed upon herself, this distinction she saw in her personality, became the defining meaning of her life, the assured purpose of her future. It wasn't an expression of arrogance or conceit but rather an absolute determination to escape the central trauma of her life and to evade the appalling way in which the white community treated their Black neighbours. Later in life she told the story of how, in her late teens, she was leaving a hotel and as she did so she met a white woman who was coming into the hotel who stopped and spat on her. Such regular experiences of humiliating degradation, because of the colour of her skin, only intensified the fierceness of her life's meaning and her profound sense of purpose.

Married and divorced at the age of thirteen and married again at fifteen her two young husbands played an inconsequential role in her life, except for the fact she kept her second husband Billy Baker's name for the rest of her life.

When Josephine lived with Grandma Elvira the older woman often talked about her days as a slave on a tobacco plantation in Arkansas. Josephine always felt ambivalent about her grandmother's origins, feeling both proud and ashamed that she had been a slave. As we have seen, Carl Jung wrote about the trauma that is passed on from generation to generation and I have noticed how many of my clients are trying to change the karmic providential direction of their family, ending a lineage of repeated behaviour patterns. For instance in my own case my paternal great-grandmother committed suicide and then two of her sons, my great-uncles, did the same, followed by my aunt and her son, my cousin – all ending their own lives prematurely. Part of my own therapeutic task was to unravel this pattern of self-destruction which had taken four successive generations of my father's family.

In Josephine's family her great-grandfather and her grandmother and no doubt previous generations even further back had all been slaves and, once freed, Elvira had barely managed to survive the restrictions of racist, segregated St Louis. Carrie had attempted to break free from the clutches of this inheritance but finally had had to leave it to her daughter Josephine to cut these karmic tendrils.

This process of Josephine's liberation from the trauma

of American racism, with its endemic brutal misogyny, began at the Old Chauffeur's Club in St Louis. While she served customers, this pretty fourteen-year-old waitress would improvise little dance routines and, encouraged by the male members of her audience, she would also sing. These improvisations were good for business and Josephine started to take part in unrehearsed impromptu performances with the Jones Family Band. The house band leader, Old Man Jones, was impressed by the raw natural talent of this fledgling entertainer and invited Josephine to join the band when they performed for the queues waiting to buy tickets at St Louis's largest theatre, the Booker T. Washington Theatre, where one night the Dixie Steppers were top of the bill. By chance a few hours before the evening's show this vaudeville act had lost their lead singer due to a marital spat and the Dixie Steppers' agent, Bob Russell, who had noticed Josephine, invited her and the Jones Family Band to fill the gap.

In her 1935 autobiography Baker wrote of the audience's response to her first theatrical performance describing 'the cheers, the lust of the men in the audience, the whistles, the laughs and the cries'. For the rest of their St Louis run Josephine became the lead singer with the Dixie Steppers. At the end of the fortnight Bob Russell invited Josephine and the Jones Family Band to join his touring company for concerts throughout the South. This was Baker's first experience beyond the familiar streets of St Louis and although the performances were a great success, she found the daily humiliation of racial segregation excruciating.

Her appearances on the touring circuit with the Dixie

Steppers began to develop her reputation and by the time she was sixteen she was hired to join the chorus line in the touring production of the Broadway hit *Shuffle Along*. The dance director of the show immediately recognised Baker's talent and placed her at the end of the chorus line where she took all sorts of comic liberties, which were greatly enjoyed by the audiences. When the tour arrived in Brooklyn the show's producers – impresarios Noble Sissle and Eubie Blake – having heard about Baker's exploits, attended a performance and when the Broadway production went on tour Baker was given a substantial role for the huge salary of $125 dollars a week. The tour started in Boston and ended in St Louis, much to Baker's delight. After the tour Sissle and Blake immediately engaged Baker for their new musical *The Chocolate Dandies*.

While Baker's reputation was gathering pace, on the other side of the Atlantic the director of the Théâtre des Champs Élysées, André Daven, was having trouble filling his enormous venue. The impresario, Caroline Dudley, a friend of Daven's, suggested that he might like to consider what was then called 'a Negro Vaudeville'. He liked the idea and Dudley travelled back to New York to assemble a cast. She visited the back nightclubs and cabaret venues and came across Baker who was performing at the Plantation Club, having just finished her run of performances of *The Chocolate Dandies*. Caroline Dudley was immediately won over by Baker's natural charm, her comic timing and her erotic charisma. By mid-September 1925 at the age of nineteen Baker was aboard the S.S. *Berengaria* on her way to France. On the 22 September she arrived in Paris and was met by André

Daven, at the Gare St Lazare, who planned to open his new show *La Revue Nègre* ten days later.

As the hectic rehearsal schedule began, the artist Paul Colin watched intently as he had been commissioned to design the poster for *La Revue Nègre*. He found that his eye kept returning to one particular dancer of whom he later wrote: 'Her body was so beautiful. I never saw anybody move in the way she did. She had the perfect figure for the poster.'

Paul spent an afternoon drawing and sketching Baker as she posed for him. Despite the fact she spoke no French and he no English that evening they became lovers. Five days before the opening of the show Paul Colin's posters, featuring a near-naked Baker, appeared throughout Paris. The show's choreographer Jacques-Charles refined Baker's raw electric performing talent pairing her with a tall, muscular giant called Joe Alex.

On the night of the first performance the show's opening number featured the Afro-American clarinettist from New Orleans Sidney Bechet and then, in front of a backdrop depicting the Mississippi and the moon shining through trees draped with Spanish moss, Baker appeared. She was soon followed by Joe Alex who joined her in a primal mating dance. The audience were electrified but remained in stunned silence until the dance reached a rapturous climax. An explosion of clapping, cheering and whistles filled the theatre.

The *New Yorker* Paris correspondent Janet Flanner wrote of the evening:

Within half an hour of the final curtain the news and meaning of Josephine Baker's arrival had spread by the grapevine
up to the cafes of the Champs-Élysées, where the witnesses
of her triumph sat over their drinks, excitedly repeating
their report of what they had just seen. Her magnificent dark
body, a new model to the French, proved for the first time
that black was beautiful.

After *La Revue Nègre*'s success in Paris, the show's
impresario, Caroline Dudley, decided to take the production
as soon as possible to Berlin. However just before setting off
on the Paris–Berlin express Baker had had a visitor. Paul
Derval, the director of the Folies Bergère, had turned up and
persuaded the 'Ebony Venus', as she was now being called,
to sign a contract to star at the Folies Bergère.

La Revue Nègre opened at Berlin's Nelson Theatre ten
days later and the German audiences were electrified by
Baker's performance. On the opening night the over-excited
audience stormed the stage and carried the near-naked star
of the show back to her dressing room. The next day the
entire six-week run was sold out. Returning to Paris in mid-
March 1926 Baker immediately started rehearsing at the
Folies Bergère, where – determined to out-compete his old
rival André Daven at the Théâtre des Champs-Élysées – Paul
Derval had thrown half a million-dollars at his production
of *La Folie du Jour*.

On the first night the curtain opened and Baker
appeared in a huge golden cage. Her costume was perhaps
the most famous and notorious garment she ever wore: a
waistband girdling her hips was decorated with a dozen

jewel-encrusted bananas which bobbed up and down as she danced the Charleston. Apart from some flamboyant jewels this belt of bananas was all she was dressed in. After her routine Baker returned to her cage and was hoisted into the roof of the theatre. The frenzied audience, calling her name, had little appetite for the supporting cast and their demands for Baker's reappearance were rewarded by her return on a trapeze, then a reappearance with armfuls of flowers which she tossed towards her fans. Again and again she returned in a new guise with a new dance, teasing, almost taunting, the overexcited audience.

The Ebony Venus's greatest asset in France was now the colour of her skin, while in America it had been her defining liability. As Baker said: 'Whites now try to do all they can to look like me. They put oil on their whole bodies and bake in the sun all day long.' One such oil 'Valaze Waterlily Cream' appeared on posters with the caption YOU CAN HAVE A BODY LIKE JOSEPHINE BAKER IF YOU USE VALAZE CREAM.

As if to fulfil everyone's expectations of her, a stream of lovers visited her apartment, but these erotic infatuations only made her feel more and more alone. After fifteen months of triumphant success in the French capital, she was missing her family in St Louis; most of all she missed her grandmother, Elvira. As enticing as these sexual encounters initially seemed, she could sense how the men she slept with were only briefly dazzled by her beauty and showed her little tenderness or even kindness as they disappeared from her apartment as soon as the sex was over.

Baker had no father to encourage her. As has been said, when an individual suffers this parental void, they often develop a powerful natural charm which they use to recruit a number of surrogate fathers and often post-pubescent young women will use sexual allure to do so. As Baker moved through her adolescence, she amplified and refined this carnal charisma.

This charming, erotic, beguiling alchemy, which the barely literate young girl of nineteen managed to generate, didn't take into account her vulnerability and loneliness when facing all the complexities of her super-charged chaotic new life in Paris, having only a year or two previously escaped the squalid slums of St Louis. How frightened and intimidated she must have been, her nervous system swamped with adrenaline and at the same time denied the serotonin and the dopamine so readily available when in the company of her loving family. With none of this reassurance, no wonder she repeatedly fell in love with so many glamorous Parisian libertines to compensate. Again and again she would become infatuated with her latest suitor, most of whom only wished to boast to their friends that they had spent the night with the notorious Josephine Baker. As her friend and first biographer Marcel Sauvage said 'She was a woman constantly pursued by men, but not because of affection but rather sexual curiosity. It was not tenderness. And she was looking for tenderness.'

Into this vacuum there emerged a strange character who called himself Count Pepito de Abatino. This slim, good-looking man in his mid-thirties was in fact originally a stonemason from Palermo in Sicily who – like Baker – had managed to transform himself into someone altogether more glamorous. He had become a dance instructor at the famous club Zelli. On meeting him Baker recognised a kindred spirit and the two spent an evening at the nightclubs and bars of Montmartre, getting to know each other. Initially Baker kept Abatino at a distance and wouldn't invite him back to her apartment to share her bed, although it was quite clear that he adored Baker. Every evening after every performance he would be by her side, looking after all her whims and wishes, covering her with a depth of genuine affection she wasn't used to. As one biographer noted 'Josephine fell in love with being loved.' As her relationship with Abatino deepened she gave up her wild life of sexual promiscuity.

Soon Abatino became her manager, promising to help her develop her vocal and choreographic technique which still lacked a certain finesse and sophistication. Since arriving in Paris, Baker had always wanted to open her own nightclub and it emerged that Abatino had certain entrepreneurial talents and turned out to be an astute businessman. The couple opened Chez Josephine just before Christmas 1926 and the club became a great success, soon appearing on tourist itineraries. By the time of her twenty-first birthday she had become a much more settled, less chaotic, happier individual, thanks to Abatino's affectionate guidance.

Abatino then persuaded Baker that they must capitalise on her great success in Paris and they should consider a world tour. He seemed to know exactly who to contact in the cities he approached, although Baker was extremely reluctant to return to America, even after they received offers from a New York promoter. The European leg of the tour included Athens, Barcelona, Budapest, Vienna, Prague,

Copenhagen, Stockholm and Helsinki. Without exception Baker charmed and delighted audiences in all these European capitals. Then it was off to South America, visiting six different countries and ending with triumphant runs in São Paulo and Rio de Janeiro.

As she travelled throughout all these diverse and different places she was struck how not one of them seemed to have the culture of virulent racism that was so prevalent in her own country. This wide experience of so many cultures provoked within Baker the early stirrings of her ideas and thoughts about what she would come to call 'the brotherhood of man'. This conviction, which would grow and develop and become the central mission of her life, saw humanity as one immense family that would eventually mature and evolve into a world community where the colour of a person's skin was of no importance. Increasingly the meaning of her existence would become this quest for racial harmony, particularly in the country of her birth.

After her world tour's Brazilian finale, Baker and Abatino boarded the SS *Lutetia* in Rio for the return journey to France and on the long voyage home she agreed to perform in the ship's saloon. Every evening a middle-aged, balding man wearing thick horn-rimmed spectacles sat in the front row, enthralled by Baker's performance. Finally, he introduced himself as Le Corbusier, the world-famous Swiss architect who was returning from a lecture tour of South America. He was a great fan of American jazz and asked if he could draw her. Despite Abatino's presence, a shipboard romance ensued, though Baker kept this infatuation brief. She knew only too well how much she owed Abatino: he had shaped her, honed her and was committed to perfecting every element of her unique personality.

As soon as they were back in France, Abatino signed a contract for Baker to star in the autumn revue at the Casino de Paris. The show *Paris qui Remue* was another resounding hit. The city's authorities decided to organise a celebration of the racial diversity of French colonial culture. Baker was deeply gratified when she was elected 'Queen of the Colonies' by the Colonial Exhibition Committee. This great honour conferred on her by the French authorities made her consider that she should renounce her US citizenship and become a French national because of the generosity of her adopted country, who only saw the colour of her skin as a significant element of her natural beauty.

This disappointment in the US reached a bitter climax in 1936 when Abatino persuaded a reluctant Baker that she should finally return to America after a ten-year absence. The visit got off to an ignominious start when they arrived at New York's Hotel St Moritz where Abatino had booked two large penthouse suites. As soon as the manager saw the colour of Baker's skin, he told them that they could stay at the hotel on the strict understanding that they never entered the hotel's main lobby and must always use the service entrance at the rear of the hotel, as they had many guests from the southern states, who would not be able to accept this kind of indignity.

Baker appeared in a new production of *Ziegfeld Follies* at the Winter Garden Theatre in a cast that included Fanny Brice, Bob Hope and Eve Arden, who all received glowing reviews. Yet Baker's performance was slated by the critics with critical barbs which included 'Miss Baker has a dwarf-like voice' that reminded the reviewer of 'a cracked bell with a padded clapper'. Another critic pronounced that 'although she might appeal to jaded Europeans, to Manhattan theatre-goers she was just a buck-toothed young Negro woman, whose dancing and singing might be topped practically anywhere outside Paris' while a third stated that: 'Miss Baker has refined her art until there is nothing left of it.' It was as if the high-minded, arrogant New York critics resented Baker's global success.

Inevitably Baker was humiliated and she turned her disappointment into an angry attack onto Abatino, insisting that he had chosen completely the wrong vehicle to showcase her talents. Devastated by her aggressive onslaughts, Abatino took the next liner back to France, while Baker went onto St Louis for a reunion with her family. During the voyage home he became ill and soon after his arrival back in Paris he was diagnosed with advanced cancer of the kidneys and died several months later.

With Abatino's death Baker would never again find another man so completely committed to her prosperity and welfare. He had put up with her regular infidelities and her taunting criticisms of him when things didn't go smoothly but without him, she felt lost and lonely. Back in Paris, she threw herself into her work where Paul Derval of the Folies Bergère booked her for another production, after which the leading Parisian nightclub La Frontenac presented her for a long run and there was another Colonial Exposition.

Then in the spring of 1937 she met Jean Lion, a rich, blond aristocrat, with a definite flair for business. At only twenty-seven he owned and managed Jean Lion and Company, which traded in sugar and other commodities on the international markets. Baker was besotted with Jean Lion. Her friend Jacqueline Stone said: 'She was in love with him to the point of craziness. She had to have that man and she was willing to do anything to get him.' Within a few months the couple were married. Baker now longed to have children but sadly, after two years, she had a miscarriage and the marriage then started to collapse. Jean Lion was constantly absent, travelling on business and by spring of 1940 they had divorced. Two months later the Germans invaded France and Baker's life changed forever.

The powerful sense of meaning and purpose with which Baker always filled her life created the capacity to formulate ambitions and aspirations that fell into three distinct phases of contrasting adult experience. The first of these periods was devoted to refining a unique performing style with its particular erotic emphasis, a talent that she used to escape from the cruelty and racial abuse that had traumatised her childhood and adolescence. She did this by absconding to France where racial discrimination held little sway and where her particular theatrical gift thrust her into the spotlight of fame and celebrity. In the second of these phases she was determined to repay her adopted country for all it had done for her by serving the French cause when Nazi Germany invaded France. From 1940 until 1945 this engaged all her energy, time and strength, and yet the trauma of the war and a grave illness, which almost killed her, forced her into a severe midlife crisis that radically transformed the direction of her life. During a third and final phase of her life she stopped prioritising her theatrical career and pursued two new twin obsessions: leading the civil rights movement in the country of her birth and the adoption and upbringing of over a dozen abandoned young children from varied ethnicities that she came to call her 'rainbow tribe'.

When Germany invaded France in May 1940 and overran its capital without a shot being fired on 13 June, Baker knew only too well what Paris was in for. She so easily remembered how when she had performed in Berlin, Nazi stormtroopers had thrown ammonia bombs at her as they ranted 'go back to Africa'. It was after that experience when she became a member of the International League against Racism and Anti-Semitism.

In the spring of 1938 Baker had been holidaying in the Dordogne when she came across a beguiling fifteenth-century chateau called Château des Milandes. When she heard that the owner was looking to rent the property she immediately signed a long lease on what would become her home until she was forced to sell the property in 1969 due to bankruptcy. As the Germans closed in on Paris, Baker took her maid, Paulette, and an assortment of pets and drove her packed sedan in a southerly direction, eventually reaching Les Milandes where she was to take refuge for the next six months.

She had already been recruited into the French military intelligence when she had entertained the troops manning the Maginot line with Maurice Chevalier. During these performances her ardent patriotism had come to the notice of Jacques Abtey, a young intelligence officer who had been instructed to recruit any notable personalities who might prove useful to French army intelligence. Baker was immediately attracted to the handsome, dashing young captain and was only too pleased to help her adopted country. As a neutral American she was able to make regular visits to the Japanese and Italian embassies where she regularly attended diplomatic receptions, occasions that gave her an opportunity to gather useful information about likely German intentions.

After her flight to des Milandes she discovered that Jacques Abtey was hiding nearby and she invited him to stay with her at Les Milandes, an altogether more secure refuge. Throughout that summer she and Abtey helped members of the Free French army escape to Spain. French intelligence now regarded Jacques and Baker as a formidable unit and they were sent together on intelligence-gathering trips to Marseilles, Spain, Portugal and eventually Vichy-held French Morocco. Jacques pretended to be Baker's manager as she appeared on stage in all these countries, but on these trips the espionage duo gathered essential information that helped the Allied cause as they prepared for the North African landings.

She and Jacques inevitably became lovers which resulted in a pregnancy. In a Casablanca hospital, Baker gave birth to a stillborn baby and then fell desperately ill. Despite an emergency hysterectomy her condition became even worse and for the next six months – from December 1941 until June 1942 – Baker fought for her life, nearly dying from peritonitis and then blood poisoning. Rumours of her condition circulated until press reports appeared saying Baker was dead.

As Matthew Pratt Guterl says in his book *Josephine Baker and the Rainbow Tribe*: 'She needed to die before she could be reborn.' What died in that Casablanca hospital was that ego-driven, attention-seeking compulsion that drove her celebrity and her seductive sexual allure with its blatant eroticism that she had sold to French impresarios who promoted her vaudeville carnality. In its place a new vision of life emerged, a new sense of meaning and purpose that Pratt Guerl calls 'multiracial cosmopolitanism', or what Baker would come to call 'the brotherhood of man'.

Yet before she returned to the country of her birth to undertake the work she now had to do, she had to first help her beloved adopted country in its ongoing fight against Nazi tyranny. In 1943, now fully recovered, she continued her work for the Free French army intelligence as well as entertaining Allied troops in North Africa. This included intelligence-gathering visits to Cairo and Beirut, with regular concerts for Allied soldiers. Her work continued in Jerusalem, Corsica, Sardinia and Italy where she raised over 3 million francs for the Free French forces. Finally, after the liberation in France, she returned to Paris in 1944 wearing a French military uniform complete with gold epaulettes. For her invaluable intelligence work, for her numerous concerts entertaining Allied troops and for the very considerable amounts of money she raised for the French cause, she was awarded the Resistance Medal, the Croix de Guerre and the Chevalier of the Légion d'honneur, presented to her by General Charles de Gaulle himself. And finally in May 2021 Baker was moved from the Monaco cemetery where she was initially buried to the Panthéon in Paris.

*

As hostilities came to a close in 1945 Baker saw the war as a valiant attempt to rid the world of racism, fascism and xenophobia and yet as she performed for American troops she had witnessed how the pestilence of racism was still deeply embedded in the US military. By 1942 there were 500,000 Black Americans in the army, but only 5 percent in combat units. Black soldiers were primarily used in construction units and as mess attendants and stewards. Baker was appalled that when performing for the American army units white soldiers took the front seats while Black soldiers were only allowed to stand at the back of the audience and while fraternising with the troops she said that she never met a single Black officer. During her performances she would increasingly insist that Black soldiers were seated at the front and after the show she would immediately make her way across to the Black sections of the audience and introduce herself.

On returning to des Milandes she began to consider turning her chateau and its estate into a multicultural conference centre that was committed to her vision of racial diversity. However des Milandes was in a dilapidated state of chronic disrepair. She and her new husband, band-leader Jo Bouillon, decided to take up the American impresario Ned Schnyzler's lucrative offer of ten thousand dollars plus expenses per week for a three-month tour of America in the spring of 1951 with concerts in San Francisco, Los Angeles, Las Vegas, Chicago, Miami and New York. Raising funds to refurbish and redevelop des Milandes was an essential priority and so Baker and Bouillon signed the contract, although

Baker insisted on a number of clauses to ensure that all her concerts would permit integrated audiences. If curfews or segregation orders were in place, these had to be suspended and all the stage crews had to have both Black and white personnel. She also refused to perform in front of all-Black audiences. Although these anti-racist requirements were reported unfavourably in many Southern newspapers she succeeded in her groundbreaking demands and the sell-out tour made her a fortune. Her single-handed personal civil rights crusade made such an impact that a few weeks after the tour the National Association for the Advancement of Coloured People (NAACP), the leading civil rights movement of the day, organised a 'Josephine Baker Celebration Day' which involved parades, performances, street parties and numerous tributes to this first great champion of de-segregation in a number of American cities. And the NAACP awarded Baker their 'Outstanding Woman of the Year Award'.

After the tour was over she returned to St Louis to be reunited with her family. She immediately invited her mother, brother Richard, sister Margaret and the younger members of the family to come back with her to des Milandes to help her turn the chateau into the thriving home of multiculturalism that she longed for.

Baker and Jo Bouillon finally arrived back in Paris just in time for her to speak out at the International League Against Racism and Anti-Semitism. Returning to des Milandes she threw all her energy for the next few years into the regeneration of her chateau and in 1954 she adopted Jean-Claude, the first of her children. A few months earlier *Le Monde* reported that Baker was about to become 'the mother of a family of all colours', describing her as 'an ardent proselyte of the antiracial struggle' in her bid to create her 'rainbow tribe'. During the next decade, eleven further abandoned children would arrive to join the tribe from nine different countries and ethnicities. The first international event that Baker hosted at des Milandes was the 'Conference Anti-Raciste' in January 1957. After the success of the conference she was determined to establish 'The College of Universal Brotherhood' at the chateau and to finance this venture she set up a foundation through which she channelled all her performance fees.

In the mid-fifties she was a lone voice amongst theatrical celebrities advocating this revolution in civil rights, desegregation and multiculturalism. The American activists of the 1960s were yet to find their voice. Then in 1962 and early 1963 plans were being made to arrange a march on Washington by a coalition of civil rights groups to demand that congress pass a civil rights bill banning segregation and other such human rights violations. One of the organisers was the Black activist Jack Jordan who was determined to invite Baker to take part in this historic occasion, but her US visa had been revoked because of accusatory FBI reports that she was a communist. With Attorney General Robert Kennedy's help her visa was renewed and on 28 August 1963 Baker joined 200,000 protestors on the historic march on Washington, dressed in her French military uniform, complete with all her decorations. The finale of this great gathering was Martin Luther's 'I have a dream' speech, but before this Baker was asked if she would address the enormous crowd. She came forward, completely unprepared, to the sound of resounding cheers and applause and launched into a spontaneous informal speech, unaided by notes or text. Her address included the following words:

> I have walked into the palaces of kings and queens and into the houses of presidents. But I could not walk into a hotel in America and get a cup of coffee and that makes me mad. And when I get mad I open my big mouth. And then look out 'cause when Josephine opens her mouth they hear it all over the world.

Josephine Baker died twelve years later. During the last decade of her life she struggled to keep her Milandes project financially solvent. Exhausting herself she gave performance after performance in Europe and America to pay her accumulating debts, but in 1969 she was ignominiously evicted. She moved to more modest accommodation in Paris and in order to clear her remaining debts and to continue to financially support her twelve children she went on performing in Paris and in America. In June 1973 she appeared in four final concerts in New York's Carnegie Hall and each night the cheers and applause that followed the performance seemed endless. The reviews were ecstatic. John Wilson of the *New York Times* wrote: 'there is about her something of the aura that Duke Ellington has. They both have the style and wit and a confident knowledge of who they are. It stems from basics – Miss Baker moves the way Ellington plays.'

I think John Wilson's review sums up perfectly the mature Josephine Baker. She had such a confident understanding of who she was – such self-awareness, such certainty, such poise. And in this certainly lay an integrity, a compassion and an infectious life-enhancing joy that encouraged and inspired almost everyone she met. No wonder when she died in April 1975 the streets of Paris were filled with cheering crowds as her funeral cortege made its way to the church of La Madeleine, to the sound of a twenty-one-gun salute, making her the only American woman ever to have received such an honour.

In 1977, two years after she died, her last husband – Jo Bouillon – published Baker's memoirs. As if speaking from beyond the grave she described the very mission of her existence:

> My life, like that of so many others, has been a constant struggle. On one side of the scales I've placed my worldwide reputation as an artist and on the other side human justice. The choice was easy for me because I've always placed justice above materialism.

This quest for 'justice' became the central driving force, the quintessential meaning and purpose of her life during her last twenty-seven years.

In stark contrast to Josephine Baker's theatrical world I would like to end these thoughts on our need for and reliance on a sense of meaning by considering the extreme case of the psychoanalyst Viktor Frankl, who avoided a descent into futility during the months he endured while incarcerated in Auschwitz. This harrowing experience provided the compelling content of his book *Man's Search for Meaning*.

Viktor Frankl was born in Vienna in 1905 to Jewish parents. As a precocious teenager he became interested in psychology and sent a letter to Sigmund Freud, who replied with a thoughtful, sympathetic response. The correspondence continued for several years and as a result Viktor enrolled as a medical student in 1923 at Vienna University, where he specialised in neurology and psychiatry. After graduating he organised youth counselling centres, funded by the city of Vienna, due to the large number of teenage suicides. He soon began his psychotherapeutic practice and by the late 1930s, he was head of neurology at the Rothschild Hospital in Vienna where, despite the Nazi's Anschluss, he continued to work until 1942 when he and his entire family were arrested and sent to Theresienstadt. Here his father soon died of starvation and pneumonia. In 1944, aged thirty-nine, Viktor and his mother, wife and brother were sent to Auschwitz. Frankl came to regard this agonising experience as a developmental opportunity which forged not only an exceptional individual but also a new brand of psychoanalysis which he called Logotherapy. He was later to write of his experience in Auschwitz: 'I could see beyond the misery of the situation and thus turned an apparently meaningless suffering into a genuine human achievement. I am convinced that, in the final analysis, there is no situation that does not contain within it a seed of a meaning.'

While in the concentration camps, Viktor conducted a form of psychotherapy on individuals who appeared to be close to committing suicide which he called 'life-saving procedure'. In *Man's Search for Meaning* he writes about two cases where both men talked repeatedly of their intention to end their own lives, because they had nothing to live for. Viktor succeeded in preventing them from committing suicide by 'getting them to realise that life was still expecting something from them; that something in the future was expected of them'. One of these men had a child he adored, who was waiting for his father in the safety of another country. Viktor convinced the man that his deep love for his son gave meaning to his life, despite the depth of his suffering, and his life's mission was somehow to stay alive so he could be reunited with his adored son, to spare his child the trauma of losing his father. This suggestion saved the man from committing suicide.

The second of these men, who seemed to have lost all hope, was a scientist who had written a series of books, but an important aspect of his work remained incomplete and could not be completed by anyone else. Viktor managed to persuade this individual that despite the horrors of his current existence, he had a duty to stay alive so he could eventually return home to finish this work.

From time to time, Viktor used to conduct group therapy sessions and after one particularly bad day he gave a significant impromptu lecture. Earlier that morning it was announced that someone was guilty of sabotage, punishable by immediate execution. Unless the person responsible was given up, the whole camp would be punished with a day's starvation. That evening the camp authorities not only deprived the inmates of food but also light, when all the electric lights were turned off. Viktor's senior block warden, also an inmate, was a wise man and in the dark gave a talk, in an attempt to improve the depressed mood in the hut. Having

finished he then turned to Viktor and asked him to say something to sustain them. Once underway Viktor insisted that
'whoever was still alive had reason for hope. Health, family,
happiness, professional abilities, fortune, position in society
– all these things could be achieved again or restored'. He
quoted Nietzsche: 'That which does not kill me makes me
stronger.'

He then went on to say even in these terrible circumstances, human life never ceases to have meaning. He wrote
of that evening: 'I asked the poor creatures who listened
to me attentively in the darkness of the hut to face up to
the seriousness of our position. They must not lose hope
but should keep up their courage in the certainty that our
shared struggle had dignity and meaning.' It appears that
with these words Viktor managed with the intimacy of their
shared affliction to soothe the battered souls of his fellow
inmates. His comforting words offered hope and a possible
final release from their suffering. He facilitated a solidarity
among his fellow victims, which despite everything, invigor-
ated their will to survive – to endure, to persevere, to survive
and eventually look forward to a new life, beyond the horrors of the camp.

While in Auschwitz, Viktor was involved in one of the
most unusual psychotherapeutic relationships that I have
ever come across. The daily work parties were led by Kapos
who were often the most cruel and sadistic of the camp's
warders. But Viktor's Kapo seemed particularly drawn to
him, as he had serious difficulties in his marriage and a range
of other emotional troubles. Having heard that Viktor was
a psychologist he started to confide in him and on the long

daily marches to and from the worksite, he positioned Viktor alongside him so he could benefit from his psychotherapeutic advice. As a payment for Viktor's services, the Kapo gave Viktor extra food and he was given the less strenuous, easiest tasks on the worksite. Viktor had no doubt that this psychotherapeutic work with his Kapo saved his life.

It is quite clear that Viktor's extraordinary optimism and hope, and his ability to find a sense of purpose in the prisoners' shared misery, sustained and kept alive many of the camp's inmates, who encountered him. His ability to use his experience as a victim of the Holocaust is profoundly inspiring, particularly for anyone suffering insuperable difficulties in their lives. He often quoted another of Nietzsche's famous maxims: 'He who has a why to live for can bear almost any how.'

Melanie Klein's Theory of Ambivalence
and The Depressive Position
(Melanie Klein, Emma Jung, Cary Grant)

A s we have seen, Freud's opening gambit – as he launched his psychoanalytic enterprise to inaugurate the new century in 1900 – was his monumental *The Interpretation of Dreams*, a pioneering text which went well beyond the realm of the subject of its title. A superfluity of principles and concepts that he had been furtively formulating in the previous decade were now paraded onto the public stage.

This montage of psychotherapeutic theory included the first proclamation of 'the Oedipus complex', which was to have such purchase on his future disciples in the century to come. In his play *Oedipus Rex* of 429 BC Sophocles describes how his hero Oedipus inadvertently kills his father Laius and then marries his mother Jocasta. Freud takes this ancient drama and insists that early in life the male infant is so intoxicated by his mother, while at the same time so threatened by the predatory presence of his father, that he wishes to kill this unwanted male rival.

While so much of Freudian theory is prescient and forward-looking, the Oedipus complex feels anchored in the 2000-year patriarchy of phallocentric male dominance which implicitly had such an impact on his legions of female patients. This very considerable gender imbalance, which is so blatantly apparent in Freud's initial formulation, was obviously a lapse which he felt needed addressing. He therefore suggested in his 1908 paper 'On Sexual Theories of Children' that parallel to the infant male's desire to be erotically entwined with his mother was the infant female's anxiety upon realising that she suffered from a humiliating genital deficiency, which Freud described as 'penis envy'.

Freud goes on to suggest that the baby girl feels resentment towards her mother, who has neglected to provide her with a penis, and senses that the mother is somehow incomplete when compared with the father, which leads to a traumatic sense of inferiority. This phallocentric confirmation of the age-old patriarchy of Western culture held sway in the opening decades of psychoanalysis's development, which was dominated by male practitioners, but in the years following the First World War a group of exceptional women, led by Karen Horney, Helene Deutsch and Melanie Klein, criticised Freud's formulation of both the Oedipus complex and penis envy and suggested a very different sequence of early infantile experience, which configured itself almost entirely around the mother, while paying almost no attention to the father.

Of these various women Melanie Klein stands out as the most influential and significant theorist who contributed so much to the ongoing debate regarding the emotional development of children and the subsequent impact of early infantile experience on adult psychology.

Near the end of her distinguished career Klein wrote a paper called 'Some Reflections on the Oresteia' which was published three years after her death, in 1963, and was, in essence, a comprehensive summary of her psychoanalytic beliefs. Following Freud's example of using Sophocles'

Oedipus Rex to argue the case for a father-centred account of infantile emotional development, Klein chooses Aeschylus's drama concerning Electra's murderous hatred for her mother in *The Oresteia* to position early child psychology around the infant's polarised feelings of both love and hate for the mother. This deflected almost all attention away from the father onto the tiny child's traumatic confusion between their love and hate for their mother which has all but superseded Freud's Oedipus complex and his subsequent consolation prize of penis envy as the primary emotional challenge of our earliest years.

Melanie Klein's work and life exemplifies one of the fiercest and most exacting polarities that humans have to endure: the duality of both love and hate that is almost always aroused in children's early experience of their mother, a polarity between two extreme emotions that becomes a permanent challenge throughout our lives.

In her pamphlet published for a lay audience in the year of her death entitled 'Our Adult World and its Roots in Infancy' (1959), Melanie Klein gives a clear and simple account of her theories, shorn of the convoluted language that is so often a feature of psychoanalytic theory.

> I have formed the view that love and hate towards the mother are bound up with the very young infant's capacity to project all his or her emotions onto their mother, thereby making her into a good as well as dangerous object.

Unlike Freud, Klein spent many hours (using her play technique therapy) in the company of infants, observing their states of what she described as 'persecutory anxiety'. She watched as they displayed a succession of painful emotions – 'states of rage, lack of interest in their surroundings, incapacity to bear frustration and expressions of sadness'. Comparing these early emotional expressions to those displays of feeling conveyed by her adult patients, she observed the manner in which the mental life in all individuals is crucially influenced by their earliest environments and inevitably by their relationship with their mothers, who are the architects of their first emotional experience, which becomes the primary root of their developing psychology.

In the earliest stages of their relationship the mother conveys her love and understanding by the manner in which she handles her baby. But this love and understanding will inevitably never provide permanent protection against all the baby's frustration, discomfort and pain, as the mother will frequently be distracted by her own needs and the needs of other family members. Yet as the infant experiences all emotional responses through the channel of the maternal relationship, the mother will be seen as the originator of the entire range of the infant's conflicting emotions. Therefore the mother will be perceived by the tiny child as the source of all contentment and discomfort, of all pain and pleasure, of all anxiety and repose, of all harmony and calamity. As the infant encounters all those conflicting dualities the emotions felt towards the mother will range from intense love to violent hatred.

I had one client whose first baby received the highest level of maternal love and attention and as a result was a very happy and contented infant throughout her first eighteen months. Then my client became pregnant again and her baby suddenly became much more irascible and unsettled. Although there was no outward evidence of this important event, the client felt quite sure that her baby's sudden change of mood was ignited by the fact that a very significant change in the family's constellation was about to take place and her baby sensed this would have an impact on her relationship with her mother. It was as if she and her firstborn had such a well-attuned relationship that her baby was picking up the most subtle modulation in her mother, now that her thoughts were beginning to consider her future second child and were no longer completely absorbed by her toddler, a distraction in maternal attention that was making her decidedly unsettled.

In such cases, the mother − being the monopolising presence in the baby's existence − then becomes the intense focus of its agonising ambivalence and the object of the tiny child's two conflicting primary emotions of love and hate, generating the most troubling polarity of uncertainty, confusion, equivocation and anxiety.

Klein stresses how this ambivalence − this polarity between these two primary emotions − confronts us all with the ultimate psychological challenge of our lives, intimating that this is the principal aim of psychological maturation: to accept, and in this acceptance, to resolve this polarity that we first encounter in our earliest years. She declares that to reach this resolution is to achieve what she calls 'the depressive position', a state of psychological maturity which can provide us with a peace of mind and a sense of wellbeing that no longer suffers the discomfort of this most chaffing tension between love and hate.

Once we are parents, we will inevitably experience both the love and hate that our children feel towards us. Since becoming a parent myself I'm sure that the greatest gift we can give our children is to allow them to express negative emotion, particularly if it is directed towards us as a parent. These eruptions of hatred towards us arise from the ambivalence with which they regard us, an understandable confusion that – as Klein makes clear – has been present from the earliest months of their lives. Such displays of hatred, expressed in a great plume of anger, are a fundamental aspect of our repertoire of emotions and if they are blocked, prohibited and covered with shame they will be repressed deep in our children's unconscious, where they will fester and become a toxic presence, fermenting into a loathing of the parent who has so disastrously misunderstood their child's need to express this hatred. Such vehement explosions of rage and hatred, once expressed, must be met not only by this parental allowance but also by a well-judged boundary, to prevent the rage becoming a kind of permanent collateral damage to the emotional economy of the family. And more often than not, as the hatred and rage abate, the allowance of these negative emotions will result in a swing back to expressions of love and affection.

So many of my clients start their therapy by shamefully admitting a level of hatred they feel towards their parents, which was never allowed or expressed and has been repressed into their unconscious where it has morphed into a depressive tendency that has become a disabling liability in their life. The unearthing of this hatred and the shedding of the shame it engenders is so often the initial task of the therapy, which invariably relieves the depression. Once this is achieved, the rekindling of some kind of affection towards the parent can begin and the aim of therapy then becomes to reach an acceptance of the ambivalence, acceptance that we will both hate and love our parents, our life-partners, our children and our closest friends. In this way the opposite of love is not hate: the opposite of love is indifference. Love and hate are a duality that we must embrace as a whole.

In their book *Faces in a Cloud: Intersubjectivity in Personality Theory* Robert Stolorow and George Atwood present their proposition that the leading pioneers of the psychoanalytic movement produce theories and concepts which emerge from their own psychobiographies. They suggest that Freud and Jung and other such luminaries chose models of psychological development and emotional trauma which describe their own early traumatic experiences. Unconsciously, almost inadvertently, they construct complex and often labyrinthine descriptions of psychological states of being which match their own early woundings.

If Stolorow and Atwood are right, and I find their thesis both eloquent and compelling, did Klein's experience of being mothered, and her experience of being a mother, result in the particular nuances and modelling of her own theories? Indeed is Klein's life an excellent case study that exemplifies the cogency and credibility of her influential ideas?

Melanie Klein was born in 1882, the fourth and youngest child of Moriz and Libussa Reizes, who lived in one of the poorest quarters of Vienna. Moriz was twenty years older than his young wife and was employed as a dental assistant, earning insufficient income to support his family, which forced Libussa to open a shop in which she sold a range of products, including live reptiles, an occupation she felt was way beneath her dignity. But then Moriz won a substantial amount of money in the National Lottery, bought a dental practice and moved his family to a more respectable suburb of Vienna.

Melanie displayed a high intelligence and talent at school and at the age of sixteen was enrolled in the Vienna Gymnasium, hoping for a career in medicine. Although she longed for her father's attention, he always remained a distant figure who showed a marked preference for his eldest child Emilie. However, her father's lack of interest was compensated by her mother's obsessive focus on her youngest child.

If we look at the various accounts of Klein's mother, the larger-than-life figure of Libussa Reizes, we are confronted by a bewildering array of contradictory descriptions. In one account she is described as 'a Slovakian beauty, witty, smart and passionate about learning' and in another 'Melanie remembered her mother as an outstanding beauty and much more alive than her father. Most of all she admired her mother's interest in art, her thirst for knowledge and dedication to learning.' Yet she was also an intrusive overbearing parent, who interfered in every aspect of Melanie's life. In her authoritative biography of Klein, Phyllis Grosskurth describes Libussa as 'tough and domineering', writing that 'from the envy, aggression and sibling rivalry within her own family, Melanie had abundant material from which to formulate her later theories'. As Melanie grew up, Libussa would instruct her daughter 'whom to see, what to do and what to wear'.

In December 1902, Melanie's much loved elder brother Emmanuel – whose intellectual and artistic prowess greatly influenced her – died of heart failure at the age of twenty-five. Devastated by this tragedy, a grieving Melanie agreed to marry Arthur Klein, a chemical engineering student, who had proposed to her eighteen months earlier. The wedding took place two months after Emmanuel's death, an event that Phyllis Grosskurth describes as 'the first great mistake of her life' since 'she was not in love with Arthur and sensed in him a certain rigid inflexibility and a will as strong as her own'.

Just over a year later her eldest child Melitta was born. In her autobiography Melanie's ambivalence towards her daughter is evident. It is clear she loved Melitta, and yet she writes: 'I threw myself as much as I could into motherhood and interest in my child. But I knew all the time that I was not happy but saw no way out.'

Throughout Melitta's childhood, Melanie suffered from increasing irritability, nervous exhaustion and deepening depression. Her general mood was clearly affected not only by the demands of motherhood but also by the stresses and strains in her troubled marriage to Arthur, made worse when the family in 1908 moved to the small, drab town of Krappitz in remote upper Silesia where Arthur had become the director of a paper mill. A year earlier Melanie had given birth to her son Hans and it was quite clear that the family was now in a state of crisis. In response, Libussa was only too pleased to intervene and she arrived in Krappitz determined to provide some order to her daughter's dysfunctional household.

For the next two-and-a-half years Melanie spent more time away, attempting to find relief from her psychological difficulties, than at home looking after her children with Libussa, who treated her daughter as if she was a permanent invalid. Arthur was encouraged by his mother-in-law to make regular trips to Vienna to attend business conferences and visit his company's headquarters. Invariably he would return home to find that Melanie had been sent off to yet another sanitorium to try to recover from her depression and nervous anxiety. The sheer power of Libussa's control over her daughter's family had a detrimental effect on Melitta, who disliked and distrusted her grandmother, and Libussa responded by making it clear that she preferred Hans to her sulky granddaughter.

Melanie appears to have feared most the possibility of a further pregnancy and Libussa used this anxiety to persuade her daughter to remain apart from Arthur as much as possible. Libussa's strategy of 'divide and rule' worked perfectly and her dominion over the Klein household was complete. She went so far as to tell Melanie that her husband and children were better off without her. Phyllis Grosskurth comments: 'It is a chilling conclusion that Libussa did not want her daughter to be happy, that she did not want her to find fulfilment, that she begrudged her the enjoyments of which she herself was deprived of when she was young.'

The situation improved in 1910, as did Melanie's state of mind, when the family returned to Budapest. And then four years later Melanie experienced a momentous year after she read Freud's *The Interpretation of Dreams*, which had a profound effect on her. Soon after she began psychotherapy with Freud's close friend and collaborator Sándor Ferenczi. As this new phase of her life began, two other pivotal events occurred: the birth of her son Erich and, towards the end of the year, the unexpected death of her mother. In the early months of 1915 this despondent incapacitated woman, who had been oppressed by a dominating mother, who was stuck in a loveless marriage, who was finding her own experiences of being a mother overwhelming, suddenly found her bearings as her therapy with Ferenczi and her continued immersion in Freud's writings began to liberate her from the depressive paralysis that had plagued her adult life.

Ferenczi remained her analyst and mentor for the next five years and quickly became aware that his patient was a talented, creative woman who appeared to have a voracious appetite for Freud's books and papers, which he would regularly recommend to her. As this process gathered pace and her depression lifted, she felt an unfamiliar freedom now that the mother – whom she had both loved and hated – could no longer interfere with her life. Ferenczi, helped by Freud's close colleague Otto Rank, had created the Hungarian Psychoanalytic Society in 1913. Regular meetings were held in the cafés and coffee houses of Budapest to discuss Freud's theories and Melanie was invited to these gatherings. Of her mentor she wrote: 'During my analysis with Ferenczi he drew my attention to my great gift for understanding children and my interest in them and he very much encouraged my idea of devoting myself to analysis, particularly child analysis.'

Encouraged further by Ferenczi she wrote her first psychoanalytic paper, based on a case study involving a four-year-old, who was in fact her son Erich, although this anomaly remained a secret. After her formal entry into the psychoanalytic profession, she separated permanently from her husband Arthur, who then went to live in Sweden. Soon after these two events, Ferenczi wrote to Freud informing him of his brilliant young patient, who had such an insightful aptitude for treating disturbed children. Until her death, Libussa had often been the primary carer for her three grandchildren but now – as if to compensate for her previous neglect – Melanie Klein took an intense interest in her children's development.

In the same fashion that Freud analysed his patients' dreams, Klein analysed children's play, providing her child clients with an array of toys. She noticed how these young children projected strong feelings onto certain toys, which seemed to represent siblings, parents, child peers or indeed themselves. As they expressed anger and dislike or conversely love and affection for certain toys, their anxiety and other neurotic symptoms would subside and as the conscious expression of these strong feelings were tolerated and allowed by her, the surrogate parent, shameful feelings felt by the child could be released, easing their anxiety.

In the years following the First World War Klein published a series of papers describing both her techniques and findings. Then, in September 1920, she attended the first post-war international psychoanalytic congress held in The Hague. Here she met her second great mentor, Karl Abraham, the founder of the Berlin Analytic Society and Institute, who was regarded by many as Freud's most stalwart and brilliant colleague. Attracted by this charismatic figure, a number of eminent pioneering psychoanalysts moved to Berlin: Hans Sach from Vienna, Alix Strachey and Edward Glover from London and two talented women analysts Karen Horney and Helene Deutsch from Göttingen and Vienna.

Shortly after she met Karl Abraham at the Hague conference in 1920, Klein moved to Berlin where she was made an associate member of the Berlin Psychoanalytic Society. The Hungarian analyst Michael Balint, a fellow member of the Society, describes Klein's rather awkward presentations during Berlin Society meetings:

> She already was an analyst of repute even though she still had an uphill fight being the only child analyst in the midst of a very 'learned' German society. Time and again she brought her clinical material, using very naïve expressions of the nursery used by her child patients, which often caused the learned and reluctant audience embarrassment, incredulity and even sardonic laughter.

However, the English contingent of the Berlin Society, led by Edward Glover, Sylvia Payne and Ella Sharpe, warmed to this eccentric woman with her colourful presentational style and idiosyncratic theories regarding early childhood development. From now on, Klein would always polarise her colleagues. She was destined to make many enemies who hated her dominating, rhetorical style, and yet she would always attract devoted followers who found her charismatic, charming and a woman of high originality and considerable capacity. It was as if in her very manner and personality she attracted both love and hate, the two primary constituent elements of her most significant theoretical achievement – her 'depressive position'.

Klein had become a familiar and striking figure at the congress in Berlin in 1922 and in Salzburg in 1924, where she gave her first congress paper, 'The Technique of the Analysis of Young Children', to a large and enthusiastic audience. After this success in Salzburg she was invited by the leading British analyst James Strachey (Lytton Strachey's brother) to give a series of lectures to the British Institute of Psychoanalysis during the summer of 1925, which were all warmly received. After the death of Karl Abraham in December 1925, and when her ideas were being met with more and more opposition in Berlin, Klein moved to England where she would spend the rest of her life and where she was destined to make an indelible impact on the development of psychoanalysis. Indeed, the leading historian of the British psychoanalytic movement, Richard Wollheim, stated Klein had more influence on the entire psychoanalytic movement than anybody else, apart from Freud himself. And yet despite her notable success and the high reputation of her theories and concepts, she continued to have problems in her family life. She found being a mother as difficult as her experience of being a daughter, as she always managed to constellate in her relations with her children the double bind of both love and hate. Particularly painful was her relationship with Melitta, her eldest child.

In 1928 Melitta joined her mother in London, having graduated with distinction from Berlin University. For several years mother and daughter lived together in relative harmony until, during Melitta's training to become an analyst herself, she started therapy with Edward Glover, with devastating consequences. Presumably in the early sessions of their work together Melitta was empowered by the strong paternal transference she projected onto the commanding presence of Edward Glover, who was quite unlike her own ineffectual and disinterested father. With this idealised father figure eagerly listening to her stories of her dysfunctional family and her mother's state of almost permanent emotional collapse, Edward Glover no doubt began to form a very different view of Klein and clearly encouraged Melitta to vigorously separate from her mother's dominating presence. In the summer of 1934 Melitta wrote a letter to her mother declaring her independence. She insisted that throughout her adult life she had been neurotically dependent upon her mother and that from now on their relationship had to be drastically different and if they were to maintain any semblance of a friendship Klein had to regard her daughter as a colleague rather than a dependent child. She ended her letter: 'I am now grown up and must be independent. I must be allowed to have interests, friends, feelings and thoughts which are different or even contrary to yours.' It was the letter that Klein should have sent Libussa but was never brave enough to write.

Yet this proclamation of Melitta's independence now turned into something altogether more malevolent. At meeting after meeting of the British Society, Edward Glover and Melitta began to openly attack her mother. Glover's relationship with Melitta went way beyond that of therapist and patient. His admiration for Klein entirely evaporated as he listened to Melitta's accounts of her maternal inadequacies and both Glover and Melitta's high regard and love for her now swung in an extreme polarisation to expressions of enmity and hatred. Members of the Society watched in horror and embarrassment as Melitta and Glover continued their vendetta of loathing towards the most revered member of their organisation. As Melitta mounted onslaught after onslaught, Klein maintained a dignified silence, leaving her supporters Joan Riviere, Susan Isaacs and Paula Heimann to defend her. Ernest Jones was particularly distressed at this civil war which had suddenly erupted in the Society and suggested that Melitta and her husband Walter should move to America, but to no avail. Glover and Melitta would be seen holding hands at meetings and at conferences and there was a general feeling that Glover now saw Melitta as the daughter he had always hoped for.

Melitta's hatred for her mother peaked when her brother Hans died in a climbing accident in the Tatra Mountains and Klein was so distressed by this tragedy that she was unable to travel to Budapest to attend her son's funeral. Yet Melitta was merciless. She insisted on telling all those who would listen that her brother had actually committed suicide due to his deep depression as a result of his mother's neglect throughout his childhood.

After Hans's death, Klein's work was monopolised by examinations of loss, grief and loneliness – emotional experiences that now filled her life. Yet somehow she managed to sublimate her suffering into both her theoretical and clinical work in a manner which allowed her to come to terms with her own bereavement, anguish and disappointment.

She used these insights to transform such misfortune into a process of development which produced a rare level of emotional maturity, psychological repose and a series of books and papers on these subjects that are revered to this day.

Throughout the rest of her life, Melitta's opposition remained implacable and in 1945 she moved permanently to America. Melitta returned to England briefly in July 1953, but mother and daughter never met. Klein's friend and colleague Betty Joseph recalls how during the 1953 London congress she and Klein were sitting on a bench outside Bedford College and Melitta walked by, yet mother and daughter pretended not to notice one another, which visibly upset Klein. They were never reconciled, although a photograph of Melitta remained on Klein's bedside table until she died. Perhaps from Klein's point of view, hate had not completely won the day.

In her great redemptive paper 'Love, Guilt and Reparation', Klein maintains that both love and hate are an inevitable polarised reality in our psyche. As we have seen, this is because in infancy our first experience of love, towards our mother, becomes fused with our first expression of hatred, as we feel certain that our mother is the source of all discomfort and pain. We take the reality of this polarisation, with all its painful ambiguity, from our earliest years into our childhood, adolescence and eventually into adult life. And yet we can, in our later years, experience a full measure of 'reparation' by finding a way to moderate our frustration, envy and resentment by utilising what Klein describes as 'the innumerable ways of taking in beauty, goodness and love from without'.

By doing this we continuously add to our happy memories and gradually build up a store of values by which we gain a security that cannot be easily shaken, and a contentment which prevents bitterness of feeling. The more true satisfaction we experience, the less do we resent deprivations and the less shall we be swayed by our hatred. Then we are actually capable of accepting love and goodness from others and giving love to others and again receiving more in return.

I believe these words from the conclusion express Klein's inspiring optimism, which is not a naïve idealisation, but a realistic, obtainable hope that the inevitable polarity between love and hate can, through this developing maturity, reach a state of mind when compassion, empathy and humility combine together and place love in an unassailable position above the hectoring voice of hatred. The last line of her perceptive and insightful paper is an aspiration I hope all my clients eventually achieve, when she writes: 'If we have become able, deep in our unconscious minds, to clear our feelings to some extent towards our parents of grievances, and have forgiven them the frustrations we have had to bear, then we can be at peace with ourselves and are able to love others in the true sense of the word.'

I hated and resented my mother throughout much of our long relationship, but I do remember as a small child thinking how beautiful she was and how much I loved her and being terrified that some accident or misfortune might befall her. When I was sent away to boarding school at the age of eight I missed her terribly. Much later, when I was in my twenties, I experienced repeated bouts of depression and in my quest to understand this anguish I found my way to a therapist who offered me a second experience of being mothered. In my many sessions with my surrogate mother I encountered my hatred and anger towards my actual mother. This hatred remained in the ascendancy until old age and infirmity produced, in my mother, a late unexpected tenderness. Her toughness, her intolerance, her harshness faded as a touching vulnerability began to emerge and in her last years she once again became lovable and the hatred in me faded. The sense of Klein's 'reparation' between us changed everything and allowed us an intimacy that I remember being at its most complete when I held her hand as she died.

Most of my clients fall into one of two categories: those in search of a life partner and those who are married or in a long-term relationship, which in almost all cases involves an assortment of issues and tensions which provides significant material in our therapeutic work together.

Often my clients from the first group are in their thirties or forties when they arrive for their initial session with me, complaining that they are unable to sustain a close and committed emotional relationship. Frequently, relatively soon after starting therapy, they meet someone new, fall in love and in a state of bliss announce that the therapy has already worked magnificently and – having met their perfect soulmate – all their problems are solved.

I have watched as time and again the idealised relationship, fuelled by oxytocin, runs its course and then the couple collide with romantic love's nemesis: a state of raw vulnerability, with its feeling of being over-exposed, painfully insecure and unprotected from the likely wound of abandonment. All too often the supposed soulmate suddenly appears unreliable, unpredictable and a dangerous liability to the client's security and prosperity. Petty jealousies, familiar insecurities and other unwanted pernicious feelings coalesce and the once idealised partner loses his or her perfection and becomes a vessel for both love and hate. This is the return of Klein's 'depressive position', the reappearance of that polarisation of love and hate felt towards the mother in the earliest years, an echo of how we – when we are tiny infants – blame the much-loved mother for every infringement to our comfort and happiness.

The romantically attached couple are now faced with three options: they can end their relationship; they can continue to blend and fuse their lives while repressing their negative feelings towards each other; they can express both their love and hate for each other and weather the inescapable confrontations, rows and arguments which will intrude into the harmony of their partnership. The last option at least honours the reality of the challenging duality which sits at the core of their union even though they will have to face the disturbance of the emotional turbulence that will erupt from time to time. This third option would seem to be the most honest, the most mature, but perhaps the most difficult, to assimilate. Klein's depressive position is no more than the acceptance and working through of the polarity of love and hate, in a fashion that tolerates this ambivalence and the inclement emotional weather that it will stir up in every child-parent connection, in every romantic attachment, in every marriage, in every sibling relationship, in every intimate friendship.

However, the majority of my clients are married or in a long-term relationship. I had one client who arrived for sessions in a bid to save a faltering marriage at the age of eighty-eight. Inevitably many people feel that their marriages have lost forward momentum, have become arid and listless and an edge of disappointment seems to affect all aspects of their shared lives. They miss the days before the banalities of day-to-day family routine had cauterised the idealisation that had once marked their relationship.

This ennui and tedium is often the repressed, unexpressed anger of Klein's depressive position and what Klein is asking us to accept is the inevitable fact that the flipside of love is hate and in our culture that regards hate and anger as unacceptable emotions, these primary feelings are repressed and morph into the secondary emotions of boredom and disappointment.

One model or metaphor that my clients find helpful is the comparison between the Greeks' concepts of Eros and Agape. Eros is the erotic life-force, the supercharged ecstasy of being in love, as high-octane oxytocin surges through our neural pathways, illuminating and emblazoning the joys and blessings of life. These elated states are, however, ephemeral: they have a lifespan that is unlikely to survive the drudgery of raising a family. There is also a barely conscience selection process taking place during this courting stage when we are assessing whether the new partner will make a suitable parent for our future children. While Eros is primarily a love that is concerned with the gratification of one's own needs, Agape is a devoted love that is less demanding in its needs, more altruistic and empathetic in the benevolence of its expression. Agape is concerned with the welfare and fulfilment of the beloved, a love that is focused on the partner, rather than on one's own narcissistic needs. A successful long-term relationship which develops into a successful marriage will pass through the initial phase of Eros which in time will morph into a wider plateau of Agape, when neurologically the oxytocin changes into a steady flow of serotonin and dopamine, providing the high levels of contentment that a successful marriage can provide. Parenting becomes the firm foundation of the marriage, its mortar and its ballast, as the love for the children of the marriage is one of the most profound shared experiences an individual can have. Yet to get to that equilibrium, to that calm reassuring embrace of Agape, Klein's depressive position has to be achieved, with its acceptance that love and hate will reside in all our closest, most intimate relationships, particularly in the excessively close proximity of a long marriage.

To examine and explore the nature of Klein's depressive position I want to compare two individuals and their lifetime's experience of love and hate, particularly in their respective marriages. The first of these individuals is Emma Jung and the second is Cary Grant, who was married five times.

Carl Jung was undoubtedly an infuriating man to be married to. In her middle-age, Emma Jung told her close friend Susi Trüb that she came close to divorcing her husband Carl on three different occasions. As we have already seen, one of the most important days in Jung's life was his first meeting with Sigmund Freud on 3 March 1907, when he and Emma were invited to lunch at 19 Bergasse, the Freud family home. But this significant meeting had been hard to arrange as the Jung marriage was under considerable strain and finding agreed dates and suitable travel arrangements for the visit to Vienna took some time. It seems likely that during the four-day visit to the Imperial Capital, encouraged by her sister Gret, Emma had decided to confront her husband with an ultimatum that unless he agreed to three specific conditions, she would seek a divorce. The first of these conditions was her insistence that he leave his job at the Burgholzli Mental Hospital and devote more time and attention to her and his growing family. Secondly, she required a new house in which they could bring up their three children, as their small, cramped flat in the Burgholzli was completely inadequate. And thirdly he had to give up his relationship with his patient Sabrina Spielrein in order to end all the humiliating rumours that he was having a brazen love affair with his young Russian patient, whom he had been treating since the autumn of 1905.

Although it seems that she had intended to deliver her divorce ultimatum during their trip to Vienna, Carl's immediate infatuation with Freud had hijacked the visit as the two men insisted upon spending the entire three days in intense and prolonged conversation, ignoring any family obligations they might have. Yet it seems that a disconsolate Emma, egged on by her sister, did deliver her ultimatum soon after they arrived back in Zürich. Carl, terrified at the possibility of Emma leaving him, agreed immediately to end his time at the Burgholzli and begin a private practice. He also showed enthusiasm at the prospect of finding more suitable accommodation in which to house his family and, most importantly, he promised to end his relationship with Sabina Spielrein.

Carl first met the seventeen-year-old Emma in 1899 and decided there and then that he wished to marry this attractive, intelligent young woman. There is no doubt, judging by the many accounts of their marriage, that Carl deeply loved Emma, but perhaps the fact that she was the daughter of one of Switzerland's richest industrialists added to the persistence of his courtship and they were married in 1903. After their wedding they moved into the apartment in the Burgholzli. Emma thoroughly disliked living right in the centre of the busy mental hospital, which she regarded as a kind of gossip-ridden 'goldfish bowl' and where her husband's flirtatious manner with so many of the female staff and patients fuelled a continual rumour mill. As she wrote to Freud, who had become somewhat of a father figure to her: 'Of course the women are naturally all in love with him.'

Yet when they moved into their newly built, beautiful lakeside villa in Küssnacht, Emma's dissatisfaction appeared to get worse. She had hoped that once Carl had given up his hospital obligations and was running his private therapeutic practice from home they would hopefully spend more time together and as a consequence become closer, but so quickly did Jung's extensive practice develop and so busy was he giving a thriving lecture series at Zürich University – not to mention all the work and travelling involved in his new role as President of the International Psychoanalytic Association – Emma seemed to spend even less time with her husband. In the words of Jung's biographer Deirdre Bair: 'He wanted Emma to be primarily a contented "Hausfrau" who would step out of that role only when he required her considerable charm and intelligence to ease professional situations.'

In her letters to Freud she admitted she was lucky to be married to a man like Jung, but nonetheless she was 'tormented with conflict' because she desperately wanted a position or purpose in life, separate from her husband's charisma and reputation, in which her own intelligence and potential could thrive. She complained to Freud: 'I find I have no friends and all the people who associate with us really only want to see Carl.' She felt she had become a domestic drudge whose only role was to look after her distinguished husband and care for his brood of children, whom he had no time for.

Jung's response to Emma's misery was to become her therapist, a strange suggestion completely unacceptable to modern psychotherapeutic rules and protocol. Once back from his US lecture tour, which he and Freud undertook together in the summer of 1909, he began regular sessions with Emma as if she was just another patient. This did have one favourable consequence in that Emma became interested in the emerging psychotherapeutic literature and studied Freud's work closely. These early beginnings resulted in her becoming a most effective psychotherapist herself and an author of two excellent books entitled *Animus and Anima* and *The Grail Legend*. However what she really wanted to discuss in this odd therapeutic arrangement was the increasing rumours that her husband had once again taken up his affair with Sabina Spielrein, whose diaries of 1909 and 1910 reveal that Jung had indeed resumed the romantic and erotic attachment that Emma inevitably found so painful. Once again thoughts of divorce filled Emma's tormented mind, but then late in 1909 she became pregnant with her fourth child Marianne who was born in September 1910 and the idea of separating from her husband subsided.

Despite Emma's pregnancy and the birth of Marianne, it appears that in the autumn of 1910 Jung had become infatuated with a Dutch doctor called Maria Moltzer who had worked at the Burgholzli and was now in private practice. This crush on Maria Moltzer coinciding with Emma's fourth pregnancy was to be repeated when she became pregnant with their fifth and last child in 1913. It was now that Jung began his most consequential extramarital relationship with Toni Wolff, which immediately cast him into an acute midlife crisis.

It has been repeatedly remarked upon by all his many biographers that whenever the shadow of divorce was raised by Emma, Jung would fall ill and Emma would always nurse him back to full health. And yet his collapse in the autumn of 1913 was so serious and complete that it lasted four years and had the profoundest impact upon both Jung and Emma, which required her to somehow contain and accept both her deep love for her husband and the extreme anger and hatred she felt towards him, when once again he presented her with yet another marital infidelity. How she dealt with the appearance of Toni Wolff in her husband's life is a prime example of Klein's depressive position in that this brave and formidable woman managed to bear this harrowing polarity of both the love and hate that she felt for her husband with all its tormenting ambivalence.

Toni Wolff had become a patient of Jung's in the summer of 1910, soon after her father had died, a trauma that plunged her into a deep depression that went beyond the normal contours of bereavement. Jung was later to tell a friend that from their very first meeting he felt he was linked by a 'golden thread' to Toni. With her new father figure taking such an intense interest in her and showering her with compliments, Toni made a rapid recovery. Jung was later to write that he had at last found a woman with whom he would converse at 'the very deepest level of the psyche' and as soon as Toni's depression lifted, he elevated Toni to the role of his assistant. In 1911 he invited her to the Third International Psychoanalytic Congress in Weimar where he proudly introduced her to Freud as 'a new discovery of mine'. Yet despite these strong feelings he had for Toni he knew that his marriage to Emma was the most important relationship of his life.

Two years after the Weimar conference, Jung had his terminal altercation with Freud and the severance of this central relationship increased his dependence on Toni as his intimate confidante. This conflicted triangulation with these two women tipped him into the lacerating breakdown that now overwhelmed him.

In this misery and despair, with the complete collapse of his professional life with all its high status and achievements, the only person who seemed to soothe his chaotic, battered state of mind was Toni. After sleepless nights he would spend the first half of his mornings scribbling feverishly away, into what he called his 'black book', eventually published in 2009 as *The Red Book*. He would then spend an hour or two with Toni and discuss what he'd written about in his febrile emotional mood with all its visions, fantasies and dreams. During these dysfunctional years Toni became Jung's therapist, as she seemed the one person who could empathise with his fractured psyche. Emma later wrote with magnanimous humility 'I shall always be grateful to Toni for doing for my husband what I or anyone else could not have done at that most critical time.'

By the time Jung recovered in 1918 Toni's daily visits to the house in Küssnacht had been accepted by Emma as a necessary reality. There have been many comments and observations about this unconventional triangular relation-ship which lasted thirty years. Ruth Bailey, a family friend, described Emma as 'a woman with a deep sadness in her eyes' while Laurens van der Post described his friend Toni Wolff to be 'repeatedly in the grip of great distress', while Emma herself wrote in a paper she gave to the Psychological Club of Zürich in November 1931: 'In the course of one's life sometimes one must face the distressing fact that unforeseen circumstances have caused one's previously uncomplicated life to completely disintegrate.'

Emma, who had always longed to be her husband's collaborator in his psychological work, now had to watch as Toni came to her home to talk to her husband about his developing ideas concerning individuation, Anima and Ani-mus, Persona, Extroversion and Intraversion, Archetypes, the Collective Consciousness and Dream Theory. Indeed Toni became his creative partner as he developed all the ideas and concepts that filled his seminal book *Psychological Types*, which was published in 1921. Liliana Frey was later to write: 'Toni grasped the essence of Jung's psychological ideas even before he understood them.' I suspect this synergistic aspect of Jung's relationship with Toni was more painful for Emma to bear than their physical infidelity which, by the early 1920s, was virtually over.

Yet these two women had a compassionate sympathy for each other, so much so that they would talk together openly about their shared unhappiness. They reached a stage when they both agreed that they had to find a way of easing the pain of this extremely uncomfortable situation by asking Jung's colleague C. A. Meier to undertake a three-way therapy arrangement where, without the unwanted presence of Jung, they would discuss and explore their dilemma. This most unconventional therapy must have been efficacious as it wasn't long before Jung arrived at the regular Psychological Club of Zürich meetings with Emma on one arm and Toni on the other, as if symbolising his intense need for both women equally, a situation that Emma and Toni had come to accept.

By the mid-1920s Jung had encouraged Emma to develop her considerable skills as a therapist and began to send her patients. Her maturity and spirit of generosity, which she had established when faced with Toni's continual presence in her home, created among her friends and colleagues a tremendous respect and admiration and they too would refer patients to her. Invariably they noticed how these fortunate individuals would benefit from her wisdom and experience.

Her consulting room was located on the first floor next to her husband's in their house in Küssnacht and over lunch they would engage in some impromptu supervision. Their relationship deepened further when their respective mothers died in the same year and then their adult children began to provide them with grandchildren, a shared experience they both delighted in. Emma became president of the Psychological Club of Zürich and they both travelled together on lecture tours and to international conferences. So finally Emma became her husband's colleague. The leading Jungian Joseph Henderson who came to Zürich in 1929 to be analysed by Jung, reported: 'Jung told me personally that the most valuable thing in his life was his marriage. He would give up anything before he would give up his marriage.'

During the twenty years between 1905 and 1925, Emma Jung somehow reconciled herself to the infuriating, reprehensible, reckless behaviour of her husband Carl Jung. The fury and hatred she felt for her intemperate, philandering husband was matched by the intense love for him, that – despite his infidelities – never faded. By bearing these two extreme emotions for so many years she developed a wisdom and a composure that comforted and encouraged all those people who knew her. Despite the sheer power of her husband's personality, she was always able to hold her own with a self-possessed equanimity that quietly reproached her husband, with humour and amusement, when he showed signs of that inflated pomposity, which she was so familiar with.

In the autumn of 1954 Emma was diagnosed with stomach cancer. Surgery was performed, followed by chemotherapy and radiation treatment. She only spoke to her husband about her illness and insisted that no one else be informed of her condition. During the first half of 1955 she seemed to recover and was able to organise and take part in the considerable celebrations that marked Jung's eightieth birthday and she was helped with this demanding task by an old family friend, Ruth Bailey, who visited the Küssnacht house every day. Sure that the cancer had returned she asked Ruth to become her husband's housekeeper in the event of her death. By the beginning of that autumn she had further tests and her doctor told her that the cancer had spread and that she only had a few more weeks to live. She greeted this news with her customary stoicism and graciousness. On her last morning, she said to her daughters Gret and Marianne: 'I am going to die now. I am going to say goodbye to you right now.' She died a few hours later, with her distraught husband sitting by her.

There is a widespread view among psychotherapists that depression is often a result of a surfeit of repressed anger. It is certainly a view that I share and I have a rather more positive view regarding the expression of anger than our collective culture does, which generally views it as an inappropriate and shameful emotion that should be kept well under control.

Often a new client, whose presenting symptom is depression combined with a debilitating low self-esteem, spends their first half a dozen sessions giving an account of all their faults, foibles and frailties. Frequently these new clients are talented, often charming, personalities who seem completely unaware of their array of fine personal qualities as these aspects of their nature are savagely belittled by a voluble inner critic. These fierce inner critics are almost always bestowed upon them by parents whose own neuroses and disappointments have congealed into a tendency to shower their children with criticism, which results in a childhood and adolescence full of censure and disparagement.

As we examine their parents' psychological histories and emotional discontents the client starts to understand that these parental criticisms that they had to bear through much of their childhood originated from their parents' inadequacies and disappointments and as we traverse their difficult childhoods, the client begins to realise the sheer unfairness of this constant parental tongue-lashing. After a while a critical mass of furious indignation is reached and the client, for the first time, has an eruption of volcanic rage directed towards the parents. Such an explosion coming from a timid client, who has never before expressed anger, is a major breakthrough. I had one docile, compliant client tormented by savage low-esteem because of overbearing, judgemental parents, who finally discovered an incandescent rage which developed into a dramatic fantasy about how she had to murder both her parents, specifically using a long carving knife she kept in her kitchen and which on one occasion she brought along to one of our sessions. As we explored this anger and she acted out her fury, her inner critic began to loosen its grip. Her depression and low self-esteem started to evaporate as she realised that she was a gifted, talented young woman with all sorts of potentials and capacities that she could now start to develop.

More often than not, when this unconscious rage and hatred remains locked in the unconscious, it will eventually emerge and be directed not towards the neglected parents but in the direction of other innocent targets close at hand, which normally means the spouse or life partner and the individual's own children. This anger, which should have been focused on the offending parents, is now projected onto innocent family members who are bruised and battered by the collateral damage from the misdirected hatred.

All too often marriages and relationships with children falter because this anger cannot be contained or directed onto culpable parents who are now out of reach. In such circumstances effective psychotherapy can save these relationships by redirecting this projected anger onto its rightful target, the original offending parents. Where marriages do break down in such circumstances the individuals involved have been unable to locate the safety of Klein's depressive position where love leads to hatred but where this uncomfortable duality is now accepted.

Someone who only eventually achieved this emotionally enlightened duality in his fifth marriage was one of Western culture's most debonair charmers: the Hollywood icon Cary Grant.

Archie Leach was born in a suburb of Bristol in 1904. He was the only child of parents who were entirely unsuited to each other and had a fractious, ill-tempered relationship. Three years before Archie was born, his mother gave birth to her first son. When this first child was two she accidentally closed a door on his thumb and he developed gangrene and died, for which she blamed herself for the rest of her life.

He wrote of his mother:

> She wasn't a happy woman and I wasn't a happy child, because my mother tried to smother me with care. She and my father fought about me constantly. I never spent a happy moment with them under the same roof. Then when I was ten, I came home from school one day and mother was gone.

My father told me she had gone to a local seaside resort. This seemed rather unusual, although I accepted it as one of those unaccountable things that grown-ups do. However, the weeks went by and there was no further explanation for mother's absence and it gradually dawned on me she wasn't coming back at all. There was a void in my life, a sadness of spirit that affected everything I did. I always felt that my mother had rejected me.

Unbeknownst to Archie his father had had his mother committed to the local Bristol insane asylum in Fishponds and then had moved to Southampton to spend time with his mistress and the child they had had together. Archie was deposited with his paternal grandmother who frequently left him alone in an unheated house with a minimal amount of food.

Three years later Archie managed to get a part-time job as a 'call boy' at the Hippodrome, Bristol's premier theatre. Within a year, having been expelled from school, he joined a troupe of theatrical vaudeville players known as 'The Pender's Knockabout Comedians'. After eighteen months touring England, the troupe travelled to New York where they featured in the review *Good Times* at the New York Hippodrome, which ran for the next nine months.

As I have said, I have noticed how individuals who have been poorly parented develop a considerable natural charm which they use to great effect in their attempts to recruit surrogate mothers and fathers to fill the void left by their negligent parents. Archie Leach, in those early years in America, developed a magnetic, seductive charm. Combined with his handsome good looks and tall, slim body, he radiated an attractive urbanity and a discreet yet alluring sexuality. He also had a way with words that was full of wit, poise and empathy: indeed he became irresistible to everyone he met. Buoyed up by his growing confidence in his charismatic persona he moved to California where he was determined to become a Hollywood actor. Within a handful of years his leading ladies included Mae West, Marlene Dietrich, Ginger Rogers and Katharine Hepburn. Archie Leach had successfully turned himself into Cary Grant.

And yet this charming, sophisticated persona didn't ease the emotional pain caused by his bruised psyche, as the shadow of his past continued to plague him. He later wrote:

> For many years I have cautiously peered out from behind a face of a man called Cary Grant. The protection of that façade was both an advantage and a disadvantage. If I couldn't see out, how could anyone see in? All my life I have been going around in a fog. You are just a bunch of molecules until you know who you are. You spend your time being a big Hollywood actor but then what? All my life I've been searching for peace of mind. I want to rid myself of all my hypocrisies . . . Everyone wants to be Cary Grant. Even I want to be Cary Grant.

Why everyone, including Archie Leach, wanted to be like Cary Grant becomes clear if you just watch his films. Time spent in the company of this seductive, debonair, self-possessed figure makes you feel better. He seems to breeze through life with a nonchalant, easy-going charm and a magnetism that combines humour and sophistication with a certain mysterious edge of inscrutability. In his company life seems more of an adventure, more fun, more exhilarating, altogether more interesting. Cary Grant's persona can trigger an extra flow of dopamine and serotonin within our brains, giving us all an unaccountable lift. No wonder in the dark, forbidding days of the late 1930s and 1940s everyone flocked to see his films and felt better for having done so.

Yet there was a small group of individuals who took a very different view of Cary Grant: those women who had the misfortune to become one of his wives. Away from the public domain, Cary Grant stepped out of the limelight and Archie Leach, with all his troubles, and loneliness took centre stage. Each time Grant got married, Leach would elbow the charmer to one side and the new wife would be faced with a very different personality to the man she had thought she had married.

His first marriage to the actress Virginia Cherrill lasted seven months. The moment they were married Archie became insanely jealous, feeling certain that his new wife would leave him for another man, insisting when they went to parties that she spoke to no other men. The glamour, the urbanity, the savoir faire disappeared and in its place a kind of monster emerged. As Virginia Cherrill told a Los Angeles court in 1934: 'He drank excessively, choked and beat me and threatened to kill me . . . he was sullen, morose and quarrelsome in front of guests.' Cary Grant had disappeared, pushed to one side by an angry, depressed paranoid little boy who now took centre stage. In years to come, after insights gained in therapy, he wrote: 'I realised that I was trying to kill my mother through my relationships with women. I was punishing them for what she had done to me. I was making the mistake that each of my wives was my mother.' Of Virginia Cherrill he wrote: 'My possessiveness and fear of losing her brought about the very condition it feared – the loss of her.' When an interviewer later asked him what happened to his first four marriages he answered: 'They all left me. I didn't leave any of them. They all walked out on me. Maybe my marriages were heavily influenced by something in my subconscious that's related to my early years and the way I envisioned my mother.'

These constant breakdowns in his marriages and in numerous other relationships he had with women is a perfect example of Freud's repetition theory. In *Beyond the Pleasure Principle*, Freud writes:

> Patients repeat all their unwanted situations . . . the impression they give are of being pursued by a malignant fate or possessed by some extraneous power. But psychoanalysis has always taken the view that their fate is for the most part arranged by themselves and determined by early infantile influences.

Freud then goes onto give four specific examples: the patron who is always cast aside by his protégés; the individual whose close relationships end in betrayal; people who always end up nursing their partners through medical problems; and finally the neurotic repetition that Cary Grant was addicted to, which Freud describes as 'the lover each of whose love affairs passes through the same phases and reaches the same conclusions'.

In my own practice virtually every client displays this perverse unconscious desire to repeat patterns of behaviour first experienced in childhood, which tend to be painful, difficult episodes often involving parental rejection. Freud's repetition theory is now often known as 'trauma re-enactment' and one such almost inevitable trauma of early childhood is the deeply unsettling realisation that an infant has when it first feels hatred and rage towards the mother whom he or she loves.

In fact Melanie Klein insists that it is not the mother that the baby, in the earliest weeks of life, loves and hates, it is only a part of the mother: the breast. The baby experiences the mother's breast as either providing nourishment, warmth and love (the good breast) or as being absent, unavailable and rejecting (the bad breast), causing pain, discomfort, hunger and feelings of abandonment. As the baby grows it realises that both breasts belong to the mother who is alternatingly loved when she is present, available and nurturing but hated when she disappears and is absent and unavailable because of her other inevitable obligations.

As we have seen, to deal with this traumatic clash of opposite emotions the baby uses Melanie Klein's 'splitting' defence which can be used from our earliest weeks, right through our lives, but it will serve us poorly. If you want to understand Klein's concept of 'splitting' listen to any of Donald Trump's speeches: everything is black and white; everything is either good or bad; there is no ambiguity or ambivalence, no shades of grey; everything is labelled as either idealised and perfect or hated and defective.

To staunch the anxiety of opposing duality of love and hate, the defence of splitting is used and those aspects of the mother that feel bad are repressed into the unconscious. So only love remains in the baby's conscious mind but the hate still exists in the depths of the unconscious.

In later life when Cary Grant met an attractive woman whom he would idealise, the oxytocin would begin to flow and he would fall in love and be the charming, irresistible, alluring Cary Grant. When the love affair felt complete, marriage would ensue. But then the oxytocin would begin to subside and be replaced by the fear that his new wife would desert him. The oxytocin would change into adrenaline, which would then ignite Archie Leach's ancient rage and hatred towards his mother, reappearing from the unconscious, and he would become impossible to live with as Freud's 'repetition theory' would revive the old childhood trauma and the latest partner would abandon him, just as his mother had done, when she was locked away in the Fishponds asylum when Archie was eight.

Yet as Melanie Klein says, redemption and reparation from this endless wheel of repetition can be achieved. If we can release our anger and hatred from our unconscious, we won't project our rage and loathing onto others close to us but instead begin to understand that it is possible to love and hate the same person and that our hate and anger does not have to nullify the love we feel for them.

Quite suddenly, on 1 December 1935, Grant received a letter from a solicitor in Bristol informing him that his father had recently died and asking whether he knew that his mother was still alive and living in an asylum in Fishponds on the outskirts of Bristol, where she had been taken all those years previously. This was shocking yet miraculous news for Archie who immediately made the journey back to England to be reunited with his mother who of course was delighted to see her now famous son. Archie was urbane and friendly but somewhat ambivalent in this first meeting, but in the years to come he would make regular trips back to Bristol, although he could never persuade Elsie to come and live near him in Los Angeles. He provided for her financially and played the part of the attentive son, but it seemed unlikely that they would ever become close or intimate and Cary Grant went on having faltering, fractured relationships with a succession of wives and partners.

Then in the 1950s he met Dr Hartmann, a pioneering, radical psychoanalyst, who used LSD with his patients until it was made illegal in 1968. Under the influence of this hallucinogenic drug, the client would undergo a five-hour session, delving back into the memories and emotions of their earliest years. Cary Grant later wrote of the experience:

> I took LSD with the hope it would make me feel better about myself. I wanted to work through the events of my childhood, my relationship with my parents and my former wives . . . At first I found it unbelievably painful. I would run the gamut of emotions from deep pain with tears running down my face to light-hearted, almost drunken laughter. I learned to accept the responsibility for my own actions and to blame myself and no one else for circumstances of my own creating . . . The experience was just like being born for the first time.

He estimated that he had 'about a hundred sessions' over a three-year period: slowly Archie Leach was becoming Cary Grant. The fusion of Shadow and persona eventually produced someone of rare emotional intelligence. You can detect this integrated, mature, authentic personality, at last at ease with himself, in his later films and in his rare public appearances. He retired in his early sixties and at the age of sixty-two became a father for the first time, a role he relished like no other. Then finally at the age of seventy-seven he married for the last time and enjoyed six years of mutual devotion before he died in 1986.

By all the accounts given by friends who knew him in his later years, he became a man of gracious, self-effacing courtesy, who retained the humour and charm of his persona which had become a natural part of his personality and no longer the mask he wore to hide the Shadow of Archie Leach's forlorn and anguished wounding. He had found a gift in his wound that he was brave enough to encounter fully in his therapy, which resulted in an uncommonly well-lived life.

John Bowlby's Attachment Theory
(Virginia Woolf, Franz Kafka)

One of the most frequent emotional dichotomies felt by my clients is that inconvenient disparity between our need for security and our desire for adventure. In our adult lives we tend to entrench ourselves in the comfort zones we surround ourselves with, in our professional occupations, in the familiarity of our homes, in our marriages and closest relationships, in our financial planning, our hobbies and leisure pursuits and in the reassuring banalities of our daily routines. Yet at the same time we long for adventures that take us beyond the constraints and limitations of these carefully constructed bastions of security, which provide our lives with a sense of reassuring structure.

The psychotherapeutic writer who most extensively wrote about this uneasy contrast in the human psyche was Michael Balint. A Hungarian from Budapest, Balint trained with renowned psychotherapist Sándor Ferenczi but then moved to England in 1939 when the Hungarian government became rabidly antisemitic. His underrated book *Thrills and Regressions* (1959) starts with a chapter entitled 'Funfairs and Thrills' which – in a playful manner – uses the pleasures and amusements to be found at funfairs as a means of examining this polarity between security and adventure.

The three most significant gratifications to be found at

a funfair, he maintains are food, aggressive pleasures such as throwing, shooting or smashing things and fairground rides such as swings, roundabouts, ghost trains and switchbacks. The food is always sweet and cheap and the aggressive games provide tests of strength and destructive contests where, for instance, stacks of porcelain are smashed up by hurling wooden balls at them. Balint says these two groups of amusement provide regressive pleasures: the indulgence of infantile oral treats and the expression of early destructive and aggressive instincts, allowing the individual the gratification of expressing violent and angry behaviour. The third group comprises vertiginous and frightening fairground rides. What Balint is suggesting is that the funfair provides us with adventures within a familiar, predictable setting, which meets these two contrasting needs of excitement and a reassuring sense of safety.

He then moves on in his examination of our need for security and our desire for adventure by introducing us to two types of human behaviour experienced by what he calls 'ocnophils' and 'philobats'. The word 'ocnophilia' is a Greek word meaning to cling, to shrink, to hesitate or to hang back, which has as its premise some reservation such as fear, risk-aversion or apprehension that restricts and constrains the actions of an individual, who prefers to remain within the safety of familiar surroundings and people. As Balint says, the ocnophilic world consists of objects (familiar places, people, activities) 'separated by horrid empty spaces. The ocnophilic lives from object to object, cutting his sojourns in the empty space between the objects, as short as possible. Fear is provoked by leaving the objects and allayed by rejoining them.'

In contrast, philobats find objects restrictive, almost claustrophobic, and prefer the spaces between objects where they feel most comfortable and contented. Balint gives the example of the pilot who is safe in the sky, the sailor who finds freedom on the high seas, the driver enlivened by the open road, the skier thrilled by the mountain descent and the parachutist falling through the sky. In the words of Balint: 'the philobat world consists of friendly expanses dotted with dangerous and unpredictable objects that have to be negotiated.' As a consequence the philobat distrusts dependency and commitment while the ocnophil fears independence and spaciousness.

Yet Balint emphatically states that ocnophilia and philobalia are not polar opposites but 'two different attitudes branching off the same stem'. I agree with Balint that they are two styles of temperament and behaviour which are not opposing polarities but rather two reactive attitudes that are found in all of us. Ideally we should embrace aspects of both ocnophilia and philobatism, although one of these attitudes usually dominates. The compliant, risk-averse ocnophil will perhaps need to be nudged out of their restricted, sequestered comfort zone, while more risk-inclined philobats who distrust commitment may need to find a more settled life.

In endless hours studying babies, infants, children and adolescents, Donald Winnicott, the distinguished analyst and paediatrician, was well qualified to understand the origins of this chaffing between the polarities of security and adventure. In a chapter entitled 'On Security' from his book *The Family and Individual Development* (1965), Winnicott writes:

'Whenever an attempt is made to state the basic needs of infants and children, we hear the words "what children need is security." Yet parents who are over-protective cause distress in their children, just as parents who cannot be relied upon make their children muddled and frightened. Evidently then, it is possible for parents to give too much security.' I think Winnicott is right. I call this tendency that some parents have to be anxiously over-protective 'parental engulfment'.

Winnicott goes on to say that healthy development requires the child to find an early spirit of adventure that provides them with a challenge, which – when the time is right – they must use to somehow break out of this constricting over-protection. When this first happens during infancy, this tension between the need for security and the desire for adventure is ignited and the creative tension it creates can last a lifetime. The elderly individual accommodated in a care home will feel the tension of this polarity just as strongly as the ten-month old baby who has just developed the physical ability to crawl away from the maternal protective grasp.

Winnicott stresses that the essential self-confidence which each child needs in order to develop 'the capacity to live imaginatively, which brings out the best in people' requires a safe 'environmental provision'. This provision is initially provided by the parents, but then by the playgroup and early schooling, as the child discovers the adventure of social interaction, beyond the safety of parental care. As Winnicott writes: 'It is their surroundings that make it possible for each child to grow and without adequate environmental reliability the personal growth of the child cannot take place or such growth will be distorted.' This 'adequate environmental reliability' is a feature we all try to find as we need this safe foundation from which to kindle our spirit of adventure and explore the world beyond our comfort zone. The partners we bond with, the homes we create, the reliable profession providing financial security, the nuclear family, the extended family and our local communities can provide this safe environmental provision, from which from time to time we feel the need to leave, in the knowledge that these secure aspects of our life are there for us to return to.

One of Winnicott's most well-known ideas is his concept of 'transitional phenomena' which developed after he noticed that at an early stage of development infants became obsessively attached to pieces of rag, a blanket, a teddy bear or doll, which was an essential element of the safe environment provided by their parents. He observed how many infants are at their most animated and confident when they are being fed and when they are in close intimate contact with their mother and then increasingly with other significant carers, such as a father or grandparent. But between these moments of connection and intimacy infants would focus their attention on these transitional objects which represented the absent mother or carer. These transitional objects allow the child to cross this threshold from total maternal dependency into a new world, as they explore their first adventures as a separate individual, allowing them their earliest fledgling experiences beyond the embrace of the mother.

One of the most well-known transitional objects was a teddy bear called Archie which belonged to John Betjeman.

Archie was given to his owner when he was eighteen months old and was the poet's constant companion all his life. When he died at the age of seventy-seven, Archie was securely tucked under the Poet Laureate's arm.

Winnicott outlines the transitional object's primary features. It must belong exclusively to the child, who can treat it in any fashion whatsoever, allowing love and hate to be expressed freely. Sometimes it will be the victim of brutal physical violence, which must be permitted. It must have a distinctive personality and temperament, which means it can never be copied or replaced. Its importance lies in the fact that it stands in for the mother, yet is not the mother. Indeed, a family anecdote that I grew up with recalled how as a toddler I owned a beloved teddy bear called Augustus. One day Augustus was inadvertently left in a shop and was lost forever. Apparently I was inconsolable, so deep was the trauma of losing Augustus. I refused a number of proffered replacements and became morose, sullen and disinterested both in food and parental affection as I clearly blamed my mother and father. Refusing all alternatives, it was then that I discovered some relief in sucking my thumb, an anatomical transitional object that I used to good effect when facing moments of stress, well into my adolescence.

Winnicott contends that transitional phenomena remain with us for a lifetime, providing us with symbols of security which extend our capacity to have adventures. For instance each morning I get up early and brace myself for two to three hours writing. This daily event always feels like a risk because if the writing goes well, the dopamine in my brain will be given a boost and I will feel good all day. If the writing is a struggle and I achieve little, the dopamine will subside and I will feel grumpy and forlorn, and so I surround the experience with transitional objects. I must have a fortifying cup of tea in a particular mug, which belonged to my father-in-law, with whom I had a particularly close relationship and who held me in a high regard that my own father never expressed. I can only write sitting in a particular chair, with a specific wooden plank across my knee, in Roald Dahl style. I can only write using a special pen. These illogical rituals have nothing to do with superstition but are all transitional phenomena that fuel my capacity to begin that exciting adventure that I have always found writing to be.

These objects give us a feeling of empowerment, a confidence to meet the challenges that we face in our lives as we stray beyond our carefully arranged defences into unfamiliar territory and experiences. Our spirits of adventure tempt us to return to the excitement of the big city, to embark on the foreign journey, to begin some new unfamiliar undertaking or to enter a new relationship. As we age and time becomes more and more precious, we should continue to honour these pendulum swings between periods of rest and relaxation in places and situations where we feel safe and secure, but also need to leave to embark upon another adventure, which adds to the thrill and excitement that a full and imaginative life can provide us with.

What I believe both Balint and Winnicott are suggesting – and what I seek to achieve with my clients – is not the settled acceptance that we are either an ocnophil or a philobat but a blend of both. This idea is beautifully described by the father of attachment theory, John Bowlby, who wrote in his book *A Secure Base: Clinical Applications of Attachment Theory*: 'All of us from the cradle to the grave are happiest when life is organised around a series of excursions, long or short, from the secure base provided by attachment figures.'

One of our greatest writers, loved and admired by her devoted readers, Virginia Woolf, was throughout her life constantly engaged in attempting to blend her divided personality that exhibited this tension between her ocnophil and philobat nature, a tension that no doubt fuelled her great literary achievement.

The balancing of these two conflicting needs of security and adventure requires very precise calibration. Too much security and life becomes tedious, monotonous, leaden and dull, but too much adventure can lead to exhaustion, overreach and burnout. The first twenty years of Virginia Woolf's adult life was a constant swing from excessive amounts of stimulus, excitement and challenge to periods of mind-numbing, demoralising and overprotective recuperation. But then, at around the age of forty, she began to find an equilibrium and steadying balance between periods of quiet, restful solitude and phases when her invigorating spirit of adventure was in full spate.

Quite suddenly in 1922, as she started writing *Mrs Dalloway*, she felt a spasm of confidence and self-belief. 'I feel as if I had slipped off all my ball dresses and stood naked' she wrote in her diary and she described this nakedness as the backbone of her existence, as if she had found, in her naked individuality, a strength and authority that quelled the storms and turbulence of her mental illness. 'I have to control my excitement as I push through the screen; as if something beats fiercely close to me. What this portends I don't know. It is a sense of the poetry of existence'.

Other diary entries from this period describe this excitement as she gathers up her self-belief in her own unique vision and this burst of self-confidence as her creativity expands, proliferates and uplifts her, produces – in the next six years – a sequence of literary masterpieces.

The greatest calamity of Woolf's childhood was the death of her mother Julia when she was thirteen which pitched her into her first breakdown. Then in 1904, when Woolf was twenty-two, her father died. This second loss was equally harrowing, yet far more complicated. She describes her bereavement as also a kind of liberation. In a diary entry dated 28 November 1928, when she was writing *A Room of One's Own*, she speculates that had her father lived into a prolonged old age 'his life would have entirely ended mine . . . No writing, no books – inconceivable.' As Hermione Lee writes in her biography: 'Virginia wrote and rewrote her father all her life. She was in love with him, she was furious with him, she was like him, she never stopped arguing with him and when she finally read Freud in 1939 she recognised exactly what he meant by ambivalence'. Clearly Virginia would have identified with the polarity of love and hate that characterised Melanie Klein's depressive position.

Indeed, the months following Sir Leslie Stephen's death were a kind of celebration of a newly found freedom felt by his children. Even before he died, Vanessa, Thoby and Virginia had agreed on the need to escape the family home at Hyde Park Gate and immediately after the funeral this plan was activated. Initially they went to the ethereal castle of Manorbier on a beautiful stretch of the Pembrokeshire coast followed by a journey by train through Switzerland to Lake Como and then onto Venice. Quentin Bell describes his aunt's first visit to Venice: 'Virginia, who had hardly been further afield than Boulogne, was amazed and delighted . . . indeed all four of them were in a state of childlike astonishment and joy; they could hardly believe that the place was real.'

The next destination was Florence, followed by a finale in Paris before returning home. And yet this pilgrimage, celebrating their freedom, was a delight felt most by Vanessa, while for Woolf it was all becoming too much and her fragility was beginning to show. It was too much adventure, too much excitement and her sense of insecurity increased as her sister Vanessa became more and more thrilled by the newly discovered treasure-homes of Europe. As they returned to London, an exhausted Woolf experienced the loss of her father not as a freedom but as a catastrophic abandonment. Her subsequent breakdown led to six months of depression, extreme anxiety, fainting fits, chronic insomnia, suicidal thoughts, self-imposed starvation and auditory hallucinations: an entire glut of symptoms that would mark these periods of 'madness' which would reoccur regularly during the next eighteen years.

Her recovery in the spring of 1905 was followed by a four-year period of relative stability. She even weathered the unexpected sudden death of her elder brother Thoby in the autumn of 1906. Vanessa reacted to Thoby's death by marrying her late brother's best friend Clive Bell, a matrimonial slap in the face for Woolf who felt abandoned not only by her elder brother but now by her sister. Although Woolf liked Clive and was stimulated by his company, Vanessa had been her life's companion and now she had to live with her younger brother Adrian, who Quentin Bell describes as 'maddeningly lethargic, lamentably silent, unable to find interest in anything except the constant rehearsal of old family reminiscences'. To make matters worse Woolf was developing a reputation among her male admirers as a frigid, sexually unapproachable ice maiden, despite her obvious beauty. Becalmed by this reputation, her lack of any literary progress and the torpor of her companions – Adrian and his even more listless friend Sidney Saxon Turner – Virginia embarked upon a series of excursions throughout 1909. These adventures included trips to Florence, Cambridge, the Wagner Festival at Bayreuth, Dresden, Studland and Cornwall. To add to the year's excitements, she met and formed a tantalising friendship with one of the premier hostesses of the day, Ottoline Morrell, and met many of Ottoline's colourful friends. Once again, overdosing on all this adventurous activity she collapsed into a state of nervous exhaustion and all the familiar hellish symptoms returned. This breakdown lasted until the autumn of 1910.

The next notable step beyond the confines of her comfort zone was when she allowed herself to be courted by Leonard Woolf, whom she went on to marry in August 1912, an act of courage given her chaste, sexual diffidence. This adventurous gamble was followed by an equally adventurous honeymoon, eight weeks travelling through France, Italy and Spain, but after these exertions Woolf inevitably collapsed and throughout the winter she was in a parlous, fragile state. She rallied briefly in the spring but then in the summer she descended into her deepest, most severe breakdown, which culminated in a suicide attempt in September 1913.

During 1914, a year of recovery, Leonard turned out to be the perfect companion and (using Bowlby's concept) attachment figure. Quiet, solicitous, empathetic, yet stimulating company, he devoted himself to Woolf's wellbeing and realised that salvation would be found in the sustenance of her creativity. Leonard felt she needed seclusion, her adventures limited to those to be encountered in her literary endeavours, and so in March 1915 he rented a house in Richmond, where, free from the vibrant excitement of London and the distractions of exhausting over-stimulation, Woolf plied her literary talents within a cushion of security that Leonard, Hogarth House and Richmond would provide.

Yet the move unsettled Woolf and in spring 1915 she had a serious relapse and their first months in their new home were spent in the company of four nurses who provided her with round-the-clock care. But by the summer she began to recover and the nurses were no longer needed. Having published her first novel *The Voyage Out* (1915), Woolf steadily developed her literary career over the next six years. She regularly wrote for the *Times Literary Supplement*; she lectured at the Richmond branch of the Women's Cooperative Guild; she wrote her diary and worked on her second novel, *Night and Day* (1919). There was no foreign travel and Leonard carefully regulated their social life. Increasingly periods of time were spent in rural Sussex, in a rented house called 'Asham' situated in a remote fold of the South Downs.

During this period of seclusion Woolf wrote the short story 'Kew Gardens', prepared *Night and Day* for publication and felt the first stirrings of *Jacob's Room* (1922), but progress on this short novel was slow and while it met with much enthusiasm from her friends when it was published, the critics were lukewarm.

In the two months that straddled Christmas 1922 three important events occurred in Woolf's life: her friend Katherine Mansfield died, she met Vita Sackville-West and she wrote a short story entitled 'Mrs Dalloway of Bond Street'. The vivid personality of Clarissa Dalloway would fill Woolf's creative imagination for the next two years until this novel, which depicted one day in the life of her heroine, was finally published in May 1925. With the crucial encouragement of her new friend Vita the slowly emerging manuscript began life under the working title *The Hours*.

In the summer of 1922, as Woolf began to formulate her ideas for the novel that would become *Mrs Dalloway*, her diary entries reveal the tensions around the clash between ocnophil and philobat elements of her personality.

> I now sit down baffled and depressed to face a life spent mute and mitigated in the suburbs, just as I had it in mind that I could at last go full speed ahead. For these capacities in me will never after forty accumulate again. And I mind missing life far more than Leonard does . . . To always waste time, to sit here and wait for Leonard, when alternatively I might go and hear a tune, or have a look at a picture, or find something at the British Museum or go adventuring among human beings. But here I'm tired, imprisoned and inhibited.

She then complains:

> I foresee, as I return to *The Hours* that this is going to be the
> devil of a struggle . . . The design is certainly original and
> interests me hugely. I should like to write away and away at
> it, very quick and fierce, but needless to say I can't . . . But
> one thing I do feel pretty certain about and here I confide to
> my diary – we must leave Richmond and set up in London.

But as she considered escaping the dull inertia of Richmond her mood changed, as her ideas for *Mrs Dalloway*
began to emerge, and she was filled with a spasm of confidence and self-belief. Within four months she had finished
writing *Mrs Dalloway* and within six months they had left
Richmond and settled in 52 Tavistock Square, Bloomsbury.
Her spirit of adventure had prevailed and during the next
eight years she would publish a sequence of books that
included *Mrs Dalloway*, *To the Lighthouse* (1927), *Orlando*
(1928), *A Room of One's Own* (1929) and *The Waves* (1931)
that transformed her into one of the most important writers
of the twentieth century.

In Woolf's case, a growing abundance of love, devotion and empathy, provided by her husband Leonard and
a number of devoted friends, created a sufficient flow of
dopamine and serotonin to provide her with a feeling of creative expansion that she was unfamiliar with. Particularly
significant was her close relationship with Vita Sackville-
West. Sackville-West was determined to help Woolf develop
her self-esteem, insisting that she wasn't some ailing recluse
who must avoid all mental exertion, but rather a writer of

wit, insight and intelligence who must fully engage with her artistic gift. From the age of fifteen, her father and doctor had condemned reading and writing as an aggravation of her nervous temperament. They also denounced Woolf's artistic ambitions as the primary cause of her instability. Sackville-West reversed this diagnosis and convinced Woolf that her reading and writing could provide a cure for her condition. Indeed, Sackville-West insisted that it was her father's attempt to prohibit her love of writing which set up a dreadful sense of conflict within her that caused her psychological troubles: that she was simply being prevented from being her true self by her father, whose dominant authority bore down on her so detrimentally.

Woolf's exact contemporary, Franz Kafka, was scribbling away in Prague unrecognised and unread, at the same time as the first sentences of *Mrs Dalloway* leaked from her pen. He would have understood her predicament, as he persisted in his own tedious but secure job at the Workers' Accident Insurance Institute, allowing only the evenings and occasional weekends to indulge his literary adventures. Kafka's understanding of the way his neurotic need for security constrained his desire for existential freedom is well conveyed in his one paragraph short story 'My Destination', which contains advice he found difficult to follow. The story reads:

> I called for my horse to be brought from the stable. The servant did not understand me. I myself went into the stable, saddled my horse and mounted. In the distance I heard a

bugle call. I asked him what it meant. He knew nothing and had heard nothing. At the gate he stopped me, asking:

'Where are you riding to, Sir?'

'I don't know', I answered. 'Only away from here, only away from here. Always away from here, only by doing so can I reach my destination.'

'But you have no provisions with you', he said.

'I don't need any' I replied, 'the journey is so long that I must die of hunger if I don't find any along the way. No provisions can save me, for it is a truly immense journey.

Virginia Woolf would, I'm sure, have identified with Kafka's single paragraph short story. Indeed, their respective lives followed a similar trajectory. Woolf was born in 1882 and Kafka a handful of months later in 1883. Their childhoods and emotional development were dominated by the daily presence of an overbearing father who significantly harmed their happiness, yet this paternal oppression was perhaps the very origin of their literary genius. In 1912 as Virginia was struggling to write her first novel, Kafka was also making a faltering first attempt at novel-writing in a work that would eventually be published posthumously under the title *Amerika*. In the same year Kafka also wrote 'Metamorphosis', one of the most celebrated short stories ever written. In 1917, as Woolf began her second novel, Kafka was still trying to put some order and shape to his manuscript of *The Trial* and in 1921 and 1922, as Virginia was constructing her experimental novel *Jacob's Room*, Franz was attempting to find the time and energy to complete *The Castle* as he battled with the tuberculosis that would kill him two years later.

It seems a strange coincidence that these two troubled souls unknowingly shadowed each other during the first forty years of their lives as they went on to become two of the greatest literary figures of the twentieth century. This accolade would have amazed Franz Kafka, who published only a few fragments in his lifetime. As a kind of literary Van Gogh he scribbled away, barely noticed and unregarded. When he realised that his life was nearly over he asked his closest friend Max Brod to burn his entire literary output. This bashful self-effacement reminds me of Donald Winnicott's famous aphorism 'A joy to be hidden, a disaster not to be found' and Kafka was certainly found by posterity and became one of those few individuals whose name is transformed into an adjective.

Providence bestowed on Virginia Woolf two considerable advantages not enjoyed by Kafka. Firstly she was given sixteen more years of life, which allowed her the gratification of seeing her work published. But more significantly she was blessed by her father's death when she was only twenty-two, giving her an independence never enjoyed by Kafka who suffered the misfortune of being outlived by his tyrannical father.

Both Viginia Woolf and Franz Kafka would have understood the sombering infidelities of Melanie Klein's 'depressive position'. How they both loved and hated their fathers, whose towering presence so shaped and moulded both their emotional miseries and their epic talent.

As far as his son was concerned, Hermann Kafka was a monster. Broad-shouldered, fat-bellied, bull-necked, this bellowing self-made, self-congratulatory Prague-based entrepreneur ruled his family with a loud-mouthed arrogance which was always at its worst during family meals, when he would constantly tell his compliant, cowering children: 'You have it so good', a refrain that always concluded with his endless tales of his tough, miserable childhood. As Franz recorded in his diary:

> It is so unpleasant to listen to my father take incessant swipes at the good fortune of people today and especially of his children while recalling the sufferings he had to endure in his youth . . . How gladly I would listen to him talk about his youth and parents all the time, but to hear all this in a tone of boastfulness and petulance is agonising.

Although his father's presence was, as he wrote in his diary, 'agonising', this paternal expansiveness somehow provided him with a stable, reliable security, protecting him from the predatory, antisemitic, pitiless world that he felt he was surrounded by. Although his father was the creator and origin of Kafka's emotional difficulties, he was also his protector. It was a double-bind from which he never escaped until the very end of his life but my goodness, how it fuelled his stories with their high-octane sense of irony.

Hermann, who came from the Bohemian village of Wossek, had arrived in Prague in 1882 and by Christmas he had met and married Julie Löwy, the daughter of a successful local brewer. Within ten months of their wedding, their first child Franz was born. Almost immediately after the birth Julie returned to work in Hermann's haberdasher's store, leaving her newly-born infant in the hands of a nurse, soon to be replaced by a second nurse. So no time for any 'primary maternal preoccupation' or maternal bonding, no soothing exchange of oxytocin, no breast-feeding: just a glass bottle with a teat to nourish the baby.

To make matters worse, the Kafka family moved five times during Franz's infancy. And to then make matters even worse, Julie gave birth to another son, Georg, who died in his second year. Worse still, another brother, Heinrich, arrived but lived barely six months. The causes of death were measles and an inner ear infection, minor conditions that shouldn't have proved fatal. Julie complained to Hermann that if she had stayed at home rather than being stuck in the family shop her two sons might have lived. Hermann took little notice of his wife's complaints although Julie did employ a more competent nanny, Marie Werner, who remained with the family throughout Franz's childhood and adolescence. But the damage was done. The atmosphere of trauma, loss and constant change that marked the Kafka household throughout Franz's early years scarred the young boy, who became a nervous, troubled child and who found life in his unpredictable home full of uncertainties and agitations.

He described his earliest years in a letter to his fiancée Felice Bauer in December 1912: 'I lived alone for a very long time, dealing with nurses, old nannies, spiteful cooks, unhappy governesses, since my parents were always in the shop.' Indeed the haberdasher's and fancy goods store was open from eight in the morning until eight at night, six days a week, as well as Sunday mornings and Franz found himself 'alone' with a succession of incompetent disinterested strangers, a maternal abandonment which would have had a considerable impact on his neurological development.

A baby's brain contains a fearsome, dominating feature much like Hermann Kafka: the amygdala – our flight and fight response – is always telling us what to do, galvanising us into action because of some perceived threat or danger that we must respond to immediately with vigorous, pre-emptive action. To propel us into running faster or jumping higher to outpace the perceived predator, the amygdala commands its servant, the adrenal glands, to pump adrenaline into our nervous system so we can accelerate our escape from the jaws of the encroaching threat. In a baby's brain this becomes an agony of anxiety and fear but it has no leg muscles to propel itself forward, so the unused adrenaline coagulates into an unpleasant substance called cortisol, which pollutes the baby's neurological circuitry, slowing down and impeding the fast-growing development of the infant's brain.

Because the amygdala is hyperbolically and manically over-active, the brain – over a long period of evolution – has developed a seahorse-shaped mechanism known as the hippocampus (the Greek word for seahorse). The job of the hippocampus is to reign in the catastrophising amygdala, whose alarmist tendencies – if left unchecked – would bind us to a frightening, chaotic view of the world, and fill us with an endless deluge of anxiety and terror.

The hippocampus is quite capable of subduing the amygdala's predictions of imminent disaster but suffers one great disadvantage: although the amygdala is fully developed by the first eight months of pregnancy and becomes immediately operational at birth – jolted into action by the trauma of the birth process – the hippocampus, on the other hand, is not fully formed until the end of the infant's third year. The situation is made worse because once the adrenaline has turned into cortisol, this toxic substance prevents the hippocampus from growing into a champion that can take on the amygdala.

There is, however, one contrivance available to staunch the adrenaline and the predictions of calamity barked out by the Cassandra-like amygdala. This one saviour, this one protector, is an ever-present, ever-vigilant, loving mother who can provide for her baby with hourly infusions of oxytocin, dopamine and serotonin, a rich brew of hormones which combined together will easily stem and arrest the spine-chilling warnings of the amygdala and its corrosive gift of cortisol.

But the mother must be there, nursing her tiny child throughout the day, being close at hand as her baby sleeps, with her ever-available breasts providing a flow of nourishment, as she remains perfectly attuned to every one of her infant's needs, soothing all anxieties and fears as they arise. If she succeeds in these tasks her child's hippocampus will grow and prosper and become – at the age of three – a fully formed and effective ally up to the job of meeting the amygdala's alarming premonitions.

Of course mothers have other duties, other obligations to attend to, but a small baby does deserve to become the mother's priority over all other competing commitments. Hermann and Julie's knowledge of infantile neurology was, however, in short supply and in the Kafka household Hermann's needs always prevailed. After three years of inadequate maternal care, frequent moves to new homes and the death of Georg with all its consequent distress, Franz's cortisol-drenched hippocampus would have been woefully underdeveloped, unable to combat his raucous amygdala. It seems probable that his hippocampus never gained its full effective stature, leaving Kafka, throughout his adult life, a timorous, anxious individual, prone to depression and self-loathing, very much a cautious ocnophil rather than an expansive, confident philobat, who never managed to achieve the aspiration he described in his short story 'My Destination'. He never did get 'Away from here, only by doing so can I reach my destination'. And yet he did become posthumously one of the great writers of the twentieth century. So how did this happen?

Max Brod introduced Kafka to Freud's work in 1911 when he gave his friend a copy of *The Interpretation of Dreams*, in which Freud discusses his theory of the child's love for the mother and the patricidal hatred towards the father.

In his diary entry from 23 September 1912 Kafka wrote: 'This story, "The Judgement", I wrote at one sitting during last night, from ten o'clock to six this morning. I was hardly able to pull my legs out from under the desk, they had got so stiff from sitting.' Kafka describes a night of literary passion which is almost erotic. Here is Franz Kafka at his most adventurous, getting 'away from here', away from the tedious grind of his work at the Workers' Accident Insurance Institute, away from his family, away from the anxiety sparked off by his recent first meeting in August with Felice Bauer. In this diary entry he lists the influences upon his story 'The Judgement', mentioning Max Brod's 'Arkadia', the writers

Arnold Wassermann and Franz Werfel and 'thoughts about Freud of course'. Given the contents of 'The Judgement' he must have been thinking of Freud's Oedipus complex.

'The Judgement' concludes with an altercation between George Bendemann and his enfeebled, ageing father, who – despite his physical decrepitude – still holds considerable power over his son. In the final paragraphs the father shouts: 'You were an innocent child, to tell the truth – though to tell the whole truth you were the devil incarnate. Therefore I hereby sentence you to death by drowning.' George immediately accepts his father's instruction and, combining the role of executioner and condemned, he quickly leaves his father's house, which stands by the river, and as he makes a suicidal leap into the cold water he cries out: 'Dear Parents, I did love you, always.'

In this strange story, of which Kafka was so proud, it is the father who is responsible for his son's death and Kafka's unconscious fear since early childhood, that is now finally expressed, is an inversion of Freud's Oedipus complex. This night of cathartic creativity seems to liberate Kafka from his inertia. In October and November he writes most of his first novel *Amerika* and then, with a masterly flourish, he writes his greatest short story 'Metamorphosis', another piece of writing about parental disappointment which results in the final abandonment and death of the story's young anthropoid hero. Within eighteen months he begins 'The Trial'. A year later, in early 1915 at the age of thirty-two, he finally leaves home.

Writing 'The Judgement' in one nocturnal eight-hour creative spasm had an impact on Kafka similar to a technique used by Jungian therapists called 'active imagination', which employs various devices to access unconscious fears, anxieties, hopes and aspirations. This can be achieved by entering a kind of reverie within which long-lost, forgotten experiences and thoughts can be retrieved. (As we have seen, Cary Grant benefitted from this technique when using hallucinogenic drugs in a psychotherapeutic setting.) But contact with significant unconscious material can also be facilitated by a guided meditation, or by drawing or painting an image, or by writing a story or a letter.

In Kafka's case the story 'The Judgement' brings into full consciousness his fear that his father has murderous feelings towards him, a fear that must have been embedded in his unconscious since early childhood. Kafka's cathartic release from this primal unconscious anxiety of Oedipal threat was achieved by formulating this story. This process acted like a purgative, releasing a spasm of creative energy which was inaccessible because of the unconscious fear of his father's murderous hatred. Once brought into consciousness and confronted, his inertia is overcome and a plume of fertile and productive energy is released. This is also what active imagination can achieve.

One kind of active imaginative act that I find very effective and frequently use with my clients is the composition of a letter to the offending parent who was responsible for the childhood wounding. All too often the abusive or neglectful parent is now in a fragile old age, their harmful transgression having occurred decades earlier. In such cases sending some furious, enraged letter would be cruel and inappropriate, yet in the penning of the letter the rage and hatred can

be consciously expressed for the first time. A letter expressing this anger and loathing for the parent concerned can
be both a necessary and liberating reparative experience,
but for compassionate reasons the letter should not be sent
but worked with in the therapeutic sessions until the emotional fury and visceral loathing can be worked through and
finally shed.

Kafka was to write just such a letter to his father in the
autumn of 1919 when he was thirty-six. Earlier that year
he had met, and become infatuated with, Julie Wohryzek,
the daughter of a Prague shoemaker. While both were convalescing in the town of Schelesen, they were reunited in
Prague. In a letter written to Julie's sister in November 1919
Kafka writes: 'When I returned to Prague, we flew to each
other as if driven. There was no other option for us. And
now came a happy and peaceful time, since it was beyond
our strength to stay away from each other.'

The prospect of being finally, happily married was closer
than ever when he proposed to Julie and she accepted, but
when he told his father about his plans to marry Julie, he
received a blunt response with Hermann refusing to give his
blessing, saying: 'Can you do no better than marrying a girl
who'd give herself to anybody. Aren't there any alternatives?'
Kafka tried his best to ignore his father's outrage. Wedding
plans were made; a flat in Prague was found to rent; the
banns were published. But then they lost the apartment and,
unable to forget his father's disdain, Kafka lost his nerve.
Two days before the wedding he ended his relationship with
Julie Wohryzek.

The only way Kafka could retaliate against his father's

insensitive, callous treatment was to write a furious one-hundred-page letter to Hermann and from the text of the letter it appears that Kafka knew that reconciliation with such a tyrant simply wasn't possible.

> Being the way we are, marrying is barred to me because it is your very own domain. Sometimes I imagine the map of the world spread out with you stretched diagonally across it. Then it seems to me that I could consider living in only those regions that either are not covered by you or are not within your reach. And in keeping with the conception I have of your magnitude, there are not many and not very comforting regions left, and marriage in particular is not among them.

This is an instructive metaphor and reminds me of many of my male clients, who sense they have lost the Oedipal struggle with their fathers and from then on always prefer to pursue a profession or way of life diametrically opposite to their dominant father. I certainly did the same, choosing two careers that were utterly alien to my father's temperament. Indeed I was only able to begin training to become a psychotherapist when my father's dementia closed down his critical faculties. He would certainly have regarded therapy as a pointless, limp-wristed activity.

Kafka, furious at his father's rebuke, was deeply disappointed by the end of his relationship with Julie and doesn't hold back in his litany of criticisms that now flood the pages of his letter. He describes Hermann's appalling table manners, his lewd, tasteless dirty jokes, his disagreeable moods, his pompous hypocrisy, the heartless, tight-fisted manner in which he treats his employees, the way he has to dominate every conversation, the sneering contempt he has for his children and his self-pity with its recurrent accounts of his miserable childhood. The charge sheet seems endless. It's as though Kafka reaches deep into his unconscious and brings out fistfuls of repressed traumas and torments inflicted on him by his odious father, in a furious tirade against his oppressor who has ruined every aspect of his life. The letter is a testament of extreme hatred, a visceral primal loathing that Freud would have relished as a perfect example of Oedipal revulsion.

And yet this protracted letter was never sent and was found by Max Brod after his friend's death, among his papers. It has always been regarded by Kafka scholars and biographers as a primary source of immense value, which is seen as evidence that Kafka's relationship with his father Hermann was the principal, most dominant feature of his challenging life.

However I would dispute this view. It seems to me that even though she is upstaged and is rendered almost invisible by the loud and deafening presence of her husband, Kafka's mother was the most significant, principal influence on the fragile psychology of her eldest child. Franz Kafka's state of mind was so deftly calibrated by his mother's neglect that he was destined to view the world through such a subtle and original lens of perception and produced a body of work that fascinated and intrigued his huge readership.

Although she remains a muted presence in most biographies of her son, her calm, understated personality had a considerable impact on not only her children but also her husband. She is regularly described as outgoing, warm-hearted and friendly, but biographer Ernst Pavel wrote of her being distant and detached. He writes of her 'corseted tenderness that must have felt like ice to the touch' and Max Brod described her as 'a quiet woman who was also extraordinarily bright and full of wisdom'. In a letter to Max Brod in October 1917 Kafka wrote of her 'prudence, calm, superiority and worldliness'. She certainly used all these qualities in her dealings with her husband Hermann, who seems to have reined in the excesses of his personality when in her presence, shedding his bovine coarseness. In the most challenging times, he would retreat behind her dignified authority, recognising that her stability and calmness was far more reliable than his narcissistic bluster. In his vitriolic letter to his father, Kafka conceded one thing: 'You were always affectionate and considerate to her.'

The defining experience of Julie Kafka's life was the death of her mother, when she was four. She was immediately cared for by her grandmother, who in turn died a year later. Such trauma at such a young age can have emotional consequences similar to adult post-traumatic stress disorder, which results in the child developing a limited capacity for emotional responsiveness and strong attachments. In its place the developing personality will have a preference for self-sufficiency rather than intimacy and in Julie's case her relationships were quite probably emotionally underdeveloped.

We have already seen that to recover from the trauma of the birth process a baby needs all the reassuring love he or she can get from a reliable and permanent maternal presence. Immediately after the birth the amygdala will be in rampant spate, deluging the tiny brain with intense fears of annihilation, which Winnicott describes as 'primitive agonies'. Only a very responsive, tender-loving mother can soothe her baby's dread.

It is only recently that MRI brain scans and brain autopsies have led us to the understanding that the mother's prolonged and reliable presence is vital for the baby's neural development. Prior to this provision of hard neurological data, psychotherapeutic theory depended upon anecdotal evidence of clinical practice, the leaders of this field being Melanie Klein, Donald Winnicott and the founder of 'attachment theory', John Bowlby.

In 1963 John Bowlby wrote: 'The evidence is now such that it leaves no room for doubt that the prolonged deprivation of a young child of maternal care may have grave and far-reaching effects on their character and so on the whole of their life.'

This defining premise of attachment theory is based on the assumption that a well-lived life will have at its foundation a series of successful attachments within the nuclear and extended family and in adulthood in social and professional contexts. The ability to form and sustain these key attachments will depend upon the success or failure of our first 'primary attachment' with the mother, although 'primary attachment' could be achieved with a surrogate mother such as a grandmother, aunt, sister or some other permanent, reliable loving carer.

During the earliest months, a baby's facial expressions, attempts at smiles, dilating pupils, crying, sucking, clasping and clinging are pre-verbal attempts to communicate his or her needs to the mother. If the mother is well attuned to her child, which will almost certainly be the case if there is a good circular oxytocin flow, then she will respond successfully to all her baby's signals. If the mother provides this 'attuned responsiveness' the baby will feel safe and secure, but if this confirmation of her ability to meet her child's needs is not provided, the baby will develop what Bowlby calls an 'anxious attachment', when the baby is never certain how the mother will respond or, even worse, whether she will actually be there at all. If this state of 'anxious attachment' prevails, the infant will invariably choose one of two strategies which Bowlby observed in hours of clinical studies with small children. The first of these strategies was what he called 'ambivalent attachment' that used obsessive clinging to the mother or prolonged periods of inconsolable crying in an attempt to communicate the extremity of the infant's needs. This could result in excessive submission or vigorous attempts at attention-seeking in a desperate bid to regain the mother's focus on the unmet need. The second strategy was very different. If their needs aren't met, the baby can become a 'coper'. The infant, not trusting the absent or poorly attuned mother who can't respond effectively to her child's needs, becomes a precociously self-sufficient stoic. I have had a number of clients who spent their earliest weeks in an incubator or separated from their mother who had been hospitalised elsewhere because of a medical emergency. These individuals often have a glacial self-sufficiency, which Bowlby called 'avoidant attachment'.

Kafka's mother, Julie, definitely displayed an 'avoidant

attachment' defence, no doubt forged by the early loss of her mother and a consequent self-sufficiency. When Franz's two brothers died it seems Julie coped well: the biographies report that she felt a sense of guilt at having been absent in the family shop when her two boys were dying, but there are no reports that she suffered a prolonged bereavement or any searing grief.

However, her son was definitely someone who could only manage 'ambivalent attachments'. He clung throughout his life to a deficient father and mother and the partial and questionable reassurance of family life. He only finally left home at the age of thirty-two and he never managed to set up a permanent home of his own. He constantly returned back to the familiar sound of his braying, censorious father and his emotionally muted mother, in the submissive mode of someone only capable of 'ambivalent attachments', and when he finally broke this personality style of repeated compliance in his one-hundred-page letter to his father which detailed all his complaints and misgivings, he simply didn't have the necessary courage to send the letter.

Although many women found him attractive, Kakfa had great difficulty sustaining emotional relationships, despite longing to get married. His first sexual encounter appears to have been with a shopgirl when he was twenty, which he later described as 'charming, exciting and vile . . . I knew I'd never forget it but at the same time knew that it was full of vileness and filthiness'. This ambivalence appears to have been present whenever he experienced sexual intimacy.

Then four years later in 1907 he met a Viennese student, Hedwig Weiler, while on holiday and began for the first time the kind of long-distance love affair conducted by a regular exchange of letters, a means of communicating intimate thoughts and feelings at a distance. The most prolonged and intense of these epistolary relationships was with Felice Bauer, whom he met at Max Brod's house in 1912. She lived in Berlin and he in Prague and this strange love affair continued until December 1917 when he ended the second of two engagements. This is one of the most well-documented and commented upon courtships in literary history. *Letters to Felice*, a collection of Kafka's letters to her, was published in an abridgement in 1973 and runs to over 450 pages. Much like his letter to his father, it is one of the key primary sources in the ever-burgeoning Kafka scholarship.

With Felice safely based 350 kilometres away in Berlin, Kafka was able to indulge in other brief flirtations and dalliances. There was Grete Bloch, an infidelity he confessed to Felice with a certain relish, who became pregnant in the summer of 1915, although his paternity was only suggested by Grete some years after his death. All this emotional turmoil seemed to ignite a spasm of literary vigour and he started to write *The Trial*, a book about the guilt of 'K', the beleaguered protagonist of Kafka's novel who can't understand why he has been branded with this guilt by the 'powers that be'.

At the end of the summer of 1915 Kafka ended his engagement to Felice, but they were reunited the following year in Karlsbad and they took a holiday together in Marienbad. The engagement was back on. But then in August 1917 Kafka was diagnosed with tuberculosis which prompted him to tell Felice that he could not marry her.

A year later in late 1918, while convalescing in Schelesen, Kakfa met and fell in love with Julie Wohryzek, whom he became engaged to in June 1919. But – as we have seen – Hermann disapproved of this supposedly unsuitable match and to the intense disappointment of his son, refused to give his blessing. Unable to ignore his father's verdict, Kafka ends yet another engagement and vents his fury in the one-hundred pages of invective he intended to send his father.

As his consumptive lungs deteriorated further, Kafka was put on permanent sick leave and had time to begin his final epistolary romance with Milena Jesenská-Polak, who lived in Vienna and wrote to him to offer her services as a translator. Despite the fact she was married, he travelled to Vienna and spent four days with her. Two months later they met again, in Grund on the Czech-Austrian border. This latest romance soothed Kafka's fury towards his father and he began to write *The Castle*, his final work. Once again a new affair propelled his literary endeavours forward. They met one last time in Prague in the autumn of 1921 when Milena, probably to Kafka's relief, informed him that she couldn't leave her husband, but several months later Milena changed her mind and wrote that she was desperate to see him. Kafka replied immediately, saying: 'Don't write and avoid meeting me. Just fulfil this request for me in silence, it's the only way I can go on living.'

A few weeks later he wrote to Max Brod, explaining to his friend why he couldn't sustain an emotional relationship with a woman. 'I'm tempted by the body of one girl out of two, but not at all by the girl in whom I've placed my hopes . . . I can love only what I can place so high above me that it is out of reach.' Love and sex have to be separated and sex is simply not possible with any woman he idealises. This double-bind made the normal convention of marriage beyond him. Perhaps this is a predictable issue for anyone with 'attachment anxiety', who then suffers from a lifetime of 'ambivalent attachment', where nobody can ever be trusted enough to embark upon the unpredictable perils of matrimony. And yet Kafka was to have one more relationship with a young woman whom he did trust, whom he did love intimately and intensely, both erotically and emotionally.

In July 1923 Kafka decided to join his sister Elli and her children on a summer holiday in the Baltic resort of Müritz. In the camp where Kafka, his sister and her family stayed, he met a nineteen-year old Jewish girl called Dora Diamant. She was immediately drawn to Kakfa and wrote the following to a friend: 'I was particularly struck by this man. I couldn't shake off the impression he made on me. I even followed him into the town.' After their first meeting on 13 July, they saw each other every day for the remaining three weeks of his holiday. Before his departure they exchanged gifts, and when he returned home to Prague he only stayed a few days before setting off for Berlin where Dora lived. Kafka managed this despite his parents' insistence that he remain at home because of his faltering health: it was as if he knew that time was short and he was therefore determined to be reunited with Dora. She later recounted to a friend that Kafka regarded this immediate departure to join her in Berlin, contrary to the wishes of his parents, as one of the greatest achievements of his life. Once together in Berlin, in the ten months left to him, Dora devotedly looked after

Kafka in a manner he had never experienced and he had no trouble giving himself over to her care and attention.

I have noticed that with some of my clients who are in their late seventies and eighties that when time is short, it also becomes tremendously precious and they aren't inclined to waste a single day being miserable. I certainly feel this need to savour each week as I move through my seventies, not squandering so much as an hour dwelling on past regrets or future fears.

Thanks to Dora's love and devotion the last ten months of Kafka's life were – despite his illness – calm and tranquil. It was as if, during these few months living together in their apartment in the leafy Berlin suburb of Steglitz, this was exactly what Kafka had yearned for throughout his adult life. With his illness placing such a large question mark over their future together he didn't have to agonise over engagements or wedding plans or placating his parents, anxieties that had so plagued him in the past: he and Dora could now live intensely in the present moment. With Dora he felt the kind of security an ocnophil always longs for while enjoying this new adventure together on the edge of the great city of Berlin, a metropolis in the 1920s worthy of the most adventurous of philobats. Kafka loved Dora's independent free-spiritedness and – having escaped the clutches of her own overbearing Jewish parents in Poland – she seemed to completely understand the subtlety and nuanced irony of his literary achievement. After his death she wrote: 'When it came to literature he was not open to negotiation or compromise. His entire existence was at stake. He not only wanted to get to the bottom of things; he was at the bottom.'

One of the most frequent disappointments that my clients complain of is that they 'have never been "got"' and what they are trying to convey through this slightly clumsy euphemism is that they want to be understood, seen and recognised in all the complex variety of their personality. They don't want to be judged, but accepted and appreciated, despite their flaws and frailties. In fact what they seem to be after is to be loved devotedly, an experience they perhaps had in their first year of life from an adoring young mother, before she turned her attention to other competing obligations.

This is what Franz Kafka had longed for and finally experienced with Dora. At last he was 'got': understood, appreciated and loved as never before. They remained together in their Berlin suburb from September 1923 until March 1924, but their seven-month idyll was brought to an end by his worsening tuberculosis. With Max Brod's help Kafka returned to Prague, but Dora remained in Berlin as he could not face the prospect of introducing her to his parents.

The larynx specialist he saw in Prague suggested that he go immediately to the very grand Wienerwald Sanatorium in Austria, which dealt with lung and throat disorders. Kafka said goodbye to his parents and made the journey to the clinic alone: he would never see his parents or the streets of Prague again. Dora followed him to Ortmann in lower Austria where the clinic was located. Five days after Kafka's arrival a senior doctor told him that they didn't have the right facilities to treat the severity of his condition and the next day he and Dora travelled to Vienna to the city's laryngological clinic, where he immediately underwent a series of tests and examinations. It seemed Kafka's 'tubercular larynges' was terminal, but Dora pleaded with the doctors that this dreadful news be kept from him.

Her request was granted and it was suggested that Dr Hugo Hoffmann's private clinic near Klosterneuburg, fifteen kilometres from Vienna, might suit the couple as guests and family members could stay in the same building, which meant Kafka and Dora could be accommodated in adjacent rooms. The informal atmosphere and delightful period house, with its pretty garden, suited them perfectly and they quickly settled into their new home, which seemed to improve Kafka's mood and general condition. It was now Dora who wrote regularly to Kafka's parents on his behalf, with regular bulletins regarding their son's precarious health, reassuring them that there was 'absolutely no reason to worry'. It was becoming clear that Kafka trusted Dora in a way he had never done before and had complete faith in everything she did for him.

Max Brod wrote in his memories that Kafka desperately wanted to marry Dora and wrote to her father, asking for his blessing, but her father refused, giving no explanation. When Max Brod visited in early May he was amazed how alert and vigorous his friend appeared to be, considering it was on that very day that Kafka had received the rude refusal from Dora's father. Brod goes on to describe how when Dora arrived, Kafka broke down and wept, embracing her time and again declaring 'that he had never wished for life and good health more'.

A few weeks later, during the afternoon of 2 June 1924. Kafka was sitting on his balcony enjoying the early summer sun, trying to write a letter to his parents. When he felt too tired to complete it he gave it to Dora, who wrote the few concluding sentences. This final communication with his parents was full of affection and optimism that they would soon be reunited once his predicted recovery was complete.

In fact Kafka only had a handful of hours left. That night, as Dora sat beside him as he slept, he woke suddenly, fighting for breath. A doctor was called and Kafka was given an injection of camphor, which seemed to have little effect. He lasted until the late morning when, having been given some morphine, he slipped away with Dora sitting beside him, clasping his hand. He was only forty years old and an unpublished author.

It is worth repeating John Bowlby's dictum from his book *A Secure Base: Parent-Child Attachment and Healthy Human Development*: 'All of us, from the cradle to the grave, are happiest when life is organised as a series of excursions, long or short, from the secure base provided by our attachment figures.'

This idea is, I believe, one of the simplest and most profound concepts that has emerged from the development of psychoanalytic theory during the twentieth century. One of our most important requirements, if we are to live a fulfilling and productive life, is that we have a secure foundation which we trust entirely and from this seat of comfort we will generate sufficient confidence to explore and satisfy our curiosity by exercising our natural sense of adventure.

Carl Jung, Carl Rogers and Donald Winnicott:
The Pressures of the Collective
(Charles Darwin, Nicolaus Copernicus, Ludwig Wittgenstein)

O ne of the most common presenting issues that my clients complain about is the persistent tension between their desire to develop their true individuality and potentialities, which seem to be constrained and opposed by the many collectives that surround them.

Collective pressures bear down upon our individuality from our earliest age as we learn to conform to the rules and conventions of our immediate environment. Firstly, we come up against the parental collective, which is quickly amplified by the family collective. Then the educational collective kicks in, followed in short order by peer-group pressure. This peer-group collective pressure will last a lifetime and once school and university are negotiated, the educational collective will be replaced by professional and vocational conformity. The marital collective often comes next, followed by the emerging collective of the new family. Other collectives include those of our community, our nation and the overall zeitgeist of the society and culture we are part of. All play their part in undermining and compromising our true, essential individuality whose pristine, elemental nature is buried under layer upon layer of this collective compliance.

Yet how do we escape all this pressure to conform when

we have to earn a living, support a family, raise children or have obligations to ageing parents? Such responsibilities are an undeniable moral requirement and this perhaps is where one of life's great challenges lies: this tension between the needs and potentialities of our true individuality and the responsibilities we all have to the many different collectives we are embedded in. Thus one of life's primary tasks is to fashion a compromise between our individuality and the contracts we have made in our professional lives, marriages, family and social lives that preserves our true nature and yet fulfils our responsibilities to those around us and how to accommodate and pacify this fiercest of double binds is a pivotal dilemma in the practice of psychotherapy.

Most schools of psychotherapy place great value on the authenticity and uniqueness of each human being's true nature. Indeed this central issue stands at the core of Donald Winnicott, Carl Jung and Carl Roger's models of psychological development.

Winnicott suggested that from a very early age the infant begins to move from a 'true self' to a 'false self', when the mother is unable to hold and attend to her baby because of the competing obligations that she inevitably faces. The child will attempt to recover the mother's full devoted attention by developing strategies of compliance that please the mother which begins the process of developing a 'false self' as opposed to a 'true self', which is degraded by the child's need to regain the 'primary maternal preoccupation' that characterises the first months of life. In his paper 'The Concept of the False Self' Winnicott gives an example:

When you teach your small child to say thank you, you do this out of politeness and not because this is what the child means. In other words, when you start teaching good manners, you hope that your child will be able to tell lies, that is to say to conform to convention to that degree that makes life manageable. You know perfectly well that the child does not always mean 'thank you'. Most children become able to accept this dishonesty as a price to pay for socialisation.

It is in all these developing family and social compliances that Winnicott suggests 'the false self' continually gains ground at the expense of the perpetually diminished 'true self' and this disparaged core becomes more and more hidden away. A Winnicott epigram that I've already mentioned is worth repeating: 'A joy to be hidden but a disaster not to be found.' As Winnicott says of therapy: 'The true self is hidden and what we have to deal with clinically is the complex false self, whose foundation is to keep the true self hidden.' It is therapy's primary task to restore the value and the dominant position of the true self.

Winnicott's 'false self' is similar to Jung's 'persona', that mask of social conformity and collective compliance. Jung borrowed the term from the Roman theatre where 'persona' was the word for the mask which actors put on: a different mask for every one of their roles. We too have numerous roles we play and for each collective we join we have a mask or persona that allows us to adapt to the roles and conventions of that particular group: it is our packaging, our personal public relations exercise. But all too easily our persona can take over our entire existence.

As we have seen, the prime task of Jung's theory of individuation is to explore and then reveal the very essence of our individuality, quite separate from the requirements and conventions of the collectives we are surrounded by, which fashion much of our personality. (Notice how the word persona is contained in personality). He sees individuation as an innate psychological drive or inner compulsion in us all to discover this unique individuality in all its complete wholeness but is too often obscured and suppressed by our persona. In *Psychological Types* Jung insists that for a culture or society to prosper and be successful it must allow an opportunity for individuation. 'Only a society that can preserve its internal cohesion and collective values, while at the same time granting the individual the greatest possible freedom, has any prospect of enduring vitality.'

In his paper 'Ego Distortion in Terms of True and False Self' (1960), Winnicott provides us with a case study of a middle-aged female patient whose 'false self' was so successful that in their therapeutic sessions her primary wound was that her real life had not yet started and that her true nature had so far never had a chance to exist. I have had a number of clients whose presenting issue when beginning therapy was that they 'didn't feel at home in their own skin'. And indeed many of my clients say they suffer from 'imposter syndrome'. What imposter syndrome suggests is that the individual has become so adept at performing the role of the persona's 'false self' that if their mask is stolen, mislaid or damaged, they fear they will be revealed to be a fraudulent charlatan, the subtext to this fear being that their 'true self' is nothing like the image that they project for all to see.

The founder of 'person-centred counselling', Carl Rogers, uses the term 'organismic self' to describe this true authentic aspect of our nature, the discovery of which he regards as the principle goal of therapy. In his 1963 paper 'The Concept of the Fully Functioning Person' he writes: 'the theoretical model of the person who emerges from therapy is a person functioning freely in all the fullness of his organismic potentialities, a creative person who is ever-changing, ever-developing, always discovering herself and the newness of herself in each succeeding moment of time.'

To consider how this polarity, with all its chaffing tension, can deeply affect an individual's existence I want to consider aspects of the lives of Nicolaus Copernicus, Charles Darwin and Ludwig Wittgenstein.

The greatest scientists of the past have frequently been timid, diffident introverts, who wished for nothing more than to be left alone to develop their theories without having to take part in the raucous, strident controversy that their revolutionary ideas so often provoke. Such self-effacing modesty often attracts powerful extraverted champions who devote their lives to promoting the innovative groundbreaking concepts formulated by these shy geniuses, whose ideas are destined to change the world. Two of the most vociferous of these outspoken evangelists were the crusading proselytisers Thomas Huxley and Georg Joachim Rheticus, who both acted as a kind of St Paul to two of science's greatest messiahs.

The young Rheticus showed such prodigious mathematical talent at an early age that he was made Professor of

Astronomy at the University of Wittenberg in 1536, when he was only twenty-two. Wittenberg had become the principal Protestant seat of learning, whose youthful, ardent scholars could – for the first time – openly question the Catholic orthodoxy without fear of the Inquisition, who were charged with eradicating any subversive new ideas that attempted to question the rigid dogma of the papal world view.

As Rheticus began his professorship he became increasingly intrigued by the rumours that in Poland a certain retired Catholic canon had produced the first formulation of a sun-centred cosmology, although no such written explanation of this scientific insurrection existed, so incendiary would such a proposition be to the Polish cleric's mother church. Even Martin Luther himself had described Canon Copernicus as 'that fool who went against Holy Writ'.

In 1539, at the age of twenty-five, the passionate Rheticus set off to Frauenburg in the small, northern state of Ermland to seek out the reclusive, enigmatic Copernicus. He had planned to be in Ermland for a month but he stayed for two years, such was the powerful synergy between these two men whose partnership was destined to have such a profound impact on human history.

When Rheticus met Copernicus, it was love at first sight and he described the ageing priest as 'Atlas who carries the earth on his back'. Rheticus's arrival, with all his ardent enthusiasm, was a great surprise to the lonely, disappointed old man, who was now convinced his life's work would disappear like him into an eternal oblivion, as death drew ever-closer to the infirm and ailing sixty-six-year-old.

Twenty-nine years earlier he had, in an informal fashion,

circulated his unpublished notes on his heliocentric insights to a few carefully chosen colleagues, presenting his evidence upon which his revolutionary idea was based. Yet he stopped short of seeking formal publication, as he knew that his ideas would be seen as an act of seditious rebellion by the Catholic Church, whom he served. Now with the providential arrival of this young scholar from Protestant Wittenberg he was filled with new hope. Perhaps together he and Rheticus could produce a book giving a lucid account of his life's work, which could be published after his death and be read by a more sympathetic readership, while he slipped beyond the clutches of the Inquisition. It was all a question of timing.

When he had first circulated his ideas he had been supported by his oldest friend and colleague, Tiedemann Giese, who was now the Bishop of Warmia. Rheticus and his master travelled to the nearby Baltic state of Warmia and the three astronomers spent a long summer discussing, debating and cajoling each other, as a coherent formulation of Copernicus's heliocentric cosmos and the evidence that supported it slowly emerged. Rheticus and Giese pushed hard for immediate publication, but the old Canon stood his ground and – desperate to preserve his anonymity while he was still alive – he continued to plead his preference for posthumous fame. The book now had a title – *On the Revolutions of Celestial Spheres* – but Copernicus remained adamant: publication must be delayed. Rheticus and Giese suggested a compromise: Rheticus, under his own name, would write a description of the unpublished manuscript, while all mention of Copernicus's name would be deleted from the text.

By the beginning of 1540, the new manuscript was completed, yet delay followed delay and the typeset text wasn't sent to Copernicus until June 1542, by which time his health was failing. As he perused it the old man discovered much he wished to change and correct but Rheticus's vital job of proofreader was suddenly interrupted when he accepted the chair of higher mathematics at the University of Leipzig. Andreas Osiander, a friend of Rheticus, was now recruited to take over the proofreading and he began to send batches of pages to Copernicus for his final inspection. In November 1542, at the age of sixty-nine, Copernicus suffered a cerebral haemorrhage, which impaired his memory, silenced his speech and paralysed the right side of his body. Further collaboration was at an end.

Throughout the winter and early spring of 1543 his condition worsened and Rheticus had arranged for the book to be published in Protestant Nuremberg. Finally the printer's task was completed in April 1543. One of the first copies off the press was dispatched to Frauenburg, where Copernicus lay close to death. On 24 May 1543 the package from Nuremberg arrived where it was immediately unwrapped and placed in Copernicus's hands. As his grasp began to slacken, those who were with him watched as the life-force ebbed away out of his frail body. Eros had somehow been kept alight until his life's work, contained in this handsome volume, had been placed in his expectant hands.

The individual had prevailed. The collective juggernaut of the day, the Catholic Church, had met its match in the shape of this dying priest whose pioneering work would now be taken up by those other valiant individuals Kepler, Galileo and Newton.

Three hundred years later another scientist, living quietly in the English shires, would – in much the same way – censor his own ground-breaking work. From 1837 until 1859 Charles Darwin refused to publish his revolutionary findings, but in his case he suppressed his innovative, radical work because he didn't wish to upset his wife Emma and a coterie of close friends and colleagues. Despite their reluctance these two men, perhaps more than any others, were responsible for dethroning God as the creator of the cosmos, our galaxy, our solar system, our planet and all life on earth. *The Revolutions of the Celestial Spheres* (1543) and *On the Origin of Species* (1859) were the work of two introverted individuals who – without wishing to do so – helped end the supremacy that this religious collective had maintained for almost two millennia and both lives were dominated by their battle between their individual genius and the presiding collective of the day. Despite their natural desire to conform with all the collectives that surrounded them, their destiny, their talent and their split nature turned them reluctantly into two of mankind's most celebrated rebels.

As has been said, the first and most dominant of collectives is the parental, family collective, which inevitably has the greatest and possibly most corrosive impact upon a person's innate individuality. The nineteenth-century Victorian father was perhaps the perfect representation of the 'patriarchy'. Indeed this word summons up a picture of an oppressive, overbearing paternal authority that towers over his children with a despotic dominance, as was the case with Charles Darwin's father, Robert, who in turn had been completely dominated by his father, Dr Erasmus Darwin, founder of the famous 'Lunar Society'.

Robert's mother Mary (Charles's grandmother) seems to have fallen into a hypochondriacal depression brought on by the loss of two other children prior to Robert's birth. She died when Robert was only four, a time during which she relied upon lavish infusions of alcohol and opium to counter the physical pain and general state of misery that filled her days. As a result Charles Darwin's father Robert enjoyed almost no maternal attention, although after Mary's death an Aunt Susannah was recruited by Erasmus to look after his three sons. His eldest son Charles was very much his father's favourite and Erasmus made sure that this preferred child followed him into the medical profession. But then disaster struck: while studying medicine at Edinburgh University, Charles cut his finger when conducting a post-mortem and the injury resulted in septicaemia. Charles was dead within a week. The loss of his favourite child at such a young age devastated Erasmus and he now placed all his hopes on Robert, whom he insisted should train to become a doctor, despite the fact that Robert had no desire or inclination to join the medical profession.

In *The Autobiography of Charles Darwin* (1887) Charles writes of his father:

> He hated his profession so much that if he had been sure of a small pittance or if his father had given him any choice, nothing should have induced him to follow it. To the end of his life, the very thought of an operation sickened him.

And yet it appears that despite his dislike for the medical profession he did have a compassionate nature and considerable emotional empathy which he brought to bear when dealing with his patients. Still, Robert Darwin's frequent depressive and irritable states of mind replicated the dominating parental collective that had pushed him so reluctantly into a medical career and he now insisted that his son Charles should also study medicine at Edinburgh University. Indeed Charles would be the third generation of Darwins to attend the country's finest medical school, following in his brother's, his father's and his grandfather's footsteps, as the family collective tightened its grip around yet another generation of reluctant medics.

Inevitably Charles disliked every aspect of his medical studies. He found the lectures he had to attend tedious, dreary and numbingly monotonous and he hated the clinical studies and ward rounds at the Royal Infirmary, which he found upsetting. The visible evidence of physical suffering disturbed him and his visits to the operating theatres filled him with dread, as he seemed to share his father's extreme aversion to the sight of human blood. The terrible drama of amputations he could barely tolerate and finally – after witnessing an operation on a terrified child – he fled from the operating theatre vowing never to return to this 'theatre of suffering'.

His aversion to medicine went far beyond that of his father's, who – having repeatedly scolded his son for his lack of diligence and commitment to the family profession – began to realise that Charles's dislike for so many aspects of the medical profession was so intense that another career would have to be found.

Robert Darwin pondered on the possibility of law or perhaps the military for his son, but understood that Charles was unlikely to prosper in such competitive professions, which required a modicum of self-discipline. The only alternative that came to mind was that safe haven for shiftless wastrels: the Church of England. With this in mind his father decided that Charles would be sent to Cambridge to study for holy orders. Robert felt sure that his son would make an amenable, perfectly acceptable English parson, in some rural parish, where he could indulge his passion for botany. Once again the parental collective had won the day.

By a quirk of fate 350 years earlier Nicolaus Copernicus was also sent off, equally reluctantly, to one of Europe's leading universities to study for the priesthood. Yet in his case it was a frightening powerful uncle who provided the parental collective authority, as his father had died when he was ten. Darwin and Copernicus also shared another much more traumatic experience. Charles Darwin's mother died when he was eight, while Copernicus's mother died when he was nine. Copernicus's mother barely warrants a mention in his various biographies, not because she had little impact on her child, but rather because there seems little primary material upon which biographies can draw their assumptions.

Barbara Copernicus, we do know, was the daughter of a rich town merchant and city councillor and her brother, a man of patrician gravitas, became the influential Bishop of Varmia. Barbara married Nicolaus's father, another prosperous town merchant, and in quick succession they had four children. It appears from what meagre evidence there is that Barbara died when her youngest child Nicolaus was nine. When his father died a year later, the four children were adopted by their rather severe maternal uncle Lukasz Watzenrode, a senior cleric, who would soon be elevated to become the Bishop of Varmia.

It's worth noting that Copernicus and Darwin shared a number of personal characteristics: they both suffered from anxiety and were prone to bouts of illness, which were probably psychosomatic, and as a result they both tended towards introversion and a nervous compliance to all the various collectives that surrounded them. They were both extraordinarily intelligent and were capable of highly original scientific work and the formulation of groundbreaking ideas, yet these innovative scientific talents were constantly stalled by a depressive tendency that I'm quite sure originated from the early traumatic loss of their mothers. I'm tempted to suggest that their respective qualities of genius also sprung from a kind of compensatory psychological dynamic which stemmed from this shared catastrophic maternal bereavement: a kind of extreme 'gift in the wound'.

In Copernicus's case, after the death of his mother, the new parental authority took immediate action. Without asking the children's opinion, the eldest daughter Katyryna was married off to Bartel Gertner of Krakow, while her sister, also called Barbara, was sent off to become a nun in the Cistercian convent at Kulm and the two boys were inevitably destined for the priesthood. Like Darwin's brush with medicine, Copernicus never really felt at home amongst the Catholic clergy and yet he still found time to indulge his passion for astronomy and mathematics.

Somehow both these great men seemed to achieve their

groundbreaking discoveries by remaining quietly, almost silently subversive in regard to the leviathan religious collectives that so nearly overwhelmed them. And yet in the last few days of Copernicus's life, and when Darwin reached his early fifties, both men gave permission for their great works to be published after their seditious discoveries had lain out of sight for decades because of their fear of the collectives which they knew would be so deeply offended by their inflammatory work.

In 1828 Charles Darwin went to Cambridge to study for the Anglican priesthood, having been brought up in an intensely religious environment. The prevailing culture of the time was predominantly organised around the settled, unchanging religious status quo. Cambridge University in the mid-nineteenth century has been described as a religious police state, where the fellows of each college could only join the aristocracy of the university if they first became priests themselves, evidence that they unquestionably follow the overriding creed of the day.

During his three years at Cambridge the notion that he would join the Anglican priesthood became less and less congenial and by the end of his first year he knew that he lacked any religious calling whatsoever. As his spiritual aspirations waned, the vacuum left was filled by an enthusiasm for natural history that turned into an obsession. Deeply immersed in his new passion, he was surrounded by some of the finest scientific minds of the day who were developing the new intellectual discipline of biology. The branch of the new science which most fascinated Darwin was entomology and each week he would embark upon trips out into the Fens in search of beetles and other insects, of which he became a compulsive collector. The great mentor and friend of Darwin's Cambridge years was John Stevens Henslow, Professor of Botany, who kept open house once a week and undergraduates interested in science were always welcome. Darwin never missed one of these evenings and joined Henslow on so many field trips that he became known as 'the man who walks with Henslow'.

After his graduation from Cambridge in 1831 Darwin returned home to Shrewsbury to consider what he should do next. And then out of the blue, in August of that year, he received a letter from Henslow who had been asked to recommend a naturalist to travel as a companion to Captain Robert Fitzroy as he commanded a naval vessel that would chart the southern coasts of South America. 'I have stated,' wrote Henslow, 'that I consider you to be the best qualified person I know of, who is likely to undertake such a situation . . . the voyage is to last two years.' In fact the voyage was to last five years and was to change how Darwin regarded the world and our place in it.

From December 1831 until October 1836 Darwin's home was to become HMS *Beagle*, a small thirty-metre-long Royal Naval brig that was totally unsuited to accommodate a ship's company of seventy and the numerable specimens that Darwin would collect during the course of the long voyage. The stated objective was to complete a survey of the Patagonian coastline of South America and chart the waters of Tierra del Fuego and the Chilean seaboard and then go on to explore a number of Pacific Islands. No one on board could have possibly realised, as they left Devonport, that they were embarking upon one of the most historic voyages in human history.

Darwin, who suffered from chronic seasickness, was relieved to reach Bahia in Brazil in late February 1832 and immediately he went ashore into the nearby rainforests. For eighteen days Darwin was in a state of rapture as he explored the tropical profusion of animal and plant life, writing: 'Turning to admire the splendour of the scenery, the individual character of the foreground fixes the attention. My mind is in a chaos of delight.'

During the next few months, as the *Beagle* roamed up and down the Brazilian coast, Darwin stayed in a comfortable house on the outskirts of Rio de Janeiro with the ship's artist Augustus Earle where he became fascinated by the range of people living in Brazil, which included the country's Indigenous people, the ruling European immigrants and the teaming African slave population. His family had brought him up in a culture of anti-slavery, the burning ethical issue of the day, and here in South America he was deeply shocked when he encountered its full horrors in the raw. Darwin began to wonder how God could possibly have created human beings with such a diversity of appearance and experience, as he compared Cambridge dons with these poor blighted beings, living in such appalling circumstances. How could God allow such terrible, cruel inequality? To see naked people his own age barely surviving in such a hostile environment shook him to his core. Later on, in Tierra del Fuego, he encountered 'miserable, dreadful savages', humans living like wild animals and he began to feel that such diversity could not be ordained by God. At the same time he was becoming more and more convinced that all human beings were related and shared the same origin.

After nearly four years the expedition reached the Galapagos Islands, where Darwin collected an immense variety of rock, plant and animal specimens that were to provide him with crucial evidence when he began to develop his theory of evolution. The journey home via New Zealand, Australia and South Africa took a further year with the *Beagle* finally reaching Falmouth on 2 Oct 1836. As Charles Darwin, still only twenty-seven, made his way home from Cornwall to Shrewsbury he had no doubt as to the direction of his future life: he was destined to become a brilliantly versatile scientist, straddling the disciplines of geology, biology, botany, zoology and even philosophy as he slowly developed these early stirrings that were to coalesce into his revolutionary theory of natural selection.

Darwin's collection of hundreds of samples of rocks, fossils, animals, bird, insects and plants far exceeded what could be accommodated on the diminutive *Beagle* and throughout the five-year voyage he had shipped these invaluable specimens back to Cambridge where Henslow greeted them with avid enthusiasm. Once home, this great collection was waiting for him, as was a considerable measure of fame within the scientific community as Henslow had made sure that his exceptional protégé would now have a platform upon which to build his future career.

The intellectual aristocracy of the day organised themselves into a series of societies, located in London's West End, that were only too pleased to invite the famous young naturalist into their ranks. In 1836 Darwin was elected into the Geological Society; in 1837 the Zoological Society invited him to become one of their members and then at the age of only thirty, in 1839, he joined the country's most illustrious scientific tribe, the Royal Society.

In these years after the *Beagle*'s return Darwin was increasingly engaged with the subject of 'transmutation', which represented his early consideration of thoughts and ideas that would eventually become his theory of evolution by natural selection. Indeed a number of his biographers have suggested that the years 1837–1839 were the most fertile of his life as he became more and more obsessed with this collation of geology, zoology, botany, biology, transmutation and theology. His restless mind filled notebook after notebook. Now that he had the hard data from his *Beagle* field trip, how could he forge all this material into a coherent theory of evolution? And how would such a theory fit into the ethical values and religious beliefs of the Victorian Society which surrounded him? How could he – a conservative by temperament – stir up such seditious ideas that would not be tolerated by his contemporaries?

This unpalatable situation was made much worse when in 1838 Darwin fell in love with his cousin Emma. The courtship was swift and very quickly he realised this was the woman he wished to marry. Rather to his surprise, she reciprocated the full extent of his feelings and in January 1839 they were married. After the rushed courtship and wedding he could see that he was faced with a problem for although he was devoted to his delightful new wife and although they shared a great many things in common, she was an ardent

Christian. At a time when he was becoming appalled by the Old Testament's accounts of creation, combined with his mounting incredulity in regard to the New Testament's description of miracles, virgin births and human resurrection, he was spending his days with a much-loved wife who regarded her faith in these Christian beliefs as the cornerstone of her life. For Darwin his intellectual passions were totally at odds with his marriage and he was faced with the ultimate double bind, which plunged him into the first of a series of breakdowns

During much of 1839 he felt unwell and his work on his expanding notebooks was regularly interrupted by a variety of physical ailments and feelings of depression. And then right at the end of the year, a few days after the birth of William, their first child, Darwin's health collapsed completely and he was unable to work for the next eighteen months. Throughout 1840 and the first half of 1841 Darwin listed his symptoms as follows: heart palpitations, flatulence, nausea, shivering, blurred vision, exhaustion, fainting fits, a fear of dying, headaches, chest pains and general depression. The one consolation in all this misery was the perpetual presence of his adored wife Emma, who seemed to have all the qualities of an expert nurse. As psychoanalyst Douglas Hubble famously wrote about Darwin's psychosomatic health issues: 'There was environmental over-care . . . the perfect nurse had married the perfect patient.'

As we have seen, one of the greatest psychotherapeutic theorists produced by our country is widely regarded to be John Bowlby. Bowlby's great contribution to our discipline was laid down by him in his three-volume work entitled

Attachment, Separation and Loss, published between 1969 and 1973, although the book which he completed just before he died was his masterful biography *Charles Darwin: A New Life*, which was published posthumously in 1990. This biography is extremely revealing and gives a fascinating account of the psychological tensions that turned Darwin into a virtual invalid throughout stretches of adult life. Bowlby maintains that this emotional frailty originates from his mother's early death, when he was eight, which was preceded by her long, protracted illness. Indeed it seems that Darwin barely knew his mother when she was fit and active and throughout his early childhood a sense of impending doom hung over the household. In addition her death was somehow made worse by his father's and sister's insistence that there was to be no mention of her thereafter, so the young boy could never express his grief and extreme distress. His reactions and feelings caused by her death, and indeed her very existence, became a shameful secret that he was prohibited from ever speaking of. To make matters worse throughout his childhood his father remained not only distant and aloof but also critical and censorious towards his son.

As an adult, Darwin faced another unmentionable secret within his own family: the direction of his thoughts and their articulation in his developing theory, which held such promise, were leading him towards a series of conclusions which would crush the religious beliefs that his beloved Emma had such need of. How could he subvert and abuse not only the creed of his wife but also the beliefs shared so passionately by his extended family, many of his friends and colleagues and the much wider society that he was so embedded in?

The double bind was tightening its grip.

By 1842 Emma and Charles were living in London, but in May of that year they travelled to Emma's parents' home at Maer Hall in Staffordshire for a month's holiday. Darwin, never one to waste an idle moment when he was fit and well, decided to use these weeks of leisure to formulate a complete summary of all the notes he had taken since returning from the *Beagle* voyage. In thirty-two pages he gave his first clear account of evolution, a kind of initial embryo, which during seventeen long years of gestation would finally become *On the Origin of Species*.

These few weeks of leisure proved to be fruitful, but the rest of the summer was taken up looking for a new home, outside London, where Charles and Emma could bring up their ever-expanding family. Within a month they found what they were looking for in the Kent hamlet of Down: a large vicarage set in a small-holding, on sale for a reasonable sum of £2,200.

Darwin's task during these initial months and years at Down House was to complete the publications arising from the Beagle voyage, works that became 'Volcanic Islands' and 'The Geology of South America'. But there could be no question of publishing any thoughts that might emerge from his thirty-two-page sketch regarding evolution: he knew exactly what the reaction would be to any suggestion that man and apes came from the same origin and that God had nothing to do with the process of Creation.

Darwin kept his thoughts to himself until finally on 11 January 1844 he wrote to a young naturalist named Joseph Hooker, who became his most devoted friend and supporter.

In this letter to Hooker he shared, for the first time, a brief account of his laws of evolution that he had sketched out in May 1842.

> At last gleams of light have come and I am almost convinced that species are not immutable . . . I think I have found out the simple way by which species become exquisitely adapted to various ends . . . It is like confessing a murder.

In this first confession, feelings of extreme guilt rose up in him, like a kind of horror that he was capable of confronting Victorian society with an act of such wickedness that it was tantamount to murder. But murder of what? Given his background, his education, the family and colleagues he was surrounded by and his depressive, anxious nature, it did feel like murder: the slaying of those aspects of civilised, ethical life that allowed an ordered society to prevail and prosper.

A few weeks later Hooker's reply arrived. What a relief that his young colleague's response to Darwin's supposed calumny was calm and reassuring, suggesting that his insights were not seditious nor unnecessarily inflammatory. Furthermore Hooker was flattered by Darwin's approach and asked to hear more. Once shared this confession had a cathartic effect on Darwin which ignited a creative surge and in a spasm of energy in the spring of 1844 he expanded his thirty-two-page sketch into a 189-page essay.

Publication, however, was out of the question. Perhaps somehow providence would eventually – if Darwin waited long enough – provide an answer to his intolerable double bind and if no solution was provided his work could always be published posthumously. Meanwhile to distract himself from his insoluble problem he turned his attention to a seven-year study of barnacles.

With this simple mollusc distracting him between the years 1843 and 1847, Darwin prospered. His new home at Down delighted him in every way: his children were his pride and joy and Emma had become the perfect wife and mother, always healthy and cheerful in spite of frequent pregnancies. But then in the summer of 1848 Darwin's health took a turn for the worse. He wrote in his diary: 'From July to the end of the year, unusually unwell, with swimming in the head, depression, trembling and many attacks of sickness.' These ailments coincided with his father's rapid decline and in November 1848 the father who had been so trenchant and distant during his childhood, yet so supportive and proud as he watched his son's professional success, finally died at the age of eighty-two.

For the next few months, stricken by grief, Darwin was unable to maintain his habitual routine and he stopped working. By February 1849 his depression and psychosomatic ailments were so severe that he travelled to Malvern and placed himself in the care of the famous Dr Gully, renowned for his success in curing nervous disorders. The entire Darwin family stayed at Malvern until the end of June, when Darwin seemed at last to be recovering thanks to vigorous hydrotherapy, and by July he was able to return to work. But any thoughts on the question of evolution were completely off-limits, given his fragile health.

The year 1850 turned out to be uneventful and Darwin

focussed his attention on his innocuous barnacles. The only anxiety was his favourite child, ten-year-old Annie, whose health during the autumn started to concern her parents. And then quite suddenly her mysterious illness worsened and in April 1851 she died, leaving her stricken parents bewildered by the speed of this terrible event.

Charles and Emma Darwin never really recovered from Annie's death. As he wrote to Hooker: 'There is nothing in the world like the bitterness of such a loss.' And yet Darwin didn't collapse into a state of psychosomatic illness: perhaps he didn't because he had to support Emma who, one month later, gave birth to their ninth child Horace; or perhaps sharing his intense grief with his wife meant that he didn't internalise these extreme feelings, provoking some psychosomatic physical reaction.

After this irreparable loss he needed to maintain his quiet, reassuringly familiar routine at Down House and therefore continued to pursue his work on his reassuringly familiar barnacles: he was clearly in no mood to enter the fray in regard to his thoughts on evolution. In the summer of 1854 the last of his volumes on barnacles was published and later that year he returned to his consideration of evolution, experimenting with germinating plant seeds and gathering evidence from other scientists and naturalists that would further inform the great work he now had in his sights.

He was also prodded into action when he received word in late 1855 from his friend Charles Lyell who sent him an article entitled 'On the Law Which has Regulated the Introduction of New Species', which had appeared in one of London's natural history journals. The article, written by an obscure, self-employed specimen collector who lived in Borneo, received almost no attention, but on reading it, Darwin found it to be a lucid, cogent account of evolution, echoing many of the ideas Darwin had already formulated. Early on in 1856 Darwin returned to the manuscript of his expanding work on natural selection. Clearly Alfred Russell Wallace's article had provoked within Darwin concerns about both priority and fame, perhaps just what he needed now that he had finally slaked his appetite for barnacles. 1856 and 1857 became years of considerable progress as the epic work took shape, but in 1858 he felt overwhelmed by the sheer scale of his undertaking and his strength and energy appeared to falter. 'I have so much to do and so precious little strength to do it', he wrote to a friend.

Then in June 1858 Darwin received, all the way from Borneo, a manuscript from Wallace, entitled 'On the Tendency of Varieties to Depart Indefinitely from the Original Type'. Darwin immediately realised that Wallace's work resembled his own conclusion to an alarming degree. Writing to Lyell, Darwin moaned: 'I never saw a more striking coincidence . . . So all my originality, whatever it may amount to, will be smashed.'

This professional crisis was, however, now over-shadowed by a situation of alarming extremity which now engulfed Down House. Just after receiving Wallace's manuscript, Darwin's daughter, Etty, was struck down by scarlet fever, passing on this highly infectious disease to the family's two nursery maids. The other children were quickly evacuated and went to stay in nearby Hartfield with Emma's sister Elizabeth, but it was too late and on 2 July their tenth and last child, Charles Waring, caught the disease and died when he was a year-and-a-half-old. In a state of near-collapse the grieving parents took the entire family off for a prolonged stay on the Isle of Wight.

Darwin was in no condition to take any decision regarding the arrival of Wallace's work and so in his absence Lyell and Hooker decided to have parts of Wallace's manuscript read together with extracts from Darwin's 1844 essay at a meeting of the Linnean Society. A prostrated Darwin agreed, writing to Hooker: 'I will do anything. God bless you my kind friend. I can write no more.'

The two papers were duly read during the Linnean Society meeting that July, but Darwin and Wallace's groundbreaking endeavours barely made a mark. Somehow the busy evening's proceedings appeared to muffle the impact of the two papers. As this was the last meeting of the season the president of the society complained 'that the year has not been marked by any striking discovery'. This muted response was probably just what Darwin needed, given the dreadful loss of yet another child.

The question of when Darwin would be able to put the finishing touches to his epic work was now uppermost in the minds of Hooker, Lyell and his other fervent supporter Thomas Huxley. By April 1859 negotiations with the publisher John Murray were well underway and it was decided that the volume should be entitled *On the Origin of Species by Means of Natural Selection*. By mid-June galley proofs began arriving at Down House and to Darwin's dismay he found his own prose style coarse and lacking clarity. As a result he poured his energies into making numerous final revisions, delivering the final draft at the beginning of October. Exhausted, Darwin then took himself and his family to a spa hotel in Yorkshire, near Ilkley, for some much-needed hydrotherapy and in his absence the great work was published on 24 November 1859, in an edition of 1,250 copies, which sold out within the week.

As a second edition was being quickly prepared it was clear that *On the Origin of Species* was being met with immense scientific and public interest alike. Huxley wrote a glowing review which was published in *The Times* and there was inevitably plenty of controversy, but Darwin's marriage survived as Emma's equanimity remained serenely intact. Similarly there was no revulsion from either family, friends or colleagues. There were – as anticipated – fierce debates about the consequences of Darwin's work, but he remained above and separate from the fray, safely behind the ramparts of Down House, leaving Thomas Huxley (who became known as Darwin's bulldog) to argue his case publicly.

On the Origin of Species is indeed one of the very few books that has revolutionised how we understand the world. Yet its author, that very reluctant revolutionary, survived the twenty-three-year-long double bind that began when he had first assembled the core material of his theory. This time he did need a prolonged period of recovery to recuperate from the professional challenges and private tragedies which marked 1859 and 1860, yet he did suffer regular bouts of depression as he continued to produce a series of books that went further to secure his international fame. His final decade was devoted to an intensive study of earthworms, of which he wrote:

The plough is one of the most ancient and valuable of men's inventions but long before he existed the land was in fact regularly ploughed and still continues to be ploughed by earthworms. It may be doubted whether there are any other animals which have played so important a part in the history of the world, as have these lowly organised creatures.

This late utterance with which Darwin ended his book *Earthworms* (1881), published a few months before his death, beautifully personifies the profound contrasts of his personality. The modest subject matter, like that of barnacles, defines the introverted humility of this great man and yet his ambition – his intention – is gloriously grandiose in its revolutionary, innovative, groundbreaking aspiration.

Ludwig Wittgenstein was born in 1889 into one of the richest families in the Austro-Hungarian empire, whose flamboyant wealth was only outshone by the local branch of the Rothschild family. His father Karl was an industrial tycoon, who owned the largest steel manufacturing conglomerate in Europe, which moulded him into a kind of Austrian Andrew Carnegie, investing – as he did – in the Netherlands, Switzerland and the US. Karl and his wife Poldi had nine children: four girls and five boys. Three of these brothers were destined to commit suicide, while Karl's youngest son, Ludwig, would suffer from repeated depressions throughout his life, casting him into regular fits of inconsolable despair. This emotional dysfunctionality that afflicted his sons was no doubt a prime consequence of Karl's heavy-handed, severe unsparing parental style, that went even beyond the paternal intimidation dished out by Hermann Kafka, Leslie Stephen, Robert Darwin and Copernicus's Uncle Watzenrode.

Karl cast across his family a net of tight collective compliance insisting that his sons would together navigate the family industrial empire through the first half of the twentieth century. In order to avoid any competing educational collective that might forge unwanted distractions, the children were not sent to school and were educated by a number of tutors, carefully selected by Karl. The composer Johannes Brahms, a friend of Karl's, visited the grand Wittgenstein palace and said of the family: 'They seemed to act towards one another as if they were at court.' Apparently a rigid formality dominated the family home, in which Poldi was so anxious and frightened that she could offer little comforting tenderness to her emotionally bruised sons.

When a family's emotional problems are particularly acute I have noticed how children of the afflicted family often deploy the defence of what I have come to call 'geographisation', whereby as soon as they become adults they go and live in another country, putting a reassuring distance between them and their troubled family. But invariably this doesn't work as their complexes and neuroses that arose from the family collective are embedded in their psyche, like some accompanying piece of toxic, psychological luggage.

For Ludwig Wittgenstein this process started early. At fourteen he was sent to boarding school in Linz where he had his first experience of formal education at Linz's Realschule. It was here that he had the dubious pleasure of sharing a classroom with Adolf Hitler, a local boy, six days younger than Ludwig. It seems that time spent in close proximity to the future Führer didn't unduly disturb the young Ludwig as on leaving the Realschule he chose to go to Berlin to study at the city's Technische Hochschule. After studying engineering for two years he then moved to England to take his doctorate at the University of Manchester. It was here that he designed a rudimentary prototype of a jet engine, forty years before a British team developed the first jet-propelled aeroplane.

Judging from his early peripatetic restlessness, it's safe to say that he found his family collective so oppressive and restrictive that he had to escape it as a matter of survival. Wittgenstein was an exceptional individual who, as we will see, fought and disliked every collective that interfered with his much cherished, individual freedom. It was this ever-present tension with the succession of collectives and this fear of restriction that dominated the life of this prime example of a philobat mentality.

It was while at Manchester that he read Bertrand Russell's *The Principles of Mathematics* (1903). Intrigued by Russell's work and knowing him to be the most distinguished philosopher of his generation, Wittgenstein immediately decided to travel to Cambridge and arriving there on 18 October 1911 he proceeded to Russell's rooms without an appointment and introduced himself. After this first unscheduled meeting he was soon not only attending Russell's lectures and seminars but also dominating them, with his brilliant, almost explosive confidence. Russell wrote to his then mistress Ottoline Morrell: 'I love him and feel he will solve the problems that I am too old to solve. He is THE young man that I've always hoped for.'

Having stayed on in Cambridge for the autumn term he

was due to return back to Vienna for the Christmas holiday, but before he left, he arrived in Russell's room in a state of great agitation and asked his mentor whether he should take up philosophy as a career. Russell told him to write a paper during the Christmas break and return with it in the spring term. And so Wittgenstein returned in January with his essay. On reading it Russell wrote to Ottoline Morrell: 'It was very good, much better than my English pupils do. Perhaps he will do great things.' Wittgenstein told his friend David Pinsent that Russell's encouragement was his salvation, ending years of uncertainty and depression, unable to see how he might spend his life, as he was so often overwhelmed by feelings of futility that conjured up repeated thoughts of suicide. He now would concentrate all his thoughts and aspirations on philosophy and perhaps an academic career.

Although Wittgenstein is regarded by many academics as the greatest philosopher of the twentieth century, he was a very reluctant practitioner of his chosen profession. He certainly realised that he had an immense talent for philosophy, but inevitably he thoroughly disliked the formalities and rituals of Cambridge academic life. He also found the astringent, empirical rigour of his philosophical work was at odds with his quest for a kind of pristine moral integrity, which was more important even than his philosophical work. In the years to come he was constantly encouraging his students to give up philosophy, which he regarded as a highly dubious profession, and he spent a considerable part of his adult life avoiding his philosophical obligations, both as a teacher and writer, despite the fame and success of the *Tractatus*, the only book he published during his lifetime.

Late in 1912 Wittgenstein left Cambridge and returned to Vienna to spend time with his terminally ill father, who died in January 1913, after which he became immensely wealthy due to an extravagant inheritance. He then returned to Cambridge for a few months before travelling to the remote village of Skjolden in Norway, where he undertook the first prolonged solitary retreat that would become a regular and necessary corrective to the demands of academic life. It was here in the lonely Norwegian landscape that the first stirrings of *Tractatus* began to emerge.

At the outbreak of war in 1914 he immediately volunteered for the Austro-Hungarian army. His military service was to fall into two contrasting periods: from August 1914 to March 1916 he served behind the lines in a variety of capacities; then in the spring of 1916 he was transferred to the front line, where he took part in active military operations.

During his first phase of army service Wittgenstein had plenty of time to continue working on what would become the *Tractatus*, a set of notes and an emerging manuscript that he had begun while in Norway. Initially he served as a search-light operator in the river steamer *Goplana* on the Vistula River, but inevitably he found the rules, regulations and brutalities of the army collective odious. He was completely at odds with the other crew members, whom he loathed and because of his isolation and loneliness he fell into a depression. Then, in a Galician bookshop, he discovered a copy of Tolstoy's *The Gospel in Brief* (1892) and he became obsessed with committing whole passages to memory. His mood lightened and he wrote to his friend Ludwig Ficker: 'You cannot imagine what an effect it can have upon a person . . . it kept me alive and left undisturbed my inner being.' As Tolstoy's *Gospel* soothed his tormented mind, he was able to return to his philosophical work. In 1915 he made the important discovery of his 'picture theory of language', which was to play such a pivotal role in the *Tractatus,* and his work on his manuscript continued.

The daily nourishment conferred on Wittgenstein by Tolstoy's *Gospel* was supplemented when he found a copy of Nietzsche's *The Anti-Christ* (1895) in a Krakow bookshop. Reading these two books led him to his lifetime conviction that our spirituality and our sense of the sacred are a set of feelings or instincts, rather than a logical reality or a belief and he felt that the teachings and example of Christ provided us with an attitude or moral compass which made the inevitable sufferings of life bearable. Throughout the spring and early summer of 1915, buoyed up by his sustaining emotional response to Tolstoy and Nietzsche, Wittgenstein wrote with renewed vigour what would eventually be published as *Notebooks: 1914–1916* and these ideas would become the basis for a considerable part of the *Tractatus.*

The beginning of 1916 was to see an abrupt change in Wittgenstein's circumstances, when he was transferred up to the front line for a mass attack on the Russian positions. As he waited to take part in a battle with the enemy, he was filled by waves of fear that he would become another victim of the senseless slaughter. He was then assigned one of the most dangerous tasks, an observer in a front-line observation post. But when his position was shelled by the Russian artillery, he felt a kind of exhilarated enlightenment. He wrote: 'Perhaps the nearness of death brings me the light of life. May God enlighten me. I am a worm, but through God I become a man. May God be with me.' After the second bombardment he wrote that the felt 'like a prince in an enchanted castle'. Despite the constant danger he survived, certain that it was God's will that had protected him. He wrote subsequentially: 'Only death gives life its meaning.'

Unlike so many of his young male contemporaries across the battlefields of Europe, Wittgenstein would survive the carnage of war unscathed physically. He had served the defeated Austrian Empire for five years, an experience that had left its haunting impact upon his personality. He even insisted upon wearing his army uniform for years after the war had ended, a kind of lingering 'transitional object' that conveyed both the trauma and fierce change that the brutalities of war had wrought on his psyche, affecting the way he viewed himself, those around him, the world at large and his life's task.

Having become a prisoner of the Italians after the Armistice he was eventually released in August 1919 and on his return home his family were appalled by the change in his physical appearance and his personality. They had assumed he would return to Cambridge and continue his work as a philosophical genius, yet such a future filled him with revulsion, with all its vanity and self-congratulatory high-mindedness.

Instead he decided to undertake a teacher's training course and become a primary-school teacher. This he did and in September 1919, after giving away much of his inherited wealth, he enrolled in one of Vienna's teacher-training colleges. Having completed the course he spent the next six years teaching in a series of remote villages in Lower Austria, fulfilling his desire for a simple and secluded life. This continued until the spring of 1926, when he left teaching and became a gardener in a monastery, just outside Vienna, and living in a tool-shed in the grounds.

It was here that he received the news that his mother had died. This unexpected watershed seemed to have a startling impact upon his mood and he immediately returned to Vienna, which marked the end of his long estrangement from his family after his father had died.

Surprisingly little has been written about Wittgenstein's mother: she barely gets a mention in Roy Monk's much-admired biography. However Brian McGuinness, in his underrated book *Young Ludwig: Wittgenstein's Life: 1889–1921* (1988), writes of Poldi Wittgenstein:

> For inner reasons and because of her marriage she was like a person holding her own in a storm and so far from giving strength to her children she was someone whom they had to support. This was more marked during her widowhood. The pattern of her widowhood itself illustrates that she needed someone to hold her up. It seems that her sons especially required more devotion and insight and individual care than she was capable of giving them.

It is tempting to speculate that three of her five sons committed suicide because of this fatally flawed maternal deficiency. It is certainly likely that Ludwig's troubled personality was a consequence of the fact that his mother was afflicted by a lifetime of anxiety and a feeling of being permanently overwhelmed by her demanding husband and eight children. When my clients have been the youngest child in large families, they are often the person that their afflicted mother turns to for consolation and support. This can often lead to what I have come to call 'maternal engulfment' whereby the child will often attempt to escape the problem by enacting out the defence of 'geographisation' by leaving the country or city where the troubled mother lives. It is therefore not surprising that as a young man Ludwig moved to Manchester and Cambridge and then spent much of his adult life away from his family in Vienna. This unconscious defensive strategy tends to have one unfortunate consequence: the individual concerned will remain, on the whole, emotionally aloof and distant in all his or her relationships and will tend to avoid strong attachments and true intimacy. As Wittgenstein's former student and longtime friend Norman Malcolm wrote in *Ludwig Wittgenstein: A Memoir* (1958): 'It was Wittgenstein's tragedy that he intensely craved affection but could rarely tolerate the way it was expressed.'

On his return to Vienna, after his mother's death, Wittenstein was welcomed back home by his two favourite sisters, Hermine and Gretl, and his career trajectory took a bizarre and unexpected turn. Gretl had decided to build a new townhouse in the centre of Vienna. Although he had no experience in house design, Wittgenstein designed and supervised the building of a large house, which – despite its stark simplicity – has an elegance of line and form that has been much admired by successive generations of architects. Today it is one of Vienna's notable buildings and for the last five decades has served as the Bulgarian Embassy.

It seems that his mother's death, his return to Vienna, his reunion with his sisters and his work on Gretl's house helped him make a partial recovery from the post-traumatic stress disorder caused by his war service. Now at last he began to respond to the extraordinary success that the *Tractatus* was having both in Vienna and back in England, where Wittgenstein had become a legendary figure among the Cambridge philosophical elite, who were desperate to persuade their most renowned student to rejoin their illustrious ranks.

In mid-January 1929 Wittgenstein returned to Cambridge. As Maynard Keynes famously wrote: 'Well God has arrived. I met him on the 5.15 train.' To celebrate the return of their 'prodigal son' Keynes organised a dinner attended by all the grandees of the Cambridge philosophical aristocracy, just the kind of occasion Wittgenstein loathed.

Wittgenstein would remain in Cambridge for much of his later adult life, forever complaining about his philosophical work, always contemplating his escape from what he felt were the vanities of Cambridge academic life, a collective whose protocol, etiquette and conversations he detested. As his friend Maurice Drury wrote: 'For the greater part of his life he was making plans to forsake his work and live an entirely different mode of existence to that of an academic philosopher.'

From 1929 to his death in 1951 Wittgenstein was tormented by his way of life in Cambridge. He realised he had a unique talent for philosophical thought and discussion and also had a charismatic intensity in his teaching style that inspired almost all his students, and yet his exceptional capacity for philosophical enquiry seemed to him to be a distraction and diverted his attention from what he felt was the prime purpose of his life: his pursuit of a moral and ethical integrity.

Maurice Drury tells us that Wittgenstein often used the words 'deep' and 'shallow' to describe not only other philosophers, but also a range of other aspects of life. He said: 'Kant and Berkeley seem to me to be very deep thinkers', yet others like Schopenhauer and his contemporary A. J. Ayer were 'shallow'. Perhaps what Wittgenstein meant by comparing 'deep' with 'shallow' was the difference between true wisdom and an intellectual cleverness that lacked any moral or ethical content.

This 'deep' moral content was for Wittgenstein found in the Gospel's account of the life of Christ and in the writings of St Augustine, Kierkegaard, Dostoevsky and Tolstoy, all of whose work he would return to time and time again. He wrote to Drury: 'I am not a religious man but I cannot help seeing every problem from a religious point of view.' And on another occasion he wrote: 'The symbolism of Christianity is wonderful beyond words, but when people try to make a philosophical system out of it, I find it disgusting.' This sense of 'disgust' seemed to be ignited by his own philosophical work and indeed was, he felt, endemic in Cambridge academic life.

It was as if his career had become a kind of torture to him, a torment he increasingly felt the need to escape from. Various escape routes were considered. In 1935 he travelled to the Soviet Union which impressed him sufficiently enough for him to consider moving to Russia permanently. While staying in Dublin with Maurice Drury he thought about training to become a psychiatrist and Drury arranged for him to visit the psychiatric unit at St Patrick's Hospital so he could meet individuals who were seriously mentally ill. For a month he went two or three times a week to visit some of the long-stay patients.

Although neither of these plans materialised, he stayed away from Cambridge for longer periods and made more solitary visits to Norway and the west coast of Ireland. Then in 1939 he succeeded G. E. Moore as Cambridge Professor of Philosophy with much reservation. During the war he famously become a porter at Guy's Hospital in London before moving to Newcastle where he worked in a medical laboratory. Finally in 1947 he gave his last lectures in Cambridge, retired from his professorship and settled in a secluded cottage on Ireland's Connemara coast, where he worked on what would become *Philosophical Investigations* (1958).

A year later he travelled to Cornell University to stay with Norman Malcolm and caused consternation by appearing unannounced in a number of seminars conducted by Malcolm, with students who regarded the *Tractatus* as a holy text. While staying in New York he fell ill and upon his return to England he was diagnosed with advanced prostate cancer, an illness that he viewed with a kind of serene equanimity even though it killed him eighteen months later

On 24 December 1949 he flew to Vienna to take part in his last family Christmas, moving back into his old childhood room in the Wittgenstein mansion on the Alleegasse. His oldest sister Hermine, fifteen years his senior, who had provided such maternal support for him was also dying of cancer. Uncharacteristically he welcomed the luxuries which the house on the Alleegasse offered, including its retinue of servants. He wrote to Dr Bevan, his Cambridge GP, whom he had befriended: 'I'm very happy and being treated VERY well.'

He finally returned to Cambridge in April 1950, but he didn't remain there long, preferring to stay in Oxford in the house of one of his favourite students, Elizabeth Anscombe. There he worked steadily on texts that would become *Culture and Value* and the first part of *On Certainty* (1969).

By January 1951 his illness had progressed to such an advanced stage that he had to return to Addenbrooke's Hospital in Cambridge. However Dr Bevan, knowing Wittgenstein's intense dislike of English hospitals, invited him to spend his last days in his own home.

During these last weeks a composed and untroubled Wittgenstein wrote over half of what would become *On Certainty*, thought by many to be one of his most lucid texts. Perhaps his very final words, spoken to Mrs Bevan, were the most poignant of his last utterances. 'Tell them I've had a wonderful life', he instructed her. This seems to me a deeply moving remark when we consider how divided and troubled his personality was as he drove himself forward and yet in his last two years he seemed to achieve a harmonious resolution to the disparate aspects of his nature which seemed for so much of his life to be in a constant state of turbulent conflict.

Intersubjectivity and Intimacy
(W. B. Yeats, Marilyn Monroe)

I n the penultimate chapter of her book *Emotional Understanding: Studies in Psychoanalytic Epistemology* (1995),
the distinguished American Intersubjectivist psychotherapist Donna M. Orange writes about a client who said: 'I
don't think I care about being understood. I don't expect
people to understand me. I want to feel loved and cared for
whether I'm understood or not', the implication being that
our clients – in many cases – harbour a hope that they might
be loved by their therapist. This is exactly what happened
when the very first patient sat down with the very first therapist and engaged in the 'talking cure'.

This pivotal encounter took place in the Christmas week
of 1880, in Vienna, when Freud's friend and colleague Josef
Breuer met Bertha Poppenheim, later known to posterity as
Anna 'O'. Recalling these meetings Josef Breuer wrote: 'Her
life became known to me to an extent to which one person's
life is seldom known to another. 'The Case of Anna "O"'
is the centrepiece of Freud and Breuer's *Studies on Hysteria*
(1895), the first book of case studies that underpinned the
psychoanalytic revolution. Breuer met this young woman
twice a day for eighteen months between December 1880
and June 1882, and he described their sessions as 'the talking
cure', while Anna 'O' used the words 'chimney-sweeping'.

Quite suddenly the treatment came to an abrupt halt for reasons that remain unclear in the 1895 case study, but later Freud was more candid. Breuer had become gripped by what we now would call an 'erotic countertransference'. Finally realising the impact his infatuation with his client was having on his marriage, Breuer brought the treatment to a close. The talking cure seemed to have a good effect upon Bertha Poppenheim, who recovered from her hysteria and subsequently had a career as a pioneering social worker so groundbreaking that she appeared in 1954 on a West German postage stamp. Freud alludes to the Anna 'O' case in an early letter to Jung of December 1906, three months before the two men met for the first time: 'Essentially, one might say, the cure is effected by love. And actually transference provides the most cogent, indeed the only unassailable proof that neuroses are determined by the individual's love life.'

A number of years after he had nursed Breuer through his infatuation with Anna 'O', Freud was having to provide similar support for his protégé Carl Jung. As we have seen, Jung began treating Sabina Spielrein, a twenty-year-old Russian, towards the end of 1905 and it seems likely that Jung realised he had fallen in love with her by the beginning of 1908. Jung wrote thirty-four letters to Spielrein and the letters of 1908 are extraordinarily passionate considering that Jung was Sabina's doctor and therapist. For instance he wrote to her: 'It is my misfortune that my life means nothing to me without the joy of love, of tempestuous, eternally changing love.' Or in the same letter: 'I am looking for a person who can love without punishing, imprisoning and draining the other person. A love that is boundless and without reservations.'

The love affair that now developed was revealed to Freud by Jung in a letter dated 4 June 1909 and is repeatedly discussed in their correspondence. Finally, taking his mentor's advice, Jung ended the relationship and Spielrein made a complete recovery from her schizophrenia and became a leading founder of psychoanalysis in Russia. Jung's affair with Spielrein was followed by his relationship with Toni Wolff and, as we have seen, Wolff began as Jung's patient before then becoming his assistant and later, his lover.

Jung was not to be the only early disciple of Freud who fell in love with one of his clients. Sándor Ferenczi met Freud in February 1908 and Freud swiftly realised that this young Hungarian psychiatrist had an immense aptitude as a practitioner of psychoanalysis. For some years before meeting Freud, Ferenczi had been having an affair with a married woman named Gizella Palos, whose daughter Elma was attractive and intelligent but appeared to be emotionally unstable. Ferenczi agreed to analyse Elma. The highly impressionable Ferenczi was quickly charmed by her and six months after the beginning of the analysis, he wrote to Freud and confessed that he had begun an affair with his new client, despite the on-going relationship with her mother. In a state of great turmoil, Ferenczi begged Freud to take Elma into therapy himself. Freud was extremely reluctant, but after observing the desperate state of his protégé, he finally agreed. Ferenczi then ended his relationship with Elma and returned to Gizella, whom he eventually married.

These experiences with Breuer, Jung and Ferenczi must have provided Freud with a compelling motive to write his seminal paper of 1915 'Observations of Transference-Love'.

Freud opens his paper by asking the question 'When the patient admits that she has fallen in love with the physician who is analysing her . . . how is the analyst to behave in this situation if he is not to come to grief and yet believes that the treatment should be continued through this love-transference?' He answers his by saying:

> The treatment must be carried through in a state of Absti-nence . . . If her advances were returned, it would be a great triumph for the patient, but a complete overthrow for the cure . . . The analyst is absolutely debarred from giving way to any romantic impulses. However highly he may prize love, he must prize even more highly the opportunity to help his patient over this decisive moment in her life. The psycho-analyst knows that the forces he works with are of the most explosive kind and that he needs as much caution and con-scientiousness as a chemist.

Having laid down the cardinal principle of 'abstinence', Freud suggests that while an erotic or romantic relationship is out of the question, the client's feelings for the therapist should not be renounced and indeed should become the central material of the therapy.

The 1915 paper was clearly influenced by Freud's experience as he tried to support his colleagues Breuer, Jung and Ferenczi when these eminent physicians became over-whelmed by their feelings for certain patients. In the early years of the twentieth century Freud was battling to establish the respectability of psychoanalysis. His explicit description of the centrality of sexuality, as the primary human drive, and particularly childhood sexuality, had created swathes of hostility against his fledgling science. Now its leading practitioners were having affairs with their patients. How could the moral and ethical credentials of his science be firmly established if there was any danger of its practitioners repeatedly falling in love with their clients? Abstinence, distance, punctilious formal relations between client and physician would have to be rigorously applied: the clinician must become emotionally absent from the proceedings.

Today, however, as we consider our own practice, there is an increasing emphasis on the centrality of intimacy as one of human being's most longed-for aspirations. The current generation of psychotherapists, practising a hundred and ten years after Freud's 1915 seminal paper, appear to be questioning Freud's rigid rules with their inflexible constraints on the client-therapist relationship. Donna M. Orange and many others see Sándor Ferenczi's works as pertinent in the new climate of Intersubjective psychotherapy, despite his unforgiveable clinical lapse with Elma.

In a diary entry dated 18 June 1932 Sándor Ferenczi wrote: 'In the end one becomes convinced that patients are right in demanding from us a genuine interest, a real desire to help and an all-conquering love. For each and every one of them, this alone makes life seem worth living and which constitutes a counterweight to their traumatic past.'

Ferenczi's influential 'clinical diaries' continually emphasise the point that although sexual and romantic entanglements must be avoided, it is the intimacy achieved between client and therapist that is the key to therapeutic success. Orange considers Ferenczi's contribution approvingly in *Emotional Understanding* and she applauds Ferenczi's emphasis on the need the patient has to be loved by the therapist. Through the therapist's direct emotional connection with the patient she praises Ferenczi's view that 'No analysis can succeed if we do not succeed in really loving the patient. Every patient has the right to be regarded and cared for as an ill-treated unhappy child.' For Orange, Ferenczi is suggesting a kind of loving re-parenting, a developing emotional bond which becomes more important than theoretical insight. It is the loving relationship itself that is the primary curative factor.

In *The Modernity of Sándor Ferenczi* by Thierry Bokanowski, published in 2017, the author makes a strong argument for a reappraisal of Ferenczi's work, whom Bokanowski feels is well in tune with the current view that the intimate therapeutic relationship between client and therapist is the royal road to cure. 'Ferenczi held that taking care of the patient with tenderness, playing the role of a loving, permissive and playful parent would check and neutralise his or her unhappy beginnings in life.'

Another important psychotherapeutic pioneer of the 1930s was the Scot Ian D. Suttie. Although largely forgotten today, Ian Suttie died in 1935 at the age of forty-six, a few days before the publication of his significant book *The Origins of Love and Hate*. Influenced by Ferenczi, Suttie asks four important questions: Is psychotherapy a technical, professional service or a personal relationship? Can the therapist's love heal the patient? If so, what is the nature of this love? Does the Freudian model deny love within the therapeutic relationship? He emphasises the significance of tenderness and affection in the psychotherapeutic relationship and writes: 'I have carefully studied both my patients and my own defences and came to the conclusion that there is a taboo on tenderness every bit as masterful as the taboo on sex. What my patients need is to be loved in a way that makes them not only secure from loneliness but also secure from their own dangerous and destructive impulses.'

Orange is also an admirer of Suttie, agreeing with his view that Freud and his leading followers had a general aversion to tenderness. She is attracted to his theory that psychoanalysis provides an opportunity to restore lost and damaged capacities to find love and tenderness and she sees Suttie's book as the first intersubjective account of psychopathology.

Carl Rogers would, I'm sure, also have been attracted to Suttie's work. I have always thought his three conditions that are required for successful therapy (and what are taught at the start of psychotherapeutic training) – empathy, unconditional positive regard and congruence – are three of the most important requirements of love and Rogers' groundbreaking book *Counselling and Psychotherapy* (1942) legitimises the therapist's concern about the quality of the relationship between therapist and client.

One of the most striking features of the earliest pioneering years of the psychoanalytic movement was the total monopoly of the male practitioner. This male dominance was primarily a reflection of early twentieth-century chauvinistic patriarchy culture. How very different is the gender orientation of our profession in the first three decades of the twenty-first century.

Female practitioners – and indeed female archetypal

features, such as the capacity for intimacy, compassion and empathy – now predominate. These qualities extend considerably the potency of nurturing maternal virtues and the emphasis on the relational within the therapeutic experience and have had a very positive impact on our profession and our philosophical outlook, creating a spectacular development and acceptance of the psychotherapeutic process within our broader culture.

Freud's safety net of abstinence, with the therapist sitting out of view of the patient, never expressing any personal disclosures and repressing any feelings for the client, is more and more out of fashion. Ian Suttie's concept of a 'taboo on tenderness', which he describes in *The Origins of Love and Hate*, and the rule of emotional abstinence, with all its professional detachment and distance, has been put to one side and replaced by empathy, unconditional positive regard, the I–Thou relationship and attuned responsiveness, all psychotherapeutic concepts greatly valued by today's therapists who use these euphemisms because of their uneasiness around the word 'love' when discussing their relationships with their clients. Tenderness and intimacy are now back in business.

As has already been said, I have noticed how individuals who have not been adequately parented have a tendency to develop a natural charm that they unconsciously amplify in the hope that they can attract sufficient surrogate parents to make up for the lack of parental love. The unconscious subtext during an initial assessment goes something like this: 'I could love you, therefore I want you to love me.' The alchemy of this most seductive sales pitch is, however, not sexual, but there is the understanding that this potential relationship could become a dopamine delivery-system, or even per-haps a fully-fledged oxytocin delivery-system: a transaction of brain chemistry that the client – having not experienced true maternal bonding – now might experience for the first time with the therapist. Several years of this benign loving environment can clear blocked neural pathways in the brain and enlarge the hippocampus with its capacity for promoting feelings of equanimity and self-confidence As Louis Coz-olino writes in his excellent book *The Neuroscience of Psycho-therapy: Healing the Social Brain* (2010): 'Psychotherapists are now applied neuroscientists who create individually tailored enriched learning environments designed to enhance brain functioning and neurological health . . . we use a combina-tion of empathy, affect, stories and behaviour experiments to promote neural network growth and integration.' Cozolino could easily have used the word 'love' here. And I am sure Cozolino is right. Inadvertently the loving psychotherapist becomes a neuroscientist, affecting brain anatomy. Unwit-tingly we use dopamine and oxytocin to dredge silted-up neural pathways allowing the free flow of health-giving endorphins, hormones and neuropeptides. This is exactly how empathy and the caring reassurances of the therapist can soothe and quieten the overactive alarm of the amygdala.

What, in effect, is going on here is that both therapist and client are unconsciously trying to break down each other's defences in a bid to deepen the intimacy between them. In terms of the client, he or she will demand both consciously and unconsciously that the therapist expresses feelings that their parents often withheld from them. This second attempt at experiencing good parenting is a bid for a kind of developmental catch-up. To use modern parlance: they desperately need to press the i-Player catch-up button to hear, see and feel the programme they missed decades previously. I'm sure that we, as therapists, must be open enough, vulnerable enough, emotionally expressive enough to fulfil this tremendous need, by offering what I want to call 'therapeutic love'. The kind of love we feel for our clients should remain characterised by what the Greeks called 'Agape'. As we saw earlier, Greek philosophy distinguishes between two kind of love – 'Eros' and 'Agape'. Agape demands nothing in return and wants only the growth and fulfilment of the loved one, whilst Eros is the hope and need for erotic experience. If this Agape, this parent-like devotion, develops into an Eros-related erotic countertransference it should never be acted out physically. This imperative has many similarities to the incest taboo.

The writer who has most persuasively written about therapeutic love is Ethel Spector Person, who was Professor of Clinical Psychiatry at Columbia University from 1981 to 1991. In her excellent book *Love and Fateful Encounters: The Power of Romantic Passion* (1988) she states

> Transferential love and romantic love do possess many features in common: not only the subjective feelings they evoke but their obvious deep connection with the subject's innermost desires and their capacity to act as powerful agents of change.

She applauds Freud's view that the emotional content of transferential love towards any parental surrogate is the child's longing for an omnipotent parent who can provide protection and safety from all the malevolent forces he or she feels surrounded by. What is projected onto the parent, and later onto the therapist, is the means of taming the terrors and anxieties that Winnicott called 'primitive agonies', the traumas we experience as infants and which persist into adult life. In almost all forms of love, and especially in romantic or transferential love, we re-experience the child's empowerment that is felt when the parent provides safety, protection, pleasure and a strong feeling of purpose and meaning. As the oxytocin and dopamine flow, the level of well-being crescendos.

With an implicit reference to Freud's repetition compulsion, Ethel Person asserts that transference love is a repetition of the extravagant and unrealistic hopes we have placed on the process of loving in real life. The narcissistic and excessive hopes we had as infants for parental love were doomed to disappointment by the fact that parental attention would inevitably be diverted towards other siblings and other emotional demands. All the many domestic and professional chores, as well as the mother's other personal pleasures and aspirations, will negatively impact on the level of attention that the emotionally ravenous infant will demand. This wildly optimistic hope of infantile love is then further inflated by the excessive romantic expectations of our culture which allow these endless repetitive cycles of disappointed emotional hopes and unrealistic romantic aspirations to deeply affect adult experiences of love. This results in a UK divorce rate of 42% and legions of clients complaining about their disappointing marriages, their repeated relationship collapses and the feeling that love is a busted flush.

In the working through of transferential love the origins of these extravagant expectations can be explored and replaced by a more realistic approach to erotic/romantic love and its potential restorative powers. As Ethel Person writes:

> Like love itself, the transference love has within it the potential for pleasure and pain, good and evil. It can mask dependency yearnings, competitive stirrings and hostile feelings. But within the therapeutic situation, it can become the basis for a transforming analytic opportunity. Transference love may offer the energy for change, but only when it is rigorously analysed can one be certain of the direction of change.

Ethel Person then goes on to warn of the perils of the erotic countertransference and she cites Jung's affair with Sabrina Spielrein and Otto Rank's sexual relationship with his client Anaïs Nin as examples. This is a particular peril when the therapist is at a low ebb, experiencing marital problems or feelings of loneliness. Therapists, as we know, are prone to depression, low self-esteem and relationship collapse: how seductive, at such times, is the gratifying feeling of being admired and idealised? How reassuring is the intimacy of the therapeutic session, with its secrecy and its high sense of joint mission? If there is also a mutually strong physical attraction, the strict boundaries of the therapeutic frame will be placed under great pressure, requiring immediate supervision to avert the disastrous possibility of the erotic countertransference being played out. We must perpetually bear in mind the maxim 'Psychotherapy is an arrangement when two people agree to meet regularly, but never to have sex.'

When reading Ethel Person's description of transferential love being a replay of the unrealistic idealised expectation of the endless flow of parental loving attention, I found myself considering William Butler Yeats' concept of 'the perpetual virginity of the soul'. This idea of the great Irish poet suggests that he longed, through love, to achieve a soul connection with another human being: a deep completely fulfilling intimacy with another, ideally with a physical as well as a soulful union, and that this hope was never realised, never experienced in its fullness, leaving his soul in a state of 'perpetual virginity'. Dialogical psychotherapists call the achievement of this soulful union an 'I–Thou experience', borrowing the term from the Jewish theologian Martin Buber. Carl Jung wrote and talked about the 'Coniunctio archetype', insisting that this particular archetype holds a pre-eminent place in the human psyche, functioning as 'a fundamental psychic factor' in human beings' desire for a transcendent union with another, a kind of soul-matedness that fills so much of our culture from Homer onwards, through Shakespeare, through Wagner into our own twenty-first-century obsession with romantic film and television drama.

Can such a deep soulful eros-related connection remain a permanent state of being between two people? Or is the Jungian 'coniunctio' just a fleeting, momentary rush of oxytocin, inevitably to be followed by 'la petite mort' of post-coital disappointment, plunging us back into our lonely singularity? Should we place our bet on the more reliable solidness of Agape rather than the ephemeral transience of

Eros? If Yeats is right, are our souls destined for an existence of perpetual virginity? To explore these questions we shall turn our attention to the life of William Butler Yeats and an iconic woman of twentieth-century fame who died early, having spent much of her short life desperately searching for an all-embracing, lasting romantic love upon which she could rest her frail and damaged personality.

Susan Pollexfen was born in 1841 and raised on the west coast of Ireland in Sligo, in a prosperous, middle-class Protestant family. She lived an uneventful life until she met John Yeats, then a law student, who she married after a brief courtship. Susan assumed – and hoped – that she was marrying a successful young barrister, but John had other ideas and finding the law slow and tedious, he decided to become an artist. Susan hadn't the slightest interest in artistic pursuits and when her husband announced he was leaving the law for the perilous uncertainties of art and bohemia, she must have shrugged her shoulders and groaned inwardly, for this career choice, so at odds with his wife's aspirations, was symptomatic of a chasm that defined this incompatible couple. Their eldest son, Willy, remembered his father talking all the time, opinionated and loquacious, while his mother was a silent, impassive presence. She did, however, talk about her great love for Sligo and its surrounding landscape, which she thought was the most beautiful place in the world.

Soon after the birth of their second child Lily, John took himself off to London where he enrolled in Heatherley School of Fine Art. Once established in appropriate lodgings he summoned his wife and children to the great Victorian metropolis. Susan loathed her new home and indeed her husband's whole way of life. As Yeats's biographer Roy Foster writes: 'She hated what she construed as the pretentious and social frivolity of "the artistic life".' After an abbreviated and impecunious stay in London, Susan fled back to Sligo with her two children. There would be further sojourns to London and Dublin, but the primary home for her and her eldest son would always remain her beloved Sligo.

John never made much of his career as an artist. What talent he had was marred by his lack of application, preferring the role of the amusing, talkative dilettante rather than the committed, focussed painter with a strong compulsion to provide for his wife and four children. He was always short of money, constantly borrowing (with a Micawberish optimism) funds from his friends, his wife's family and even from his children, when they had money to lend. All these endless disadvantages and struggles slowly wore Susan down and she appears to have gone mad. At the age of forty-seven, once again reluctantly returning to London, she suffered a disabling stroke and became a reclusive mute and morose invalid for the remaining years of her life. After her death in 1900, John Yeats repeatedly said that in marrying Susan he had given 'a tongue to the sea-cliffs' through their son William's poetry.

The distinguished American psychiatrist and psychoanalyst Harold Searles died in 2015 at the age of ninety-seven. Although Searles, who was Professor of Psychiatry at Georgetown University, Washington, has been described as a 'therapeutic virtuoso' I'm not sure his position in the history of psychotherapy has been fully recognised. In groundbreaking papers such as 'Oedipal Love in Countertransference' (1959) and 'Concerning Therapeutic Symbiosis' (1973) he – in an almost confessional spirit – becomes a trailblazer for the Intersubjectivists who followed him in their shared insistence that therapeutic healing most effectively occurs when the client and therapist achieve a close, intimate and mutually devoted relationship. In his 1959 paper he goes so far as to write:

> I have found that in the course of my work with every one of my patients who have progressed towards an analytic cure that I have experienced romantic and erotic desires to marry the patient . . . I have become increasingly convinced that the patient's self-esteem benefits greatly from their sensing that he or she is capable of arousing such deep feelings in their analyst.

This revelatory admission is explored further in Searles' paper 'Concerning Therapeutic Symbiosis' (1973) where he suggests that once an attachment has been made with the therapist and a powerful transference emerges, the client will re-enact his or her early need to heal the 'afflicted mother'. He maintains that our human vulnerability and frailty as therapists is essential if the client is to re-experience this redemptive power that he or she felt in the early relationship with the 'afflicted mother', in the therapeutic relationship with us. This level of therapeutic relatedness he calls 'Therapeutic Symbiosis'.

Searles develops this idea further in his 1975 paper

'The Patient as Therapist to His or Her Analyst' – a title full of implicit controversy – where he suggests that the client needs to feel either consciously or unconsciously that he or she is healing the therapist, as healing the therapist is part of the process of healing themselves. He emphasises the client's ability to unconsciously detect the therapist's 'ill components' as he believes that most clients feel they have 'failed' in their attempt to heal their mother and this leaves the patient guilt-ridden. This element of their development has therefore been interrupted but can be re-initiated if he or she feels they are somehow healing the therapist. As the child needs to feel that they can give as well as receive, so the client needs the empowerment of giving something curative back to the therapist.

I once had a client whose mother had to be hospitalised for bipolar disorder immediately after her birth, triggered by post-natal depression. It was decided that during her stay her recently-born baby should remain with her in the psychiatric unit when she was being treated. Throughout my client's childhood her mother continued to suffer from mental health issues and was definitely an example of Searles's 'afflicted mother', imposing upon my client a strong sense of reparative responsibility. I noticed in her attitude towards me that she was always concerned about my health and longevity and I felt that this need to heal me was a regular presence in our sessions. My client's vigorous inner critic, her depression and her extreme low self-esteem had – I was sure – originated from her feeling that as a child and young adult she had completely failed in her bid to heal her mother, having felt that the purpose of her life was to save and cure her from her dreadful affliction, and my client now brought her complex to bear on our relationship. As our sessions progressed, I discovered that it was important that I told her that I benefitted from the time we spent together and that our sessions always increased my sense of composure and self-possession, which certainly was the case.

Time and again I have clients whose mothers encountered misery and turmoil in the early months and years of their child's life and in such cases the client from that early age felt a responsibility to cure and heal their afflicted mother.

Susan Pollexfen Yeats, miserable in her marriage, diminished by her poverty, an exile from her beloved Sligo, silent and morose in the company of her husband and his artistic friends, was just such an 'afflicted mother' as far as young Willy Yeats w-s concerned.

Her near-invisibility is evident from the briefest and most cursory mentions she receives in the various Yeats biographies. Indeed, Roy Foster's is the only biography to describe the death of Willy's younger brother Robert who succumbed to an attack of croup at the age of three.

This sad, benighted woman is an extreme example of Harold Searles' 'afflicted mother'. Perhaps in his earliest months, Susan could express and convey her love for her firstborn child before she was overwhelmed by the arrival of four further children. And, as she endured her regular migrations from London to Sligo and then back to London before her husband and children wore her down, she could provide Willy with a flow of oxytocin. Perhaps this was withdrawn when she gave birth to her next child fourteen months later and he sensed the beginning of an inexorable abandonment that was to fuel the future intensity of his romantic imagination, as well as his poetic genius. This is, of course, mere speculation, but I'm sure Willy felt the urge, the compulsion and the instinct to find ways to soothe and ameliorate the misery of his mother's afflicted life and the impact it had upon him. In his book *Reveries over Childhood and Youth* (1915), written in middle age, he admitted that he 'remembered little of childhood but its pain' and when he was six his father wrote: 'I am continually anxious about Willy – he is almost never out of my thoughts. I believe him to be intensely affectionate but from his shyness, sensitiveness and nervousness he is very difficult to win.'

I have had numbers of clients whose early experiences in the daily presence of 'an afflicted mother' produced in them romantic hopes which remained uncomfortably active, even though they were in stable long-term marriages. Despite a high degree of conjugal harmony, they would be regularly attracted to – and would often fall in love with – someone whom they felt might be their soulmate, which inevitably placed pressures upon their family's life. It's as if the client concerned still persisted in their search for an oxytocin hit to arouse within them the thrill of another Eros experience, which might produce the deep 'coniunctio', the 'I–Thou' soulmate experience that they had always longed for. It seems to me that these clients all shared one early experience – the oxytocin flow with an attentive, loving mother had been suddenly terminated and they were left with a lifetime's search for this sense of fusion, this intense connection that in their earliest years has been severed so abruptly. Yet, as so often happens, as the initial ecstatic intoxication inevitably wanes, they are left with Yeats's perpetual virginity of the soul.

Nevertheless it is this experience that my clients so often seek, the same romantic longing which Yeats so intensely felt throughout much of his adult life. In his memoirs, published posthumously in 1972, he wrote of his late adolescence and early twenties:

> Women filled me with curiosity and my mind seemed never to escape from the disturbances of my senses. I was a Romantic, my head full of mysterious women . . . I had gathered from Shelley and the Romantic poets an idea of perfect love. Perhaps I should never marry in church but I would love one woman of all my life.

And then on 30 January 1889, at the age of twenty-four, he met Maud Gonne in London when he was living in Chiswick. Ostensibly she came to visit Yeats's father, whom she'd met in Dublin, but she must also have been interested in the painter's son, whose two plays in verse *The Isle of Statues* (1885) she knew and admired and whose first collection of poems *The Wanderings of Oisin* (1889) had met with some success in the literary salons of London, where his passionate readings had forged a tantalising reputation. Aged twenty-three, she was a tall, elegant woman whose dress style and deportment were contrived to attract ardent suitors and Yeats knew, on their very first meeting, that Maud Gonne was the muse he was looking for: one who would inspire reams of romantic verse, which would set pulses racing and imaginations flailing. As he said of that first evening together: 'and the troubling of my life began'. He was bewitched by what Roy Foster described as her 'fin-de-siècle beauty in Valkyrie mode' and he adored the radical nationalism which had her described as the 'Irish Joan of Arc'. She was perfect in every way.

They spent the next seven days walking, talking and exchanging confidences, secrecies and hopes for the future. And yet Gonne kept one significant secret to herself: she was having an affair with Lucian Milleroye, a journalist and politician in Paris, where she was now spending much of her time. Before the year was out, she gave birth to Milleroye's child and as a result, Yeats's letters describing his longing for her and his protestations of love made little impact upon his chosen muse. When they met again in Ireland after the death of her child in 1891, he found the prostrate and shattered young woman even more captivating and he immediately proposed marriage. She refused, giving as her excuse that she would never marry because of her morbid dread of sex. To compensate for this painful rejection the poems of love and devotion poured from his pen.

This began the pattern of their relationship for the next twenty-eight years. She insisted that their bond should be a spiritual union, a platonic mystical intimacy which never became an erotic entanglement, but inevitably the lush and tormented poems of sexual longing increased their ardent velocity. As Yeats's letters to Gonne reverberated with his complaints of unhappiness she wrote back to him: 'Because you make beautiful poetry out of what you call your unhappiness, the world should thank me for not marrying you. Poets should never marry.'

Yeats proposed to her three more times in 1899, 1900 and 1901, but his love remained unrequited, her refusal as adamant as ever. Then, to add to his misery, in 1903 she married the Irish Nationalist Major John McBridge, which devastated the poet. The marriage collapsed within two years and Yeats and Maud met again in 1908 in Paris and finally consummated their relationship. And yet it seems that this much anticipated event, which Yeats had longed for for nineteen years, fell far beneath his expectations. It's unclear whether they repeated this erotic coupling, but soon after Gonne wrote to him: 'I have prayed so hard to have all earthly desire taken from my love for you and dearest, loving you as I do, I have prayed and I am praying still that the bodily desire for me may be taken from you too.'

Years later, presumably with the 1908 erotic disappointment in mind, Yeats wrote 'the tragedy of sexual intercourse is the perpetual virginity of the soul'. It was as if his search for the merging of the spiritual and the carnal was abandoned, as he finally accepted what he called 'the antinomies of soul and body'. Yet after all these years he had the consolation that his unattainable muse, Maud Gonne, who had haunted his life, was turning him into the greatest romantic poet of his age.

He made one more bid for Maud Gonne's hand in marriage in 1917, after her estranged husband had been executed in Dublin for his part in the Easter Rising of 1916. Once again she rejected him and in his confusion, at the age of fifty-one, he proposed to Maud Gonne's daughter Iseult. The twenty-two-year-old for a moment considered Yeats's offer, but wisely turned him down. But before the year was out, avoiding any romantic histrionics, he married Georgie Hyde-Lees, a twenty-five-year-old English girl of whom he said: 'My wife is a perfect wife – kind, wise and unselfish. She has made my life serene and full or order.' Of his marriage he wrote:

> All his happier dreams come true –
> A small old house, wife, daughter, son,
> Grounds where plum and cabbage grew,
> Poets and Wits about him drew:
> What then? Sang Plato's ghost. What then?
>
> The work is done, grown old he thought
> According to my boyish plan;
> Let the fools rage, I swerved in naught,
> Something to perfection brought;
> But louder sang that ghost, what then?

The sense of relief, the feeling of fulfilment, of peace of mind resonated as he considered his life's achievements as the driving force behind the Irish Literary Revival, as the founder and director of the Abbey Theatre, as a Nobel Laureate and Senator of the Irish Free State.

His later poems are considered by many to be his greatest poetic triumph. His collection *The Tower* (1928), which includes 'Sailing to the Byzantium' and 'Meditations in Time of Civil War', was followed by *The Winding Stair and Other Poems* (1933), a montage of twenty-eight poems, and finally *Last Poems and Plays* (1940), written between 1936–1939, are regarded as some of the finest poems in the twentieth century. One wonders if this final flush of significant work originated out of the molten Eros energy forged out of his twenty-eight-year obsession for Maud Gonne or whether it was entirely the result of the tenderness and Agape love he felt for his young wife Georgie, and his two beloved children, Anne and Michael. But perhaps it was harnessing both that gave Yeats his late creative energy, for at the age of sixty-nine he underwent 'the Steinach operation' designed for sexual rejuvenation, a kind of surgical Viagra that allowed him further erotic adventures which perhaps fuelled his late poetic endeavours. This time he fell for the poet and actress Margot Ruddock and then the novelist, journalist and sexual radical Ethel Mannin. Georgie magnanimously indulged these dalliances and wrote to him 'When you are dead, people will talk about your love affairs, but I shall say nothing for I will remember how proud you were.'

He died in January 1939 while staying in a hotel near Menton on the French Riviera, having just published his translation of *The Ten Principal Upanishads*, and he was buried in the village of Roquebrune, although eleven years later his body was disinterred and delivered by an Irish Navy corvette to the churchyard of St Columba's Church Drumcliff, near Sligo. The whole operation was supervised by the then Minister of External Affairs, Sean MacBride, the son of Maud Gonne.

Norma Jeane Mortenson's tumultuous life began on 1 June 1926, in Los Angeles' General Hospital. Her mother Gladys, who had spent much of her life in psychiatric facilities, gave away her baby a fortnight later.

While Gladys was beyond fulfilling any normal maternal role, felled as she was by chronic mental instability, Norma Jeane's father remained a nameless phantom whose identity was only confirmed as Charles Stanley Gifford in 2022. This meant that Norma Jeane never had a father. The lyrics of the song 'Every Baby needs a Da-Da-Daddy' which she sang in her early film *Ladies of the Chorus*, soon after 20th Century Fox transformed Norma Jeane into Marilyn Monroe, has an affecting poignancy.

> Every baby needs a da-da-daddy
> In case she runs aground
> Every baby needs a da-da-daddy
> To keep her safe and sound.
> Yes, I feel just like Red Riding Hood
> Cause the wolves are awful hungry in our neighbourhood
> Oh every baby needs a da-da-daddy
> Could my da-da-daddy be you?

This endless paternal search, this constant refrain 'Could my da-da-daddy be you?', undoubtedly resulted in the numerous alpha males who became her partners and lovers, a formidable list that included Elia Kazan, Joe DiMaggio, Marlon Brando, Arthur Miller, Frank Sinatra, Jerry Lewis, Yves Montand and President Kennedy, with whom she had a one-night stand in March 1962. But this long list had nothing to do with sexual incontinence: rather it was an endless search for that parental loving care which she never received as a child. This constant repetition of failed relationships was the perfect example of Freud's theory of repetition about which he writes: 'Based upon observed behaviour in the transference and upon the life histories of men and women, we have to assume that there really does exist, in the mind, a compulsion to repeat that overrides the pleasure principle'. 'The pleasure principle' was Freud's euphemism for sexuality and here he was questioning the centrality of sexuality.

This presiding compulsion to repeat, as Freud maintains, is something that most therapists will observe continuously in their clinical practices and it appears that human beings have an obsessive desire to continue patterns of behaviour that are often injurious to their state of mind. The 'familiar' appears to be much more attractive than the 'curative' so that the client's natural inclination is to preserve, at all costs, the familiar. This impulse stands at the centre of our complex, that neurotic, dysfunctional response we fall back into when faced by difficult situations which trigger a regression into infantile reactions and have such a damaging presence in our lives.

Freud writes: 'Patients repeat all of their unwanted situations . . . the impressions they give are of being pursued by a malignant fate or possessed by some extraneous power. But psychoanalysis has always taken the view that their fate is, for the most part, arranged by themselves and determined by early infantile influences.'

A lifetime's experience of abandonment started early for Norma Jeane when her mother Gladys handed her over to foster parents Albert and Ida Bolender. Heavily influenced by her mother Della, Gladys maintained that she gave Norma Jeane away because she wanted to avoid the stigma of being an unmarried mother and because she needed to continue to work at Consolidated Film Industries as a lab assistant and had no one to look after her baby. As biographer Donald Spoto explains: 'Gladys was plainly terrified by the physical responsibilities of caring for an infant' and Della also had no interest in looking after her newly-arrived granddaughter. As was a common practice, Albert and Ida Bolender added to their modest income by providing a home for foster children, remunerated by the state authorities of California. Albert was the local postman, while Ida spent her time looking after her son and a succession of foster children. Norma Jeane remained with the Bolenders for seven years and seems to have been well-treated and cared for, although all the other foster children stayed for much shorter periods of time before being reunited with their families. This must have increased Norma Jeane's feelings that she was unwanted and unloved by her mother. The latter made irregular and brief visits which upset and unsettled Norma Jeane and, for much of her childhood, Gladys remained 'a shadowy visitor' at the edge of her daughter's life.

As zealous evangelical Christians, the Bolenders regarded ethical and religious observances as an essential part of life and popular entertainment was a frowned-upon indulgence. As Norma Jeane later said: 'To go to a movie was a sin', while drawing, smoking and card-playing were also regarded as wicked activities. Sunday school was a weekly necessity for the brood of Bolender children and one wonders what Albert and Ida made of Norma Jeane's future Hollywood antics.

There was one thing that relieved the austerity of the Bolender's regime and that was the family dog Tippy, who became devoted to Norma Jeane. Needless to say, she adored Tippy, who was her constant companion, but then disaster struck when a furious neighbour – angered by Tippy's barking – shot the dog. Norma Jeane was overwhelmed by an inconsolable grief, which intruded into the Bolender's strict routine, and Gladys was called for. Norma Jeane then left her austere home and joined her mother in her tiny apartment near the film studio where she worked as a freelance cutter. The greatest change in Norma Jeane's new routine was the now weekly, or sometimes twice-weekly, visit to the movies, experiences she regarded as tremendous treats.

Yet within six months of being reunited with her mother, Gladys's fragile mental health began to deteriorate and an abrupt descent into a catatonic depression completely immobilised her, which inevitably led to hospitalisation. Gladys's best friend Grace Goddard, who had always adored Norma Jeane, now briefly became her foster mother. A year earlier Grace had married Doc Goddard, who regarded the arrival of this timid, introverted little girl as both an unwanted intrusion into their lives and also a pointless additional burden to the couple's meagre budget. Doc Goddard insisted on alternative arrangements and in the summer of 1935 Grace took a heartbroken, tearful Norma Jeane off to the nearby Los Angeles Orphans Home, where she stayed for the next two years. The only consolation to this new abandonment was that most Saturdays Grace would take Norma Jeane out for lunch and a movie. One of the films she always remembered was *Mutiny on the Bounty*, starring Clark Gable whom she became fixated on, convincing herself that this matinée idol must be her father, an illusion that was given some kind of reality when twenty-seven years later they worked together on *The Misfits*, the last film for both actors before they died.

Grace's Saturday treats started to include visits to a local beauty parlour and she began to persuade Norma Jeane that she was destined to become Jean Harlow's successor after they saw the glamorous superstar in *China Seas* and *Libeled Lady*. Yet despite Grace's flattering attention, Norma Jeane longed for ordinary family life and ordinary parents and she later said of this period: 'I sometimes told the other orphans I had real wonderful parents who were away on a long trip and would come for me any time and once I wrote a postcard to myself and signed it "from Mummy & Daddy".'

Finally in the spring of 1937 Grace became Norma Jeane's legal guardian and in June 1937, a week after her eleventh birthday, Grace picked up her ward and drove her home. But the new arrangement lasted only five months because one autumn evening Doc Goddard arrived home excessively drunk and with a lewd lunge launched himself at Norma Jeane, tearing at her clothes. She fought him off and ran to Aunt Grace for protection but inevitably Grace concluded that she could not trust her lecherous husband and so Norma Jeane was shipped off to live with her great aunt and cousins in Compton, a suburb of Los Angeles. Grace continued her regular visits and the Saturday routine of lunch, the beauty parlour and a movie were revived, with Grace more and more emphatic that as Jean Harlow had recently died, Norma Jeane was destined for inevitable movie stardom, replacing MGM's blond beauty. On her twelfth birthday Grace took her off for a professional photographic session, having bought her a fancy new dress and having had her hair fashioned into a Jean Harlow lookalike style. Norma Jeane's birthday present that year was a scrapbook to place her new pictures in, as if it was a passport to future stardom.

A few weeks after her twelfth birthday Norma Jeane was moved into another foster home, one that belonged to Grace's aunt, Edith Lower, known to everyone as Aunt Ana. The move proved a success, as Norma Jeane's new foster mother was completely enraptured by her delightful new child. Norma Jeane later wrote of her Aunt Ana: 'She was the first person in the world I ever really loved and who loved me. She was a wonderful human being . . . She was the only one who loved and understood me.'

But almost predictably all this loving devotion was short-lived. In 1940 Aunt Ana developed serious cardiovascular problems and was unable to go on looking after Norma Jeane, who was returned yet again to Grace's home. This new arrangement lasted only nine months as Doc Goddard had been relocated by his employers to far-off West Virginia. Before her departure Grace gave Norma Jeane two options: a return to the orphanage or marriage to a neighbour's twenty-one-year-old son, who had shown great interest in Norma Jeane. The thought of a return to the orphanage horrified her and on 19 June 1941, just after her sixteenth birthday, she married James Dougherty, who within a few months enlisted in the US Navy.

As I work with every one of my clients, we inevitably encounter all those batterings and bruisings, all those traumas and woundings, that every child gathers up and constellates into the neuroses and complexes that afflict our adult lives. One particular psychotherapist who writes about the repressed inner child which we all carry within us is James Hollis. In his book *The Middle Passage: From Misery to Meaning in Midlife* (1993) he says:

> It is not that we have a single child within, perhaps hurt, frightened, co-dependent or withdrawn in compensation, but a whole host of children, a veritable kindergarten . . . we have to deal with our narcissistic child, our jealous child, our enraged child, whose eruptions are often embarrassing and destructive.

Of course James Hollis is right: we all carry within us the neglected, humiliated, abandoned, misunderstood, damaged children that remain lodged inside our psyche, waiting hopefully to receive the attention they long for, to be understood at last, to be cherished and loved perhaps for the first time. When Marilyn Monroe was introduced to the world with the brand-new name bestowed upon her by 20th Century Fox, she fused her new identity with all Norma Jeane's chronic childhood woundings that would intrude at regular intervals into her adult life.

This tendency for an interior forgotten child to demand attention is very common in psychotherapy and as these damaged waifs emerge they must not be turned away but instead listened to and given plenty of time and care in the hope they will be understood and accepted, perhaps for the first time. The clients concerned may be parents themselves or, if not, will almost always have a parenting capacity. These parenting skills can be effectively turned towards their own inner child, who is beginning to emerge in the therapeutic sessions. When this happens I suggest the client finds some old photographs of themselves as infants or small children and carry a favourite picture of their earlier selves around in a wallet or purse. I also suggest that a similar photo be placed on their bedside table. I find time and again that if this child, who existed decades earlier, is now brought to mind, and discussed with compassion in our sessions and in the days between, a kind of parental bond can be built up between the mature adult and the once-forgotten child. If the client's past childhood is remembered and considered in this manner, the inner child begins to become less fearful, less unsettled and can be integrated into the mature adult psyche and the scourge of Freud's repetition theory becomes far less problematic.

In her adult life Marilyn Monroe was exorbitantly successful professionally. Her image as a Hollywood victim, as a dumb blonde exploited by movie moguls, is a stereotypical view that seems to be increasingly replaced by a revised understanding that she was extraordinarily astute, streetwise and forceful. As the biographies of Donald Spoto and Sarah Churchwell have shown, Monroe was not an exploited blonde bombshell, but a shrewd manipulator of the Hollywood system. She never complied to the restrictive practices of Hollywood and she became a feminist prototype in the chauvinistic, misogynistic studio culture. And her work ethic was tremendous. According to her early mentor Emmeline Snively: 'She started out with less than any girl I ever knew, but she worked the hardest. She wanted to learn, wanted to be somebody, more than anybody I ever saw in my life.'

Her publicist Rupert Allan said: 'Under all the frailty was a will of steel' and Colin Clark, her personal assistant while she was making *The Prince and the Showgirl*, remembered that 'Marilyn Monroe was just a force of nature. She was too much for America's foremost dramatic coaching couple – the Strasbergs, too much for the top playwright intellectual Arthur Miller and too much for England's best actor Laurence Olivier.' When she was interviewed by writer and journalist W. J. Weatherly, Monroe said: 'I ask myself what am I afraid of. I know I have talent. I know I can act. Well get on with it Marilyn . . . Fear is stupid, so are regrets.' As Sarah Churchwell concludes in her groundbreaking biography: 'Marilyn's stardom was her life's triumph.'

Time and again she fought with Darryl F. Zanuck, the despotic, megalomaniacal studio boss at 20th Century Fox. When she heard that her co-star Frank Sinatra was being paid four times more than her in their film *The Girl in the Pink Tights* she walked off the set and refused to return to work until her fee matched his. Zanuck caved in. She demanded and got top billing for her next film *How to Marry a Millionaire*, out-competing Lauren Bacall and Betty Grable for the top slot, and when she married Joe DiMaggio she told Zanuck she would only continue at 20th Century Fox if she was paid more. He initially refused but then after her highly publicised tour of Korea, when the newsreel cameras filmed her performing in front of vast audiences of American soldiers, she was awarded the much coveted *Photoplay* Magazine Award for 'Most Popular Actress of 1953' and Zanuck capitulated. In 1954 when the studio refused to change her contract, giving her more control over the films she made and the directors she worked with, she left 20th Century Fox and set up her own production company. Zanuck lured her back with the promise of much more editorial control and an even larger salary. She then gave a critically acclaimed performance in *Bus Stop* and – ignoring Zanuck's pleas for a partnership – went on to make *The Prince and the Showgirl* co-starring Laurence Olivier, which was produced by her own production company. This was followed by perhaps her greatest film, *Some Like It Hot*, which was made without any help from 20th Century Fox.

It seems that the alliance between the shrewd, astute, streetwise, seductive adult and the fractious, tantrum-prone, fretful child worked well for Monroe in her professional life, although many of the directors and actors who had to put up with her chronic lack of punctuality and her childish petulance found her exasperating. As Tony Curtis, who starred with her in *Some Like It Hot*, said: 'Kissing Marilyn was like kissing Hitler due to the endless retakes she insisted upon.'

The problems Monroe experienced while filming *Some Like it Hot* appeared to inflame her insecurities. Before long, director George Cukor's irritation with his star actress and Arthur Miller's increasing exasperation with his wife's petulance left Monroe in a lonely, fragile mood, so it was arranged that she would regularly see the well-known Hollywood psychoanalyst Dr Ralph Greenson.

Romeo Greenschpoon was born of Russian émigré parents in Brooklyn in 1910. After training to become a psychoanalyst in Vienna in the 1930s he returned to the US and once he had finished serving in the Second World War, he changed his name to Ralph Greenson and started a private therapeutic practice. He was then appointed Clinical Professor of Psychiatry at the University of California and developed a considerable reputation among Hollywood directors and actors. In early 1960 Monroe had her first session with the much-admired Dr Greenson, but as their relationship developed, this highly regarded therapist found himself strangely bewitched by his glamorous patient.

Biographer Fred Guiles, in his comprehensive biography *Norma Jeane: The Life of Marilyn Monroe* (1969), claims that Greenson seemed to ignore 'necessary precautions having been seduced by her air of helplessness'. In *Goddess: The Secret Lives of Marilyn Monroe* (1985), Anthony Summers is more forgiving of Greenson, saying he was 'genuinely touched by this thirty-five-year-old waif'. Other biographers state that he was 'harmful and domineering' and 'driven by money'. Donald Spoto regards Greenson as a manipulative 'Svengali', desperate to keep Monroe dependent upon him, and another biographer goes so far as to suggest that Greenson was a Russian spy, intent on incriminating the Kennedy brothers.

None of these 'Monroe scholars' accuse Greenson of sexual impropriety, and he never seemed to have been guilty of Jung's unforgivable professional lapse with Sabrina Spielrein or Toni Wolff, or Otto Rank's sexual transgression with Anaïs Nin. However, in the countertransference, Dr Greenson obviously became obsessed with Monroe, which jeopardised his professional integrity. He insisted upon at least five sessions a week, which is already an abnormally high number, but much preferred seven sessions; he hired a housekeeper to look after Monroe; he started negotiating Monroe's schedule with the film studio; he regularly invited Monroe to his home and encouraged her to have a relationship with his children and he persuaded her to hire his brother-in-law to be her legal advisor. Apart from these breaches in professional good practice, perhaps his most insidious intrusion into her life was his attempt to prevent the significant reconciliation between Monroe and her second husband Joe DiMaggio and their plans to remarry.

Although their marriage collapsed after only nine months, all the evidence suggests that DiMaggio remained deeply in love with Monroe. In February 1961 Monroe was exhausted and behaving in a highly disturbed fashion following the break-up with her third husband Arther Miller. She was eventually taken to the Payne Whitney Clinic, the psychiatric wing of the New York Hospital. Petrified, she was placed in a padded cell, reviving memories of her mother's afflicted life. Traumatised and deeply distressed she contacted DiMaggio in Florida, having not seen him for the previous six years. Immediately he flew to New York and demanded that Monroe be released, guaranteeing that he would look after her. As a result she was transferred to the much less intimidating environment of the Columbia University Presbyterian Hospital Medical Centre. DiMaggio stayed there with her for a week before returning to Florida, where Monroe joined him a fortnight later for a period of convalescence. A friend, Lois Smith, who saw them together in Florida said: 'Joe was always there for her, she could always call on him, lean on him, depend on him, be certain of him. It was a marvellous feeling of comfort for her.' After a month with DiMaggio, revived by his care and devotion,

Monroe travelled back to Los Angeles and told some friends who she dined with on her thirty-fifth birthday that she was 'very happy to have reached this age. I feel I'm growing up. It was wonderful being a girl, but it's more wonderful being a woman.'

Throughout that difficult spring Monroe had complained about a severe pain in her right side and spasms of acute indigestion. Finally the pain became so intense that in late June 1961 she returned to New York where, at the Manhattan Polyclinic, she was diagnosed with impacted gallstones and an inflamed gall bladder. She underwent immediate surgery and after the operation, when she came round, DiMaggio was standing over her. He remained with her for a week while she recovered.

Back in Los Angeles she maintained regular contact with DiMaggio and the year ended with her devoted ex-husband returning from New York to spend the Christmas holidays with her. Most inappropriately Monroe had been invited to spend Christmas Day with Dr Greenson and his family and DiMaggio reluctantly agreed to join them. In January 1962, Marilyn went house-hunting with her therapist and under his supervision she purchased a large bungalow where she would live for the eight months that remained to her.

When DiMaggio visited LA to see Monroe in early March she was living with Greenson and his family and the therapist forbade him from seeing her. DiMaggio insisted and within a few days he had managed to extricate her from the Greenson house and return her to her new home on Doheny Drive, where he stayed with her before departing on a business trip.

During the next few months DiMaggio would return regularly and stay with Monroe, and friends who met them commented on how happy they seemed together. By the end of July, after a weekend in Lake Tahoe, they announced they were getting remarried and were planning their second wedding on 8 August. On hearing the news, actress Susan Strasberg said: 'She was getting out of relationships that were not good for her and back into one that was. She knew she needed some sort of emotional and spiritual anchor.' By the end of July Monroe was being fitted for a dress and organising flowers, wine and food for the wedding party.

On 4 August she began a letter to DiMaggio: 'Dear Joe, If I can only succeed in making you happy, I will have succeeded in the biggest and most difficult thing there is – that is to make one person completely happy. Your happiness means my happiness . . . ' The letter was never finished. On the following day Sergeant Jack Clemmons of the LAPD found her body in the bedroom of her bungalow. Despite all that she seemed to be looking forward to, something had lethally intervened.

The frenzied speculation surrounding Monroe's death circles around three possibilities: she was either murdered, committed suicide or she had made a fatal mistake regarding a cocktail of sedatives. Then came the conspiracy theories with biographies and books about her death feeding the public's fixation on the Hollywood legend. Some suggested that Joseph P. Kennedy Senior had her murdered to spare his son's embarrassment; another theory had a group of CIA renegades plotting her death in revenge for Kennedy's lack of support during the Bay of Pigs incident. Mafia godfather

Sam Giancana and teamster boss Jimmy Hoffa were both put forward as prime suspects, but all these wild accusations are rejected by the less salacious biographers.

Those writers who support the suicide hypothesis seem to ignore how, after a difficult spell, Monroe's life was getting back on track both personally and professionally. She seemed thrilled at the prospect of her remarriage to Joe DiMaggio and, with Darryl Zanuck's reappointment as President of 20th Century Fox after a six-year absence and Monroe's box-office sales skyrocketing, a new million-dollar contract had just been signed, agreeing to every condition she had insisted upon. Monroe seemed hungry for more creative challenges and her position as one of the most successful movie stars in the world seemed assured. As Sarah Churchwell observes: 'Suicide is an absolute relinquishment of authority and agency', and at this stage in her life Monroe's 'authority and agency' had never been stronger. 'When Fox rehired Marilyn she showed them who was in charge. She had finally forced them to accept her value and they agreed to a million-dollar contract and that contract must have meant more to her professionally than any other victory she achieved.'

Donald Spoto gives the most convincing explanation of her death. Dr Greenson had recently changed Monroe's insomnia medication from Nembutal, which was taken orally, to the more effective chloral hydrate, a powerful barbiturate which was administered anally via an enema, but Greenson seems to have neglected to warn her sufficiently of the dangerous consequence of mixing Nembutal and chloral hydrate. Spoto points to the autopsy's toxicology report which states that alongside the high levels of chloral hydrate there was evidence of a powerful dose of Nembutal. As Spoto concludes: 'To the horror of everyone involved, what may have been intended as Marilyn's long deep sleep became her death.'

It seems to me that Monroe had navigated a path successfully through the challenges of 1961 and the first half of 1962. Her forthcoming remarriage to Joe DiMaggio was a significant development which took her beyond her lifetime's unconscious attempt to find a permanent exchange of oxytocin, having never received this vital experience as an infant or child. The lack of both a mother and father compelled her to pursue her longing for a relationship that could provide her with this Eros-driven emotional elation. Using her unique charisma she recruited a succession of formidable males whom she could fall in love with, providing her with the oxytocin high that she craved. Despite this potent array of masculinity none of them provided what she needed and by 1961 she remained a victim of 'the perpetual virginity of the soul'.

But then her experiences in 1961 and 1962 demonstrated that there was one man who could potentially make her happy. The Eros, oxytocin hit of their marriage had lasted only a handful of months but in 1962 she was experiencing a less intense but a much more reassuring feeling of Agape, filling her brain with much-needed serotonin and dopamine that gave her the secure 'emotional anchor' which only Joe DiMaggio seemed capable of providing. With this major development in her emotional life, in this shift from Eros to Agape, she seemed destined for a much happier, more contented, more secure future, just when her professional life seemed to be reaching its zenith. But providence cruelly intervened.

On 8 August, instead of taking part in their wedding, Joe DiMaggio attended Monroe's funeral, having spent the night with his beloved, lying next to her, maintaining what Donald Spoto describes as 'a solitary vigil of an adoring knight worshipping her from twilight to dawn'.

What would have happened if Monroe, on that fateful night, had not taken that additional lethal dose of Nembutal and had been married rather than buried? It think it is quite possible that, having found the 'anchor' of Joe's love and devotion to be a stabilising and transforming influence, she could have become a woman of great capacity and depth, who – much like Josephine Baker – might have recast herself in the second half of life into an individual whose talent, energy and vision extended her reach way beyond the vanities of Hollywood stardom.

Sigmund Freud: Eros and Thanatos
(Sigmund Freud, Bert Hellinger, Ernest Hemingway)

A s we saw in chapter two, Ernest Jones had the most unusual good fortune – as Freud's first biographer – to meet his subject's mother on a number of occasions during her eighties and nineties, right up to the year of her death at the age of ninety-five, when her beloved son was in his mid-seventies. 'It was strange to me,' he writes, 'as her young visitor, to hear her refer to the Great Master repeatedly as "My Golden Sigi", evidence of the closest attachment between the two.' Even in her old age she was an elegant, charming woman, who basked in the fame and pre-eminence of her oldest child, although his success had come as no surprise to her. Ever since his birth, this vivacious, life-affirming woman was certain that her Golden Sigi was destined to achieve great things.

Similar to the manner in which Picasso's mother had idealised her son, Freud's adoring mother – whose prodigious fertility had produced eight children – conferred on the founder of psychoanalysis an indomitable confidence. It seems highly plausible she was partly responsible for Freud's attraction to his concept of Eros, which made frequent appearances in his later philosophy. He describes Eros as 'the preserver of life', that force 'which holds all living things together'. Freud takes the romantic/erotic notion of Eros (as discussed in the last chapter) and extends it to a much wider and more expansive life force so that it becomes the binding constituent of mankind. 'Eros's purpose,' he writes, 'is to gather together individuals, then families and finally tribes, peoples and nations in one great unit – humanity.'

While Eros is the life-force, it is in mortal combat with another favourite concept of his later thought: Thanatos, the death-wish. In *Civilisation and its Discontents*, published in 1930 just after his mother's death, Freud writes: 'The death drive sits beside Eros and they rule the world jointly . . . The struggle between Eros and Death is the essential content of all life.' Indeed Thanatos made a striking appearance in Freud's early life when his blissful world of undiluted maternal attention was rudely interrupted by the birth of his younger brother Julius. In letters to his friend Wilhelm Fleiss, when he was conducting his self-analysis, Freud said he reacted to this unwanted interloper with a furious malevolence and he admitted that as a two-year-old, he had welcomed the death of his seven-month-old brother. In these comments Freud suggests that as an infant he had drawn a causal link between his own enraged vengefulness and his brother's death and this aroused in him a childish belief that his murderous feelings had had the power to overwhelm Julius.

Any shame that the young child felt regarding his brother's death was soon safely repressed deep in his unconscious. Dark, forbidding Thanatos lay dormant, securely displaced by Freud's fierce sense of mission, as he relentlessly followed his mother's assured conviction that he would achieve fame and distinction, a grand ambition fuelled by the life-force Eros.

Inevitably Freud excelled at school and for six years running he was first in his class. He began reading Shakespeare at nine and mastered half a dozen languages, including Latin and Greek. As a teenager he became obsessed with Charles Darwin's work on the theory of evolution, describing it as 'the greatest advancement in our understanding of the world' and he also knew by heart Goethe's essay 'On Nature'. These two masterpieces propelled him towards the study of medicine and in 1873 he entered Vienna University. After three years he was unsure about what field he might choose in his quest to emulate 'the great Darwin', for this remained the measure of his ambition, and so from 1876 to 1882 he carried out research at the Physiological Institute of Ernst Brücke, part of the University of Vienna, with his first mentor. Yet soon he met another trusted guide who became a father figure: Josef Breuer. For the next six years Freud worked closely with Brücke and Breuer, researching the mysteries of the nervous system, as the two teachers encouraged the aspirations of their brilliant student.

This began a long process of gestation before the young neurologist was able to match the achievements of his great idol, Darwin. After working for three years in the Vienna General Hospital specialising in neurology, he was appointed a university lecturer in neuropathology at the age of twenty-nine. A year later, soon after marrying Martha Bernays, with whom he would have six children, he set up in private practice. A decade of clinical work now provided Freud with the foundation and experience upon which he would base his future revolutionary theories. In 1891 he acquired his famous couch, in 1895 he published his first important book with Josef Breuer – *Studies in Hysteria* – and in 1896 he conceived the providential term 'psychoanalysis'.

For the next two years Freud conducted an exhaustive self-analysis, after which he felt ready to produce a work which he hoped would stand alongside Darwin's *On the Origins of Species*. With his customary flair for fateful timing Freud published *The Interpretation of Dreams* in the early months of 1900, as if to herald the new century. *The Interpretation of Dreams* was designed to be the founding text of the new discipline that Freud was now pioneering and was considerably more than a book about dreams: it was his first rendition of the principles and concepts of his philosophy, his theory, his programme of treatment, his account of human behaviour which he had already labelled 'psychoanalysis'.

Over the next four years his thoughts on human sexuality and their central position in the overall architecture of psychoanalysis developed further, until they reached full expression in 1905 in *Three Essays on the Theory of Sexuality*. From then on, his theory of libido became an almost sacred creed. As he gathered around him a growing band of disciples and admirers, Freud regarded any dissent from the holy texts proclaiming the primacy of sexuality in psychotherapeutic theory as tantamount to an unacceptable deviancy.

Freud's books expounding his developing theories now appeared at an increased rate and schools of psychoanalysis opened throughout Europe and America as his ideas attracted more and more followers. In April 1908, at the Hotel Bristol in Salzburg, the International Psychoanalytic Congress (with president Carl Jung) first met. Until 1914 Freud continued his relentless schedule of seeing patients, attending conferences, giving lectures and developing his theory in further books and papers and he sublimated his own libido into his driven sense of mission. Eros surrounded him in everything he did.

But then with Archduke Ferdinand's assassination in Sarajevo everything changed: it was as if in the summer of 1914, Thanatos was making its first surreptitious entry and elbowing Eros to one side, plunging not only Europe but Freud himself into years of misfortune.

The Dresden Congress, due to take place in the autumn of 1914, was cancelled. Numerous friends and colleagues of Freud's were called up and most of the psychoanalytic journals for which Freud wrote ceased publication. The Vienna Psychotherapeutic Society, which had met weekly, now gathered only sporadically. Freud wrote to his biographer Ernest Jones: 'The springtime of our science has been abruptly broken off.' To make matters much worse, all three of his sons joined the Austrian army.

During the war Freud's creative output almost came to a complete halt. He unenthusiastically gave a series of lectures between 1915–1917 but when they were published he described them as 'containing nothing that could tell you anything new . . . They are course stuff for the multitudes.' He told friends that he was writing a book on 'metapsychology' but he was so disenchanted with what he had written that he destroyed the manuscript. However, he did write *Mourning and Melancholia*, which was published in early 1917 and which presaged a wave of personal anguish that overwhelmed him soon after the war ended.

With Austria's total defeat, heating materials and food

were in short supply in Vienna: Freud complained that even pens and paper were difficult to obtain. In a letter to his Berlin colleague, Karl Abraham, he said that he was writing in a 'bitterly cold room' and 'our nutrition is scanty and miserable, really a starvation diet'. But these discomforts were to pale into insignificance when Sophie, Freud's favourite child, died of Spanish influenza while pregnant with her third child. This dreadful calamity drove home the power of Thanatos that the Great War had generated. It was, he wrote, 'a senseless brutal act of fate, which has robbed us of our Sophie . . . it is a great unhappiness for us all.'

In a desperate effort to find some sort of comfort, he returned to his desk and wrote *Beyond the Pleasure Principle* (1920), a short book that totally deconstructed his previous system of ideas. It was as if – like some traumatised child – Freud had wantonly vandalised his life's work in an act of unhinged fury in response to what he called 'higher powers who are playing with a helpless, poor human being'.

In *Beyond the Pleasure Principle* Freud dispensed with sexuality as humanity's primary drive, which he pushed to one side, and replaced it with two new theories: his repetition theory and what he now regarded as mankind's two predominant impulses: 'the life instinct and the death instinct', or what he would come to call 'Eros' and 'Thanatos'.

> Our views have, from the first, been dualistic and today they are even more definitely dualistic than before – now that we describe the opposition as being not between ego instincts and sexual instincts but between life instincts and death instincts.

This sudden suggestion that human lives were dominated by the conflict between Eros and Thanatos, more than any other polarised tension, seemed to have a profound impact on Freud's personal life. A year after *Beyond the Pleasure Principle* was published, his favourite niece, Caecilie Graf, committed suicide. Six months later his beloved grandson Heinerle, Sophie's son, suddenly died and then Freud was diagnosed with cancer of the upper palate, a condition that he would struggle with for the next sixteen years before it finally killed him. During his constant battle with this miserable condition Freud would endure nineteen separate operations, between which he continued to puff away on his beloved cigars, even though they had undoubtedly caused his cancer. This strange impulse to feed the malignancy in his mouth with the constant application of carcinogenic tobacco appeared to exemplify Freud's new theory as his life instinct fought off the death instinct.

Freud's abrupt volte-force, as he suddenly ejected sexuality from the pantheon of his theories, presents us with two enthralling questions: was Freud right? Is the struggle between the life instinct and the death instinct the most compelling feature of human psychology? And is this drive present from our earliest years? To answer these two questions we will examine the work of Stanislav Grof, the most persuasive expert on birth trauma, and one instructive case study from my own clinical practice.

One of the most important developments in psychoanalytic theory since Freud and Jung comes from the work of the Czech psychiatrist and psychoanalyst Stanislav Grof, in particular the research and clinical work described in his book

Beyond the Brain: Birth, Death and Transcendence in Psychotherapy (1984), which was based on thousands of psychotherapeutic hours in which his patients, using LSD, remembered the very moment of their birth.

Incredibly many of Grof's patients could recall what he called 'the perinatal experience'. This included the intra-uterine experience of embryonic life in the weeks preceding birth, the actual birth itself and the weeks following. His psychotherapeutic technique, which he called 'the death-re-birth process', takes his clients back to these polarised earliest experiences with Eros's very first clash with Thanatos. So powerful is this struggle at the very beginning of life that Grof maintains these earliest experiences have an impact upon our psychological and emotional future life more acute than any other life experience.

Grof describes life in the womb as a kind of bliss or paradise and his patients would describe a state of being defined by comfort, safety and serenity with a perfect sense of deep relaxation and well-being. Yet as soon as the birth process begins, the tiny human faces a moment of extreme trauma and a terrible threat of annihilation takes over, as the fierce, violent muscular contractions of the uterus increase and the baby is pushed forward. But despite these savage convulsions the maternal cervix is still closed and the baby has no escape. The bliss of peaceful connectedness is ruptured and replaced by an overwhelming anxiety and awareness of an imminent terminal threat. Thanatos in a matter of moments replaces Eros. But then, when all seems lost, a speck of hope appears as the cervix dilates. There is now a slim chance of survival: Eros has prevailed.

Grof had a number of clients whose mothers had suffered serious illness or acute anxiety during the pregnancy and using LSD these people were able to relive the intrauterine disturbance, a discovery that then reduced depression or paranoid states of mind. One such patient with severe disruptive emotional symptoms relived the early stages of labour prior to birth. She envisaged and then drew a demonic gigantic tarantula which was trying to kill her during the birth process by preventing her escaping down the birth canal. This symbolic revelation, which returned her back to her birth, reduced these emotional disturbances.

This new approach of psychotherapy achieved extremely high levels of success, relieving persistent long-entrenched psychopathological states of mind and numerous physical, somatic illnesses. Because these perinatal experiences were all preverbal, they could only be accessed when the ego's defensive control was neutralised by the use of LSD or – as Grof discovered – by other techniques he developed that didn't require the use of powerful narcotics. These included sophisticated breathing exercises, massage and active imagination techniques, often using music and the rebirthing programmes developed by Leonard Orr and Sondra Ray.

Although I have never travelled back to the intrauterine world with my clients, at some stage in the therapeutic work I often attempt to return to their actual birth and the earliest experiences of the individual involved. We do this with the help of recollections from older family members, from dreams, from the process known as active imagination and an exploration of the likely environment the client was surrounded by immediately after birth.

Grof's perinatal journey sets up a psychological polarity that is etched onto the psyche: it is a developmental drive that is in a constant fluctuation between a state of latency and an emerging actuality. The most refined articulation of this drive for development in the psyche is Jung's theory of individuation, repeatedly applauded by Grof. This first great struggle between Eros and Thanatos is experienced again and again in our future lives and the repeated pattern is driven by the constant tension between our Eros urge to develop and our Thanatos mode that keeps us psychologically inert, immersed in a kind of emotional torpor that can so easily become self-destructive.

This perinatal struggle between life and death is the very first encounter we have with our Eros-driven compulsion for psychological development, which will always be at odds with our equally strong urge to remain exactly where we are: remaining in the psychological terrain that we are most familiar with, an emotional pattern we are destined to repeat endlessly.

In this sense the clash between Eros and Thanatos is not just the struggle between life and death: it is also two sharply contrasting moods or states of mind or dispositions or modes of being. One is characterised by energy, optimism, momentum, hope and equanimity, the other by pessimism, despondency, an inertia and absence of wellbeing. Yet such a blunt, prosaic description of this duality misses an important subtlety. I am not suggesting that the spirit of Eros is always 'better' than the spirit of Thanatos: as both Freud and Grof show us, they are both embedded in the human psyche, both firmly present in the fabric of our lives. Both need to be acknowledged, to be honoured, to be lived out as inevitable, elemental aspects of our experience.

There is, in our culture, a definite tendency to deny the saturnine presence of Thanatos and its dark colours, but to do this is to reject the damaged, disconsolate parts of our nature and it is these infernal regions of our psyche which need to be experienced and explored in psychotherapy. The spirit of Thanatos can be a kind of black gold that I encourage my clients to grasp. By entering Thanatos's forbidden territory we will discover much about our true nature which the collective culture that surrounds us wishes to avoid. The great emphasis on a prevailing youth culture and a youthful appearance; the extensive cosmetic surgery industry with its nips and tucks and Botox injections intended to deny the ageing process; the tiny proportion of the population who have been in the presence of a dying person: these push questions of our mortality deep into our shadow from where they make only rare and reluctant conscious appearances.

With my clients I try to integrate and temper the chaffing opposition of these two essential polarities in our own nature and in all life: both must be accepted and harmonised into one united whole. They are two sides of the same coin, perhaps the two most fundamental realities of our existence, as individuals and as a species. How to blend these two primal elements of our being more comfortably, by achieving some sort of symbiosis or compatibility between them is – I believe – one of the most important tasks of psychotherapy.

Among my clients I have noticed how the concept of death often makes its rare appearance, marked by fear and

extreme anxiety, at three different stages of life. This preoccupation often begins in one's late twenties and is invariably present at some point during the midlife crisis and then
frequently reappears in one's late fifties. Strangely it then
seems to recede and causes little bother to clients after the
age of sixty-five. My own concerns with death have followed
a similar trajectory and now, at seventy-four, they seem to be
unexpectedly quiescent.

The great Austro-American psychotherapeutic theorist
Heinz Kohut maintained that 'accepting life's transience' is
one of our most challenging psychological tasks, and rec-
ommends we follow Cicero's maxim: 'To philosophise is to
learn to die.' Michel de Montaigne, who said 'Let us have
nothing on our minds as often as death', suggested that
the better prepared we were for death, the freer we would
be from the fear of it. Keeping our demise in our thoughts
need not be a sullen case of morbidity, but rather a relaxed
acceptance of our inevitable fate. Montaigne, having wres-
tled with high anxiety regarding his mortality in his middle
years, then became much more sanguine and characterised
death as a few bad moments at the end of life, an inevitability not worth getting worried about. This equanimity is just
the state of mind we should attempt to achieve as we try to
resolve the tension between Eros and Thanatos.

Freud's preoccupation with death, which was so evident
in so much of his theoretical work during the 1920s, was
no doubt down to the fact that he had watched in horror as
humanity was engulfed by Thanatos during the First World
War. From its first appearance in *Beyond the Pleasure Principle* to its central presence in his final work *Civilisation and Its*

Discontents (1930), the struggle between Eros and Thanatos became his presiding concern. Perhaps this is hardly surprising given that from 1923 this mortal combat between the life-force and the death instinct was raging in his own body as the malignant growth in his upper palette slowly spread its deadly tendrils.

Freud once told his nephew Harry: 'My boy, smoking is one of the greatest enjoyments in life and if you decide not to smoke, I can only feel sorry for you.' Freud saw his love of cigars as a primal oral need, essential to maintain his capacity for hard work and original thought, stimulating his intellect and imaginative powers. He once said that his addiction was a substitute for the primal addiction of masturbation. Whatever its origin, it was an act of almost hourly repetition that was to have dire consequences.

Freud had a series of operations to treat his cancer, which included the insertion of a prosthesis, a device to keep the oral and nasal cavities separate. 'The monster', as it became known, which was both chaffing and painful, badly affected Freud's speech. Eating became difficult and Freud avoided dining in public. He became deaf in his right ear and his famous couch was moved from one wall to another so that he could listen to his patients with his left ear. Despite all these incapacities and discomforts, Freud remained faithful to his beloved cigars.

After the 1938 Anschluss, Vienna became a centre of brutal, murderous anti-Semitism. So grim was the danger Freud and his family faced that his daughter Anna suggested that it might better if everyone in the family killed themselves. Freud's response was: 'Why? Because they would like us to?' The 'old stoic' would remain belligerently defiant as he faced the vicious betrayal that his 'dear Vienna' now inflicted upon him. The betrayal not only targeted Freud himself but also his life's purpose: psychoanalysis, which was now branded by the Viennese as a Jewish abomination, tarnishing the pristine innocence of Aryan youth. Consequently, his books were banned and then ritually burnt. As Heinrich Heine, Freud's Jewish compatriot, had prophesised: 'those who burn books will in the end burn people'. Although Freud himself was to avoid this incineration, his four beloved sisters – Rosa, Mitzi, Esher and Paula – all died in the gas chambers and ovens of Treblinka and Auschwitz.

In the summer of 1938, at the age of eighty-two, Freud was forced to abandon his home and flee to England and he took with him his most implacable, his most relentless enemy: the cancer that was rotting away his upper mouth and jaw. Soon after his arrival in London the malignancy appeared rampant and he underwent major surgery which involved the excision of his cheek to gain access to the tumour. This was to be his last operation.

From February onwards the pain and discomfort increased and mention of his condition filled his correspondence. Despite the seriousness of his illness, he ignored Dr Schur's insistent advice that he must give up his beloved cigars, which had become his slow executioner, and while the pain, discomfort and dispiriting news from the continent kept coming, the old stoic laboured on. It was almost as if he had to witness the start of the next world war to confirm his prophecy that humanity was dominated by its death wish Thanatos, the ultimate evidence of his repetition theory. He died on 23 September 1939, three weeks after war was declared.

In his biography *Freud: A Life for Our Time* (1988) Peter Gay writes: 'Schur was on the point of tears as he witnessed Freud facing death with dignity and without self-pity. He had never seen anyone die like that . . . The old stoic had kept control of his life to the end.'

There is a general consensus that the German death toll after the First World War accounted for a little over 2,000,000 young soldiers and included a further 700,000 civilians, caused directly by the hostilities. Thanatos's harvest in Germany was far higher in the Second World War, with 5,533,000 military deaths, while civilian fatalities reached a figure of somewhere between 6,600,000 and 8,800,000 primarily due to the Allied bombing campaign that spared few German cities.

Historians are increasingly viewing the period between August 1914 and May 1945 as a thirty-year war which featured a prolonged ceasefire between 1919 and 1939, and yet in these two decades of 'peace' the German nation suffered near-starvation, a devastating flu pandemic (which killed another half million), economic collapse, hyper-inflation and the emergence of the Nazi Party. By the end of the Second World War not only was their national infrastructure, their housing provision and their entire industrial capacity destroyed, but the German people also faced a level of national shaming which has no historical equivalent as they came to terms with the enormity of their collective crimes.

How did such devastating collective trauma etch itself

onto the haunted individuals who, in the 1950s and 1960s, were attempting to rebuild their lives after experiencing thirty years of such torment? What was going on in the shattered psyches of these Germans who had faced three decades of escalating fear, anxiety, trauma and loss? How do human beings survive this immersion in the embrace of Thanatos?

In his preface to *The Collective Silence: German Identity and the Legacy of Shame* (1993), a collection of essays by leading German psychotherapists, the American Gestalt psychotherapist Gordon Wheeler writes: 'This is a book about shame – the shame of the perpetrators, the shame of the victims, the shame of the children, all of which is felt and known and which colours the world but which cannot be spoken.'

In the central essay, 'The Psychologist without a Face, without a History', Sammy Speier, a German psychoanalyst who was born in Israel in 1944, writes: 'The generation which carried out the systematic extermination of millions of Jews, Gypsies and other groups is the generation of the parents and grandparents of today's patients in Germany.' It appears from the essays which follow that those Germans who lived through the experience of the Second World War were not overwhelmed by their guilt and shame: suicide rates did not escalate and there was no outbreak of mass psychological breakdown. Somehow the 'perpetrators' seemed to be able to avoid the moral conflict posed by the atrocities that they had witnessed or taken part in, such is the potency of our defences. However their offspring appear to have carried the burden of their guilt, which relates to the idea of generational karma that Jung wrote about in *Memories, Dreams, Reflections*.

I think this is one of Jung's most important insights. Indeed, this proposition was to emerge most dramatically in Germany in the last decade of the twentieth century and the years following the Millennium when Bert Hellinger's family constellation theory was widely practised. This gave a new generation of Germans the means to speak of their national disgrace, allowing them to escape the clutches of Thanatos that had devoured two previous generations. Bert Hellinger was born in Germany in 1925 and brought up in the village of Leimen near Heidelberg, which he remembered had a tremendous sense of community, with all the many children of the village circulating around the numerous families 'as if we belonged to them all, like one big extended family', perhaps a posture of community consolation after the calamity of the Great War. During his early childhood he spent a considerable amount of time with his grandparents, whom he was devoted to, as both his parents spent their weeks in Cologne where they had found work. He then joined his parents in Cologne where he went to his first school, moving at the age of eleven to a Catholic boarding school run by the nuns and priests of the Congregation of the Missionaries of Mariannhill. In the 1938 national plebiscite regarding the Nazi annexation of Austria, the nuns and priests voted 'no' and as a result the paramilitary wing of the Nazi Party attacked the school, smashed all the windows and scrawled TRAITORS LIVED HERE repeatedly on the school walls. The school was closed down and Hellinger joined his parents in Kassel, where he refused to join the Hitler Youth movement and was classified as 'suspected of being an enemy of the people'.

But much worse was to befall the family just before the end of 1941 when they received news that Hellinger's older brother had died while serving in the German army in Russia. Hellinger remembers his mother as being 'so solid' on hearing the news of her son's death, vowing that the Nazis could not touch her. In 1942 he was conscripted into the German Army at the age of seventeen and in his seventies he gave an interview describing his war experience.

> Death was always with us, but somehow we got used to it. By the time I was twenty half of our friends and relatives of our generation had died. Normally it is not until our sixties and seventies that our peers die but we experienced this in our early twenties. I was in a unit with between sixty and seventy soldiers. After eight days in action only twenty of us remained. The unit was reformed to full strength and after the next action we had been reduced again down to twenty. There was no time for mourning. It was a time for dying. Death was everywhere. It wasn't only like that at the front. Because of the bombing death was just as present at home. Death was always by your side.

In early 1945 Hellinger was captured by the American Army while serving on the Western Front and spent several months in a POW camp in Belgium. Upon escaping he made his way back to Germany where he enrolled at Wurzburg university, studying theology and philosophy before graduating in 1952 and entering the priesthood.

In 1953 he moved to South Africa where he started missionary work and studied to become a teacher. But it was at this time that the horrors of his war service seemed to catch up with him and he was overwhelmed by post-traumatic stress disorder. Unable to sleep, Hellinger became chronically anxious and took refuge in a remote missionary station run by Dutch monks. After a number of months he began to recover and took on some undemanding pastoral care that seemed to help his recovery.

He remained in South Africa for sixteen years, during the last decade of which he became headmaster of St Francis College, an elite boarding school near Durban run by priests and nuns of the Mariannhill order. He described this period of his life as 'A beautiful and fruitful time for me', but went on to say:

> I got a reputation for being somewhat progressive and perhaps too interested in the new theology that was developing at that time. Suddenly I was suspected of having views that were incompatible with the teachings of the church. I was interviewed by my bishop who produced a letter that accused me of heresy. He asked me for my comments. I immediately resigned from all my positions and made it clear that I would return to Germany. Whenever I realise I can't go on I immediately go another way and do something new.

In his last few years in South Africa Hellinger had been involved in a group dynamic training course led by Anglican priests. This activated an intense interest in phenomenology and Gestalt analytic theory, which now – having returned to Germany – he began to develop further. After a period of intense self-examination he left the priesthood, met his wife

Herta and moved to Vienna, where he embarked upon psychoanalytic training at the Viennese Association of Depth Psychology. This was followed by further therapeutic training in Munich and then in the United States, where he finally qualified as a psychoanalyst.

Hellinger was nearing the age of seventy when he developed his own unique family constellation theory and it was not until 1993 that he first published a series of workshop transcripts. In his final two decades, between 1998 and when he died, aged ninety-five, in 2019, he published dozens of books which sold in their millions and travelled widely delivering lectures, workshops and training courses. Why, one wonders, has Bert Hellinger's family constellation work gained such a hold in Germany during the last thirty years?

Put simply, the theory maintains that the family into which we are born not only provides us with our genetic inheritance, it also bestows upon us a family culture, with its belief systems and organising principles. For Bert Hellinger it is an energy field, a set of gravitational attractions into which we are inevitably drawn from the moment of our birth. Our family gravitational field can have a range of impacts upon us: it can restrict or amplify our ambition and aspirations, our sense of meaning and identity, our health, our happiness, our capacity for intimacy and our ability to relate to others. Where these abilities and personal qualities are limited by the family culture, constellation theory provides us with a chance to comprehend and examine these deeply embedded, unconscious family patterns. This constellation work can bring us to a level of understanding that can liberate us from the restrictive, harmful patterns of this often toxic family culture. The family constellation is deeply affected not only by the history, geography and culture which surrounds it, but also by the psychobiography of all its family members, which includes the relationship history of parents and grandparents, circumstances of birth, miscarriages, abortions, adoptions, suicides, the death of children, change of nationality or religion and levels of prosperity and poverty. There is, if you like, a presiding sense of a family karma, a family destiny that is carried unconsciously by every family member and by each successive generation. Hellinger's family constellations allow for the possibility of a release from what he describes as 'entanglements', which more often than not are both restrictive and harmful to the individual family member. It's important to note, however, that he is not proposing an escape by means of geography or abandonment: instead he suggests a more responsible, less reactive response: a process of healing, understanding, compassion and forgiveness.

This brief description is perhaps enough to explain why Hellinger's theory and its therapeutic techniques proved so attractive to the grandchildren of the Nazi generation. Finally, German 'Collective Silence' was ended and the shame and guilt could be acknowledged and slowly worked through. The outward manifestation of this process are the numerous Holocaust memorials and museums in German cities, as well as the many television documentaries, feature films, theatrical dramas and countless books dealing with the phenomenon of Germany's Nazi past. This process of both inner and outer reconciliation has transformed the German nation into a country capable of self-awareness, compassion and endless contrition.

Inevitably Hellinger's work has been widely criticised by a number of psychotherapeutic theorists and practitioners. These complaints range from his theories not being sufficiently evidence-based to his ideas being too patriarchal and anti-feminist. His treatment of cases of incest and sexual abuse have been questioned, as have his suggestion that war criminals should be forgiven. However, I'm not concerned here with dealing with these issues of efficacy or moral probity: what I wish to emphasise is that Hellinger's techniques and theories had such a profound impact in Germany upon the descendants of the 'perpetrators' of the nation's Nazi past and the Holocaust. While it is true that much of Hellinger's theory was not evidence-based but was the result of speculation and his intuitive heuristic research of recent German history, his longevity allowed him – at the age of seventy – to disseminate his family constellation work widely. It was as if his ideas towards the end of his life somehow resonated with the German zeitgeist and profoundly touched a generation that felt they had to atone for their forebears' iniquitous transgressions.

In the final years of Hellinger's long life a series of developments occurred in the field of genetics that perhaps provide an empirical foundation for his ideas. This recent development in genetics is known as epigenetics.

Epigenetics is the study of the modifications and adaptions in organisms caused by changes in gene expression rather than the alteration of the genetic code itself. Matthew Dahlitz and Richard Hill, in their 2022 book *The Practitioner's Guide to the Science of Psychotherapy*, define epigenetics more simply: 'Epigenetics is how the DNA remembers experience.'

During the first two decades of the twenty-first century the theory of epigenetics has been expanded and has now reached the periphery of psychotherapy and the study of trauma upon human development. A phenomenon named by geneticists as 'methylation' describes how traumatic experience can glaze a gene with a coating of proteins which does not alter the DNA sequence but does change the manner in which the gene expresses itself. This coated, methylated gene can be passed on from one generation to the next in a fashion that Hellinger would have entirely understood: the gene's response is adapted through a subtle form of genetic memory that results in the DNA anticipating the likelihood of the traumatic event reoccurring in the future. For instance, if a young child experiences a deficiency in maternal attention, or if there is an early breakdown in the bond with the mother or some kind of abuse experienced, the infant will be subjected to an intense fear of abandonment, the likes of which Winnicott describes as 'primitive agonies', a terror way beyond mere anxiety. In such situations the cortisol released by the amygdala will be gathered up by the glucocortisol receptors in the hippocampus which will then methylate the infant's genes, raising its anticipation of future traumatic threats to life and limb. In this fashion the child's expectations of future trauma will be raised as the memory of a threatening environment will be 'written' on his or her DNA, which then – in this methylated state – will be passed onto the next generation.

This produces higher levels of adrenaline and cortisol in the brain which reduces levels of dopamine and serotonin, resulting in an increase in feelings of anxiety and anguish, producing a generation of pessimists who – overwhelmed by feelings of paranoia – insist they that live in a threatening, predatory world.

A team of researchers at McGill University in Montreal in 2007 investigated this by studying two groups of rat pups. The first group were placed with 'good mothers', female rats capable of high levels of licking, grooming and maternal care, while the second group were given 'bad mothers', rats which were disinterested in any form of maternal care. The pups with 'good mothers' exhibited far higher levels of serotonin and oxytocin and appeared more secure, content and less agitated than the pups with the 'bad mothers', who had much greater cortisol levels which methylated their DNA. But when the poorly mothered pups were passed over to the good mothers, the coating and glazing on their DNA disappeared over a number of weeks. This is what I have always believed happens in psychotherapy: that the client is looking for an experience of re-parenting. Unbeknownst to the client, his or her genes have this veneer or film coating their DNA that can result in an expectation of endless future trauma and misfortune, leaving the client permanently alert to threat and danger. But, like the good maternal rats, the psychotherapist can de-methylate the genes of the client if they can provide the right re-parenting, which requires the right measure of empathy, care, understanding and love.

I have already mentioned how, if a client's experience of good parenting has been delayed, this vital psychotherapeutic experience provides a kind of 'catch up', a kind of thera peutic 'iPlayer' belatedly offering optimal parenting missed in childhood. Like the good mother rats, the good therapist

can provide the equivalent to 'maternal licking' and grooming, which can de-methylate the client's genes and if this is
done successfully, these genes will not be passed onto the
next generation.

Hellinger was obviously unaware of the field of epigenetics, but his family constellation work has, as its principle
premise, that trauma experienced by an individual will be
transferred into a family's destiny, or as we know, onto the
family DNA. As we have seen, Hellinger's theory was based
upon his personal familiarity with Germany's Nazi past and
his experience of family dysfunctionality in Germany, resulting from the 'collective silence' he witnessed on his return to
Europe in the late 1960s. His hunch that the national psychological wound, resulting from the trauma of two world
wars and the shame of Nazi barbarism, had a profound
impact on successive generations of German families was at
last receiving empirical validation. Yet Hellinger had already
had his validation in the extensive response of the German
population to his particular approach to psychotherapeutic
work: the immense success of his books and theories and the
widespread use of family constellation therapy in Germany
was enough to prove the efficacy and veracity of his ideas.
It is as if Hellinger's theories were de-methylating the genes
of those Germans who used family constellation techniques.

Indeed the widespread use of a variety of psychotherapeutic practices has been a striking feature of German life in
the last thirty years. The recognition and acceptance of psychotherapy gathered considerable momentum in the 1990s
and was consolidated in the German Psychotherapy Acts
of 1998. Today their National Health Service provides and

pays for psychotherapeutic help for all patients in need and the mean duration of individual psychotherapy provided by the state lies between fifty and sixty hourly sessions, but if required this can be increased to up to 300 hours of psychoanalysis. This provides a far greater support system than the British model, which can only offer six to twelve hours of Cognitive Behaviour Therapy. Germany also has a large network of psychotherapeutic hospitals with thousands of hospital beds, contrasting sharply with the UK's 'care in the community' provision, which has resulted in the mass closure of so many of the country's psychiatric hospitals.

It seems from this evidence that the grandchildren of the Nazi generation have been naturally drawn to this broad range of psychotherapeutic opportunities and in doing so perhaps they have achieved a national epigenetic recovery, with the country's gene pool being – to a considerable degree – de-methylated by a well-trained, effective psychotherapeutic profession. Perhaps this therapeutic application has contributed to the political stability and economic prosperity that Germany achieved after the traumas and catastrophes of the first half of the twentieth century.

Since reading about the discovery of epigenetics, gene methylation and the manner in which the impact of intense trauma can be passed on genetically to future generations, I have begun to wonder how my grandfather's four years in the trenches of the Ypres Salient in the First World War and my own father's five years of combat experience in the Battle of the Atlantic and in the Russian convoys in the Second World War can have affected me. Considering their lives now I think they both suffered from undiagnosed post-traumatic stress disorder, given the brutal horrors they witnessed and the intense fear they must have felt repeatedly over a number of years. Perhaps I inherited their severely methylated genes which resulted in the prolonged periods of anxiety and depression I experienced throughout my twenties. And conversely, perhaps my beloved therapist Hella Adler, with whom I worked for eighteen years, provided me with the right kind of re-parenting which demethylated my genes. I remember having a tremendous fear of death during these difficult years and it's possible that I was re-experiencing the near-proximity of Thanatos, that lethal presence that my grandfather and father had to face.

One of the twentieth century's most acclaimed writers, who took part in both the First and Second World Wars, did – I'm sure – suffer from gene methylation, which first occurred in the DNA of his two grandfathers who each experienced the slaughter and barbarities of the American Civil War. His grandfathers and his own father, who committed suicide, undoubtedly had an enormous impact upon Ernest Hemingway, whose tormented life was constantly lived close to the saturnine presence of Thanatos.

If you were born in 1899, like Ernest Hemingway, you could easily become one of those unlucky individuals who were destined to take part in both world wars. Always relishing the adrenaline rush of combat, Hemingway managed to find a third European war to bridge the gap between 1918 and 1939, when he made a number of visits to Spain to take part in that benighted country's civil war in the late 1930s.

His various combat wounds, inflicted during these three

wars and of which he was inordinately proud, were added to, in more peaceful times, by a series of injuries sustained in car accidents, boat accidents and in two plane crashes which occurred in his late fifties. In addition to these near-fatalities Hemingway seemed to be continually involved in dysfunctional marriages and affairs. These significant injuries and emotional turmoil undoubtedly exacerbated his alcoholism and subsequent mental illness.

In his 2018 biography of Hemingway *The Man Who Wasn't There: A Life of Ernest Hemingway*, Richard Bradford writes: 'His existence was plagued by an obsession with breaking away, testing the patience of his friends, wives and fellow writers, seemingly intent on never allowing contentment or obedience to play a role in what he did and thought. Why precisely he was drawn to this incessant, self-destructive mindset is an unanswerable question.'

Being obsessively attracted to so much danger and observing so much death and destruction would be a mode of repeated behaviour that would have appeared entirely predictable if Hemingway had somehow spent an hour or two lying prone on Freud's famous couch. Indeed the American writer would have provided the perfect case study for the ageing founder of psychoanalysis to prove not only his contention that the battle between Eros and Thanatos ruled all our lives, but also the efficacy of his theory of repetition.

Anson Hemingway and Ernest Hall, who provided him with his name, joined the Union Army in their early twenties and for three long years took part in and witnessed the horrors and killing fields of the American Civil War. Hospital orderly and poet Walt Whitman wrote of the carnage:

'Future years will never know the seething hell and the black infernal background of the succession war.' The ferocity and intensity of the killing was due to the fact that the combat tactics resembled those of the Battle of Agincourt while the weapon technology matched the efficiency displayed on the Somme and at Verdun sixty years later. During the two-day battle of Shiloh, more men were slaughtered than in all previous American wars combined. And at the battle of Cold Harbour 7,000 young soldiers were cut down in twenty minutes. The carnage was excessive and those combatants who survived physically were scarred mentally for a lifetime. After taking part in the bloody Siege of Vicksburg in 1863, Anson Hemingway was promoted to first lieutenant and led Company H, one of the first Black units in the Union Army, the 70th Regiment which invariably found itself in the thick of the fighting. Ernest Hall served in the 1st Iowa Volunteer Cavalry and after seeing action throughout the Western Theatre, he received a serious wound during the Battle of Warrensburg. The bullet that lodged in his left thigh was never recovered, providing him with a permanent reminder of the bloodletting, although he refused ever to speak of the war, an elected silence common amongst those suffering from post-traumatic stress disorder.

Ernest Hall ended his life riven with pain caused by acute kidney disease and Hemingway remembered when he was only six that his maternal grandfather had asked for a gun so he could die rather than continue to face such unendurable agony. Hemingway's father Clarence, who lived nearby, retrieved the pistol that Ernest Hall intended to use, removed the cartridges and returned the gun to his father-in-law, who then – according to Hemingway – attempted to shoot himself with the unloaded pistol. He later described this 'act of mercy as the cruelest thing I could ever imagine. I could never forgive my father.'

Twenty-three years later, in 1928, Clarence Hemingway took his own father's army revolver and, having no one to remove the bullets, blew his brains out, the ultimate act of self-destruction that his son Ernest would emulate thirty years later. On this occasion he preferred the full explosive impact of a shotgun. There is a family photograph of the Hemingways taken in 1906. Of the six family members pictured four of them – father Clarence, daughters Ursula and Marcelline and son Ernest – all committed suicide. Two further children, in 1906 yet unborn – Carol and Leicester – also ended their lives prematurely. One wonders the extent to which Anson Hemingway and Ernest Hall's methylated genes, traumatised by the Civil War, were the cause of this irresistible grip of Thanatos which decimated the Hemingway family.

But the great paradox of Hemingway's life was that it wasn't a tragedy. His achievement, the scope of his artistic triumph with its glittering literary prizes and the breadth of his rich experience, were full of so much energy, so much gusto, so much celebration that the measure of Eros's presence nearly matched Thanatos's grasp of his tumultuous life and this overlap was so evidently present in the sheer exuberance with which Hemingway approached the three wars he took part in.

Having joined the American Red Cross Ambulance service in early 1918, the young Hemingway was sent to join the

Italian Army on the Northeast Alpine front where they faced the Austro-Hungarian Army. Driving his ambulance up and down the mountains he delivered wounded Italian soldiers to the nearby field hospitals. But he was disappointed in the lack of action and the tedious repetition of his trips up to the support trenches as he ferried the wounded down the mountain. Somehow he managed to leave his Red Cross duties and joined the 70th Italian Infantry regiment stationed on the front line near Fossalta di Piave. Then in early July 1918, while he was manning a forward listening post, an enemy mortar shell exploded two metres from where he was standing. A soldier next to him was killed instantly while another had his legs blown off and a mass of shrapnel penetrated Hemingway's legs and lacerated his head. The blast caused the first of the numerous concussions that he would be regularly assailed by throughout his life. Despite these injuries he managed to carry another wounded Italian to the safety of a nearby dugout, an act of bravery for which he would later receive the Silver Medal for Military Valor, one of Italy's highest military decorations.

He later wrote of this first brush with death with a kind of elation: 'I died then. I felt my soul come right out of my body, like you pull a silk handkerchief out of a pocket. It flew around then came back and went in again and I wasn't dead anymore.' Later that year he wrote to his parents, saying: 'Dying is a very simple thing. I've looked at death and really I know. If I should have died it would have been very easy for me' and he described his wounding as 'awfully satisfying'. There seems to be a complete absence of fear, as if death is a congenial embrace offered by some welcomed friend.

As stretcher-bearers carried Hemingway to an aid station, an enemy machine-gunner started firing and bullets ripped into his right knee and foot, after which he was taken to a field hospital in a converted schoolhouse near Fornaci. His wounds were so severe that a priest administered extreme unction as the army surgeons began working on him, removing pieces of shrapnel from his feet and legs. He was then transferred to a hospital near Treviso, where he lay swathed in bandages from hand to foot, and later he was taken to a larger hospital in Milan where he stayed convalescing for the next four months. He appeared to relish the whole experience, particularly as he was regarded as a handsome American war hero by the nurses and everyone who now came to visit him. He fell in love with one of these nurses, an American from Washington called Agnes von Kurowsky, of whom biographer Peter Griffin wrote: 'I think the real explosion that affected Hemingway was the broken heart Kurowsky gave him.'

He had to wait twenty years for another war that would provide the thrill and inspiration that close proximity to Thanatos seemed to give him. While he waited, he wrote *A Farewell to Arms* (1929), much of which was based on his own experiences and which turned him into a global literary superstar. So successful was this novel that in 1932 Hollywood turned it into an equally successful film with Gary Cooper playing the heroic central role. The film's success took Hemingway's fame far beyond the reaches of mere literary celebrity and he longed for another war in which he could flex his heroic muscles once again.

In May 1938 Hemingway, decked out with a glamorous

new mistress, the journalist Martha Gellhorn, arrived in Madrid and found the Spanish capital precariously perched on the front line, exposed to the incoming shells of General Franco's artillery. The hotel they chose to stay in was the Hotel Florida, which – as far as Hemingway was concerned – was ideally situated next to a loyalist communication centre which regularly attracted the attention of Franco's batteries. The writer Elinor Langer described how Hemingway took great interest in how his fellow guests reacted to the incoming bombardment. On one occasion when a number of guests requested safer rooms at the back of the hotel, Hemingway insisted they should remain where they were otherwise 'they would be running away from the enemy, capitulating to Franco'.

At this point he was receiving large sums of money from the North American Newspaper Alliance (NANA) and was delighted to be paid to join a gathering of celebrity writers and journalists at the Hotel Florida who were all eager to observe the hostilities taking part in and around the Spanish capital. There were regular trips out to watch the fighting, which included the Battle of Belchite, the trench warfare on the Aragon front and the fierce fighting around Teruel. All this was done with the greatest enthusiasm and exuberance, with lashings of alcohol lubricating the proceedings.

His friend and photojournalist Robert Capa described Hemingway as 'crackling with generosity and bursting with vigour' as he acted as the kind of ringmaster of the reporters, writers and celebrities gathered at the Florida Hotel, including the film star Errol Flynn. Each evening there would be an impromptu party hosted by Hemingway. The food was basic, but the flow of alcohol seemed endless and Martha Gellhorn – who was as fearless as her lover – made the perfect hostess. They were a magnetic, charismatic couple who injected an infectious glamour and excitement into this nasty civil war.

After two months in Madrid and on the Aragon front they returned to America and stayed briefly in the White House as Gellhorn was a close friend of Eleanor Roosevelt. Hemingway would return to report on the Spanish Civil War three more times over the next eighteen months, as General Franco's fascists slowly advanced across the entire country, describing it as 'a carnival of treachery and rottenness on both sides'. Once again he turned his Spanish Civil War experiences into an immensely successful novel. As the critic Amanda Vaill says of *For Whom the Bell Tolls* (1940): 'The novel is more truthful than the journalism.' In its final few pages Hemingway describes the last few minutes of his hero Robert Jordan's life. As he lies wounded and immobilised, a platoon of enemy soldiers moves towards him and he can't decide whether to take his own life, wait to be taken prisoner and face some fearful consequences or use his last ammunition firing at the soldiers until their bullets take their toll. In a stream of consciousness ending worthy of James Joyce he writes:

> His leg was hurting very badly now. The pain had started suddenly with the swelling after he had moved and he said, Maybe I'll just do it now . . . Why wouldn't it be all right to just do it now and then the whole thing would be over with? . . . Think about Montana. I can't. Think about Madrid. I can't. Think about a cool drink of water. All right. That's

what it will be like. Like a cool drink of water. You're a liar.
It will just be nothing. That's all it will be. Just nothing. Then
do it. Do it. Do it now. It's all right to do it now. Go on and
do it now. No, you have to wait. What for? You know all
right. Then wait.

This seems to me to be a tremendous rendition of his
closeness and attraction to Thanatos and no doubt expresses
an inner debate that Ernest Hemingway had with himself
time and again during his adult life. This sense of death
being always close by was to be experienced intensely in one
more major war.

In the spring of 1944 he was hired by *Collier's* magazine to be their sole war correspondent, covering the much
anticipated invasion of Europe, and he arrived in London in
the second half of May. But before he could join the action
he was involved in a near-fatal car accident after a party
he had attended at the Dorchester Hotel. At 2.40 a.m. the
car in which he was a passenger collided with a large steel
water tank and Hemingway was thrown through the wind-
screen, sustaining a severe head wound and bad concussion.
His friend Robert Capa visited him in hospital and found
him to be in the operating theatre with 'his skull split wide
open and his beard full of blood'. The head wound needed
fifty-seven stitches. He told his new girlfriend – and future
fourth wife, Mary Welsh – that he had lied to his doctors as
he knew that the invasion of Europe was imminent and he
had no desire to staunch his alcohol consumption which the
doctors would have insisted upon if he had told them of the
severe concussion symptoms he was experiencing.

As a celebrity war correspondent he boarded the USS *Dorothea L. Dix* early in the morning of 5 June, only a week after his premature hospital departure. From his naval grandstand he witnessed the US battleships *Texas* and *Arkansas* bombard the German positions on the Normandy shore and then watched as the American soldiers faced the withering fire that decimated their ranks as they waded ashore on Omaha Beach. Reluctantly, as the fighting was so fierce, he returned to England that evening.

Ten days later Hemingway joined General George S. Patton's Third Army in France, but he developed a strong dislike for the famous general and attached himself instead to the 4th Infantry Division commanded by General Raymond O. Barton, whom he befriended. Barton provided him with a Mercedes convertible and a driver named Archie Pelkey who stayed with Hemingway until the end of the war. But his closest friend was General Buck Lanham, who commanded the 22nd Infantry Regiment. Hemingway and Lanham were like two excited small boys, playing with their lethal toys as they shared the thrill of the fighting in the Normandy Bocage and celebrating the liberation of Paris at the Ritz hotel together. Later that autumn they fought together, leading Lanham's Regiment in the Battle of the Hürtgen Forest, just over the German border.

The dense woodland of the forest was covered with giant conifer trees with few roads that were heavily mined and targeted by German artillery and the shells that detonated among the trees sprayed the advancing Americans with shrapnel and shards from the trees. Buck Lanham later said: 'During one savage firefight men were firing and advancing and dropping and firing. Then I saw Ernest as he moved forward with the advancing wave, but I never saw him hit the ground and there was no question at all that he was armed and using those arms.' Hemingway had turned himself from war correspondent into a solider, entirely against the rules of the Geneva Convention, which forbade accredited war correspondents taking part in the action. But he was in his element: it was as if the combat zone was his natural environment where he felt perfectly at home, relishing the endless pendulum swing between Eros and Thanatos.

The Battle of Hürtgen Forest began on the 19 of September and continued until the 16 December. It was the longest single battle ever fought by the US Army and accounted for about 40,000 American dead, while the Germans lost 28,000. By the end of November Hemingway had seen enough of the slaughter and returned home to Cuba. The sights he had witnessed in the Hürtgen Forest were so terrible that they would haunt him for the rest of his life and inevitably a blanket of post-traumatic stress disorder folded over him, choking his literary potency. He wrote to Buck Lanham: 'I am absolutely homesick for the regiment and miss you very badly Buck. I don't give a damn about writing. I will have to get over that. I so miss your companionship . . . I'm drinking to go to sleep at night, I'm drinking when I wake up. I've got to stop drinking or Mary won't come home and marry me.'

In the sixteen years left to Hemingway he only wrote and published two more novels. *Across the River and into the Trees* (1950) was savaged by the critics with Donald Adams of the *New York Times* describing it as 'one of the saddest books I have ever read because a great talent has come, whether for now or forever, to such a dead end'. The short novella *The Old Man and the Sea* (1952) was received with much more enthusiasm, but after Hemingway received the Nobel Prize in Literature in 1954 it was as if he had become a spent force as he spiralled into chronic alcoholism and increasing mental health infirmities.

In 2017 Andrew Farah, the American psychiatrist, published *Hemingway's Brain*, a poignant assessment of the writer's descent into the inebriated depression that ended in his suicide on 2 July 1961. It is a sad but compelling account of Thanatos's final triumph over that unique life force that was Ernest Hemingway.

As we have seen, the emergence of epigenetics in the last decade provided us with irrefutable evidence that trauma has, as one of its consequences, the methylation of genes that then can be passed on to the next generation and can easily result in an anxious disposition. One of the most frequent consequences of depression and anxiety is for the sufferer to self-medicate using alcohol, as was clearly evident in Hemingway's case. This sequence of events inevitably stirs up the age-old debate between nurture and nature: did Hemingway's propensity for depression and alcoholism have a genetic trigger? Or was it primarily ignited by environmental factors?

We have also seen how the genetic propensity for suicide which was strongly present in Hemingway's family probably started when Anson Hemingway and Ernest Hall faced the battlefield horrors of the American Civil War. Andrew Farah refers to the suicide epidemic in the Hemingway family, stating: 'There is something powerful lurking in a genetic code that not only conveys illness but also self-destructive behaviour.' This of course is right, but writing before the evidence of methylated gene inheritance was widely known, Farah can only allude to it.

With this genetic predisposition securely in place, Andrew Farah lays down a persuasive case that Hemingway's psychological fragility was activated by a whole series of woundings and accidents. His attraction to risk and hazardous experiences inevitably resulted in severe head injuries sustained over four decades, leading to undiagnosed 'Chronic Traumatic Encephalopathy', or CTE. The first occurred in 1918 when he was nineteen and the last in 1954 when he was fifty-five.

Three of these severe head injuries were war wounds: one sustained towards the end of the First World War in Northern Italy and two suffered in 1944 in Normandy after the D-Day Landings. Hemingway's head took the full brunt of the impact in two serious car accidents, in London in 1944, the other in Cuba in the summer of 1950, both requiring hospital treatments. Later that year he fell from the bridge of his boat *Pilar* while out fishing, causing yet another deep scalp laceration and concussion. The two final accidents were the most dramatic and occurred when Hemingway and his wife Mary were involved in two air-crashes which took place within a day of each other.

In the autumn of 1953 Hemingway and Mary travelled to East Africa to visit his son Patrick and his wife Henny who had moved to Tanganyika. After the visit they set off on a seven-week safari that involved both hunting and photographing the wildlife. For Christmas, Ernest had given Mary a plane ride over the Ngorongoro Crater, the Mountains of the Moon and the Murchison Falls. On the 23 of January 1954 they took off in a light Cessna aircraft. Having twice flown over the Murchison Falls, Mary asked their pilot for one final pass so she could photograph the magnificent waterfall and as they began one last circle a flock of Ibis rose up in front of the plane forcing the pilot to change course. As a result the plane hit some ancient telegraph wires, badly damaging the tail and propellor of the aircraft, and they crash-landed. Mary was knocked unconscious and suffered two broken ribs and Hemingway injured his shoulder and received a further concussion.

A search plane had been sent out when the Hemingways didn't return and flew over the wreckage of the Cessna, but no survivors were spotted. Within a few hours word spread throughout the world that Hemingway and Mary had died in the plane crash. The next morning the newspapers in America and Europe headlined the death of the writer and the effusive obituaries described his perilous adventurous spirit which had now finally proved fatal.

The day after the crash Hemingway and Mary made it to a nearby river and had flagged down a local boat which took them to the shore of Lake Albert, where they encountered a bush pilot called Reggie Cartwright who offered to fly them onto Entebbe. But the combination of the ancient and poorly serviced twin-engine De Havilland and the rutted, rock-strewn Buti Aba airstrip proved to be too much for the luckless party. Cartwright, concerned about the condition of the pitted runway, reduced his take-off speed to the minimum, rose fifty feet above the ground and then plummeted downwards. As they hit the ground the right engine caught fire and ignited, leaking petrol. While the plane was burning, Mary and Cartwright escaped through the window but Hemingway's large frame was stuck in the plane. With his shoulder injured in the previous day's crash Hemingway resorted to using his head as a battering ram against the aircraft's locked door. Again and again he hurled his head against the door until it finally opened. When he arrived in Entebbe Hemingway was met by a great gathering of excited reporters and he told them he had never felt better and couldn't wait to read his numerous obituaries. A few weeks later he wrote: 'In almost all the obituaries it was emphasised that I had sought death all my life. Can one imagine that if a man sought death all his life he could not have found her before the age of fifty-four?'

Fortunately for Hemingway his quota of Eros, his immense life-force and his zest for excitement and adventure had always outrun his endless flirtations with Thanatos. He remained in hospital in Nairobi for a number of weeks. His battered body displayed a whole range of lacerations, contusions, damage to internal organs, first-degree burns and, most serious of all, symptoms of extreme concussion. His kidneys were injured and his liver, already impaired by decades of heavy drinking, had been further damaged. In addition he had dislocated his right shoulder and fractured two vertebrae, but this fresh round of head injuries was what caused the doctors most concern. His skull was fractured and cerebrospinal fluid leaked from his left ear, leaving him with double-vision and intermittent blindness in his left eye. His hearing, he said, 'came in and out like a radio in a thunderstorm'. In the months to come the CTE grew worse and he started to display symptoms as if he had Parkinson's, Alzheimer's and other neurological degenerative illnesses.

These numerous injuries marked the beginning of a steep decline in both his physical and mental wellbeing, accelerated by his dangerously high levels of alcohol consumption that gave him momentary relief from all his crippling ailments. He became increasingly impatient, irritable, frightened and regularly exploded into terrible rages, picking on Mary as a convenient victim of these malicious tirades. He was so abusive that Mary threatened to leave him and his son Patrick wanted nothing more to do with his father, whom he described as a vengeful, raging 'King Lear'.

Hemingway returned to Cuba with Mary and his health was so fragile that he was unable to travel to Stockholm to collect his Nobel Prize in Literature. Sightseers, reporters and autograph hunters flocked to his house hear Havana, hoping they might meet or at least get a glimpse of the famous writer, leaving him to feel that he was like 'an old elephant in the zoo'.

To counter the depressions and delusions caused by his daily consumption of alcohol his doctors prescribed an assortment of antidepressants, sleeping pills and medication to soothe his anxiety and paranoia. He also took synthetic testosterone to counter his impotence. With his fame after the Nobel Prize at its peak his lamentable physical and mental state were kept secret. It was a kind of hell made worse by the civil war that was now raging around in him in Cuba as Castro's guerillas attempted to overthrow the Batista government.

After one final trip to Spain he returned to Cuba to find that Castro had won the civil war. Anticipating this, he and Mary had bought a house in Ketchum, Idaho, in a landscape he had known in his youth. In the months after they had moved in Hemingway seemed disorientated and his fear and paranoia became more acute. He started to talk of suicide and Mary insisted he go to the Mayo clinic in Minnesota, where he registered under an assumed name, as his state of mind made him feel so ashamed. There he was given the standard treatment of the day for psychotic depression, electroconvulsive therapy (ECT), and after six weeks he was discharged, but Thanatos refused to relent. He kept going for a further six months: he was asked to write a tribute to the new, young President Kennedy, but in a fortnight he could only manage a dribble of a few faltering sentences. He complained of the effects of the ECT ('It has ruined my head and erased my memory, which is my capital and has put me out of business') and his thoughts of suicide returned to the point where Mary insisted he be treated at the Sun Valley Mental Hospital in April 1961. At the end of June he was discharged and, early in the morning on 2 July, Hemingway went into the basement of his new home, found his shotgun, loaded it, returned upstairs, put the end of the barrel in his mouth and pulled the trigger.

The immense life-force that was Ernest Hemingway was finally overwhelmed by the seductive presence of Thanatos that had haunted him ever since he came so close to death in the trenches of the First World War, when he was a young soldier of nineteen. Since then, he had been drawn into a continual dance with Thanatos and now had finally been felled by a mixture of methylated genes, acute alcoholism, a cocktail of medication, CTE caused by repeated concussions, ECT and finally the barrel of his W&C Scott & Son Monte Carlo B.

Now at the age of seventy-four I find that the proximity of Thanatos is a daily presence, and yet the feeling of Eros and a sense of the value and pleasure of life are also as strong as ever. It is as if as time gets shorter it becomes more precious and one doesn't want to waste a single day being miserable. Still there is something in this outlook that smacks of denial, as if all this optimism might be a compensatory strategy which refuses to face the closeness of the inevitable eternal oblivion of Thanatos and I've noticed how my psyche has found a way of acknowledging the proximity of death and being with the intimidating realisation that illness, infirmity and mortality are not far away.

Like many other people who are my age, I often wake up between three and four in the morning feeling a deep sense of unease. Apparently the liver recalibrates at this time of night, increasing the stress hormone cortisol in our bodies and brains, hence why intimations of my pending mortality press down upon me. In these moments my heart rate goes up and I start to ponder my accumulation of years and wonder anxiously how long I have got.

After an hour or so of fretfulness I drop off to sleep and then wake at a more acceptable hour, feeling more cheerful and ready to face the day with a degree of pleasurable expectancy. Perhaps this is my psyche's way of insisting that I must face and accept the ever-nearing reality of Thanatos, but by tucking these saturnine thoughts into the quiet sequestered hours, I am forced to wrestle with what one of my clients called 'barbed-wire thinking', which somehow clears the daylight hours of all this morbidity. It's not a bad deal: an hour or two gripped by Thanatos and then free for the rest of the day to be reassured and elevated by the presence of Eros.

In the last paragraph of his book *Staring at the Sun: Overcoming the Terror of Death* (2008), the great psychotherapeutic writer Irvin Yalom wrote:

> I do not intend this to be a sombre book, instead it is my hope that by grasping our human condition – our finiteness, our brief time in the light – we will come not only to savour the preciousness of each moment and the pleasure of sheer being but to increase our compassion for ourselves and for all other human beings.

The Shadow
(Vladimir Putin)

In 1932 Albert Einstein wrote a fan letter to Sigmund Freud, which suggests that he had read Freud's latest work *Civilisation and its Discontents*:

> I greatly admire your passion to ascertain the truth. You have shown with irresistible lucidity how inseparably the aggressive and destructive instincts are bound up in the human psyche with those of love and lust for life. At the same time your convincing arguments make manifest your deep devotion to the great goal of the liberation of men from the evils of war.

In a long pessimistic reply Freud wrote back:

> Although the common needs and habits of men who live in fellowship under the same sky favour a speedy resolution of such conflicts, the most casual glance at world history will show an unending series of conflicts between one community and another, between cities, countries, races, tribes and kingdoms, almost all of which were settled by the ordeal of war . . . The upshot of these observations is that there is no likelihood of our being able to suppress humanity's aggressive tendencies.

Yet after this forlorn foreboding Freud ends his letter to Einstein with some more hopeful sentiments: 'How long have we to wait before the rest of men turn pacifist? Impossible to say and yet perhaps our hope that man's cultural disposition and a well-founded dread of the form that future wars will take, may serve to put an end to war in the near future.'

From our perspective in 2026, Freud's hope that after a long wait humanity might 'turn pacifist' seems to be a forlorn hope, with the death toll in the Russia–Ukraine war peaking at over 1 million and the Middle East nations in a mood of acute belligerence. Why exactly have 'humanity's aggressive tendencies' prevailed far longer than Freud's optimistic view, expressed in his letter to Einstein? One answer lies in Carl Jung's formulation of the Shadow, which he first outlined in his 1920 paper 'Freud & Psychoanalysis':

> The task of psychotherapy involves a more honest encounter with ourselves and our Shadow, some deepening of the journey into places we would rather not go. Our task is to live through them, not repress them or hurtfully project them onto others. To experience some healing within ourselves we are summoned to wade through our own muck and darkness.

Following Jung's advice, it is my belief that as psychotherapists our own most pressing task is to examine this dark corner of our unconscious as diligently as possible and to help our clients face this murky, unsettling terrain. Every individual, every marriage, every family, every community, every nation will inevitably develop a powerful and unconscious Shadow.

Contained in our individual Shadow are all the aspects of our personality that we find distasteful and unacceptable and which we wish to repress or deny, but from time to time we may fail to mute. Such lapses include sudden outbursts of aggression and anger in stark contrast to an otherwise placid, equable temperament; a deep, underlying, inexplicable sadness that sits just out of view beneath a cheerful, contented exterior; the sudden eruption of fear and anxiety in someone who always appears courageous and calm. Whatever we wish to hide from ourselves and from those around us we deposit in the Shadow.

The resource we use to keep the Shadow in its hidden place is the persona, that mask of social conformity and collective compliance that we show to those around us and, to some considerable degree, to ourselves. The persona is the ego's ally in the taming and imprisoning of the Shadow and this act of self-deception keeps the Shadow safely in the dark cave of the unconscious.

Often what accompanies all this venom are feelings of guilt and shame, activated by the fact we are capable of having such repellent feelings, and yet this outpouring of toxic emotion can often be a great release, as it bubbles up from the unconscious into the light of consciousness. So often this psychic silt can lie in the unconscious for year, festering away sending tremors of depression, anxiety and agitation up into our conscious minds.

The energy and effort required to suppress all this dark effluence, keeping it restrained in its unconscious prison, is tremendous and often results in exhaustion or somatic illness, but Jung maintains that if all this dark material can be integrated and accepted into our conscious personalities, then a great potential power will be available to us. However, this process of release is full of danger: as the Shadow erupts into visible presence there may be much personal and collateral damage, including divorce, professional collapse, emotional breakdown or illness. A successful working alliance with a therapist can facilitate the emergence of the Shadow avoiding much of this potential damage, but the Shadow's release may be beyond any controlled management. Indeed the psyche may feel that a full crisis is required for the emotional, psychological transformation that the Self, that guiding force at the apex of our nature, wishes to encourage.

Jung's conception of the individual's Shadow was extended as his views on the 'Collective Unconscious' expanded and amplified. As Freud had died in the opening weeks of the Second World War, Jung emerged as the most revered sage of the psychoanalytic community to consider the global apocalypse that had destroyed so many European and Asian cities and their populations between 1939 and 1945. In 1945 he wrote an essay called 'After the Catastrophe' and a year later he broadcast a talk called 'The Fight with the Shadow' on the BBC, which he later published under the title 'The Individual and Mass Psychology'. In it he wrote:

> As early as 1918 I noticed a peculiar disturbance in the unconscious of my German patients which could not be ascribed to their personal psychology. There seemed to be a disturbance of the collective unconscious in every one of these German patients, which expressed primitivity, violence, cruelty and signs of depression and great restlessness.

Defeat and social disaster had increased the herd instinct
in Germany and made it more and more probable that they
would become a victim of a mass movement . . . A new form
of existence, with its mass psychology and social dependence
on the fluctuation of markets and wages, produced individuals who were unstable, insecure and suggestible . . . Hitler
was the exponent of a 'new order' and that is the real reason why practically every German fell for him. He was the
most prodigious personification of all human inferiorities.
He represented the Shadow, the inferior part of everybody's
personality, to an overwhelming degree. In Hitler every
German should have seen their own Shadow.

As we have seen, the German national Shadow, which
emerged in the 1930s and brought devastation to Europe
in the 1940s, had its origins in the universal post-traumatic
stress disorder that emerged after the horrors of the First
World War, the collapse of the German economy and the
hyperinflation that followed. The result of these successive
catastrophes led to unprecedented levels of near-starvation,
poverty and national humiliation and such extreme levels of
stress and trauma will inevitably bring out the worst features
of human behaviour in both individuals and entire nations.
But as I have described, in the days following the Second
World War, West Germany established a comprehensive
mental-health service that proved most effective.

The other great national victim of what we might call
the twentieth-century apocalypse was, of course, Russia,
whose population endured endless decades of suffering
throughout the last century. Yet even now under the current

autocratic dictatorship of Vladimir Putin, they appear to see no end to their national anguish. It is as if the conflation of Freud's view of the 'death instinct' with Jung's concept of the Shadow is worryingly present in Russia's current plight, as hundreds of thousands of their young men are herded off to the killing fields of Ukraine.

In Russia, after losing 2.2 million of its citizens in the Great War, the list of the dead mounted swiftly. The Spanish Flu pandemic accounted for 450,000 in 1918–1919 and the Russian Civil War saw its death toll rise to 8 million. This was followed in the early 1930s by the Great Ukrainian Famine that claimed a further 5 million lives. As the famine eased, Stalin then unleashed on his exhausted population a series of lethal political purges that resulted in 1.2 million executions and untold further deaths in the camps of the Gulag. Despite the scale of this relentless misfortune, the worst was yet to come as Europe's second thirty-years' war reignited and from June 1941 until May 1945 a further 28 million Russians perished.

How did these terrible calamities affect Russian national DNA in these dreadful years? How extensive was the gene methylation which took place as Russian individuals faced personal trauma after trauma and as they witnessed horrendous spectacles of human brutality and suffered repeated losses of loved ones?

The Russian invasion of Ukraine in 2022 suggests that we are witnessing a national spasm of barbarity which stems from the genetic damage that, unlike Germany, has been left to fester with no reparative provision, as generations of Russian paranoia cast us back into a world of carnage that we had imagined we had left behind in the early decades of the twentieth century. If only the Russians had Germany's excellent mental health services or the enlightening views of someone like Bert Hellinger. In a 2016 article in *Counselling Today Magazine* the Russian psychotherapist Anton Ivanov writes:

> In most Russian communities, simply mentioning that parents are seeking mental health services for their children or themselves could have negative consequences. When such information became public knowledge, families' reputations were jeopardised and they were often stigmatised as 'dysfunctional'. Unfortunately these attitudes remain prevalent today.

With no fresh adjustments in the national psyche, the dark Shadow of intense paranoia still inhabits the Russian population who have managed to attract yet another autocratic dictator whose individual paranoid Shadow matches the national mood.

Adolf Hitler, Joseph Stalin and Vladimir Putin were all what has become known as 'replacement children', a term coined by the psychologists Albert and Barbara Cain in 1964. A replacement child is born to a mother who has experienced the death of a previous child or children. Hitler's mother had lost two children prior to Adolf's birth in 1889: Gustav in 1885 and Ida two years later. Clearly the loss of her son and daughter had a crippling effect upon Klara and Adolf's arrival undoubtedly soothed this agonising bereavement, particularly as she had to contend with the brutal indifference of her husband Alois, who was twenty-three years older than her.

Stalin's mother Ekaterine became pregnant at the age of nineteen, a few months after her marriage. Her first-born, Mikhail, died a year after his birth and her second son, Giorgi, succumbed at a similar age. Eighteen months later Joseph was born. From the start she made him feel special and to compensate for his angry, often violent alcoholic father Besarion, she was determined that Joseph would escape the family's poverty through a good education. As Robert Service writes *Stalin: A Biography* (2004): 'Keke's disappointment in her husband was sublimated into high expectations for her Joseph – and the fact that he was her only surviving child intensified her preoccupation with him.' The family lived in Gori, the second city of Georgia, where the most highly regarded school was the Gori Spiritual School, run by the local priesthood. It was difficult to get a place in Gori's most respected educational establishment, but somehow Keke succeeded and at the age of ten, Joseph entered the seminary, where his intelligence and diligence were soon recognised.

Like Hitler and Stalin, Putin was born after two of his older siblings had died. Albert had been taken by whooping cough during infancy, while Viktor – at the age of two – was smitten by diphtheria during the siege of Leningrad in March 1942. The loss of these children devastated their mother, Maria, who had to wait, bereaved and afflicted, for another ten years before a third child was born in 1952 when she was forty-one. As a result of her previous loss, Maria was obsessively protective of her son and Vladimir did not attend kindergarten. Cossetted at home, Maria taught him reading, writing and arithmetic and it wasn't until he was eight that she allowed him to go to school and mix regularly with other children.

But how can such maternal devotion create this level of dogmatic certainty, this obsessive conviction which can eventually result in such abominations as the Holocaust, the Stalinist Gulag or the invasion of Ukraine?

As we have seen, Heinz Kohut suggests the grandiose self should ideally be just an early developmental phase which needs to be passed through successfully and then shed, but when the grandiose self does not receive sufficient acceptance, the child has no alternative but to turn up the volume even further in its desperate attempts to achieve the attention it craves. But in order for the grandiose self to be sustained, it must be continually nourished by its successful attempts to seek witnesses, who confirm the reality of its grandeur and perfection. In other words, the child becomes desperate to find any opportunity to have its fragile invincibility confirmed by those around them. If this grandiose self is carried undiminished into adulthood, one of the most perfect platforms for its expression is politics, where the acceptable qualities of attention-seeking and grandstanding are constantly displayed in the stream of political rhetoric.

During the last millennium, nationalism has served humanity extremely poorly, as it is this atavistic drive that has caused so many of the world's devastating wars. The progress we have made in the last fifty years is due to nations following the collective advantages of international organisations such as the UN, EU, NATO and World Bank, rather than always looking to find ways of extending a purely national advantage. Nationalism contains streaks of infantile narcissism that we seemed increasingly to be leaving behind us, but recently it has returned in such phenomena as Boris Johnson's Brexit, Trump's 'Make America Great Again' and Putin's invasion of Ukraine.

As the Indian Prime Minister Narendra Modi said to Vladimir Putin in September 2022 in relation to the invasion of Ukraine: 'This is not an era of war.' Of course he's right: war needs to be seen as an obsolete, unacceptable way of resolving international disagreements and Putin's invasion of Ukraine is an anachronistic way of behaving, launched by a man who is driven by an excessive paranoid sense of grandiosity. Indeed such monstrous behaviour will hope-fully be one of the last expressions of this re-emergence of the wounded inner child in global politics. Our symbolic parents – as represented by our international organisations – need to assuage and mollify any further eruptions of this brand of aggressive nationalism and we will only manage to progress as a species when we lay to rest this brutal ideol-ogy. If we can't finally achieve the full maturity of pan-global international cooperation our species will flounder under the inevitable outcome of global warming, in which case an extinction event becomes more and more likely. Ironically it is global warming that insists we must now give up the grandiosity of nationalism.

Due to a moment of providential good fortune the future Russian president's father, also called Vladimir, avoided the common fate of so many Red Army soldiers and survived the

Great Patriot War that raged between 1941 and 1945. On 17 November 1941 a German infantryman tossed a grenade into his advancing platoon, killing a number of his comrades and wounding the future president's father with a shower of shrapnel. No vital organs were affected, but for the rest of his life Vladimir Spiridonovich Putin would walk with a considerable limp, a disability that kept him out of the slaughter that disposed of so many of his generation during the next four years.

Vladimir spent that winter recovering in a local military hospital while the Siege of Leningrad took an enormous toll on the city's civilians. As a convalescing soldier, Vladimir received a meagre food ration while the majority of the population starved and he shared these slender rations with his young wife Maria and their two-year-old son Viktor, who visited him each day. In the spring of 1942 he was discharged and after he was deemed no longer fit for further military duties, he was sent to work in a local munitions factory. Two months later their little boy Viktor died of diphtheria following Albert, who had died several years before the war. Other family members who died in the Great Patriotic War included Maria's mother Elizabeta and her brother Pyotr, while both Vladimir's brothers Mikhail and Aleksei were killed in the fighting, a common death toll among most Russian families during those dreadful years.

Tales about all these lost relatives would be regularly repeated in the grimy and bleak Leningrad communal flat in which Vladimir and Maria brought up Volodya, as he was known, their third and only surviving son who had been born on 7 October 1952, when they were both forty-one.

This tiny child became the principal blessing of his mother's existence. He was without doubt the great love of her life and his adored presence lit up her otherwise bleak and near-destitute life in the devastated street of Leningrad in which her family lived. She was quite sure that her lovely Volodya was an exceptional child and was destined for great things and indeed the intensity of Maria's maternal devotion evokes Freud's words: 'A man who has been the indisputable favourite of his mother keeps for life the feeling of conqueror, that confidence of success that often results in real success.'

Volodya adored his mother in return, but found his dour, rather distant and taciturn father considerably less lovable. After the war Vladimir worked in a Leningrad railway factory and, being a member of the Communist Party, he became the factory's party delegate whose job was to maintain party discipline and loyalty and the regular achievement of production quotas. For this invaluable work he was awarded the use of a single room in which to accommodate his family. While other families in the building on Baskov Lane, near Nevsky Prospect, had to share, young Volodya – who was destined to live in a variety of palaces – was brought up in a room that accommodated the Putin family alone, although they did have to share a bathtub, toilet and rudimentary kitchen on the communal landing.

But despite these meagre living conditions Maria had her miracle child to brighten each day, the child whom she would do everything to preserve and protect in her obsessional bid to avoid the fate of her two other sons' brief lives. In order to spend the days with her beloved son, whom she refused to send to school, she worked nights as an office cleaner, washing test tubes in a laboratory and in a bakery where she delivered bread. Although her husband, as a disciplined party member, was against all forms of religion, she secretly had Volodya baptised in a ceremony at the Transfiguration Cathedral and whenever possible furtively instructed her son in the message of hope that the clandestine Russian Orthodox Church tried to impart to those many Soviet citizens who were still drawn to the comfort of Christianity. Somehow Volodya seemed able to assimilate both his mother's devotional Christianity and his father's rigid Communist Party's secular views.

As I explored the mountain of material covering the life and mind of Vladimir Putin I was struck by how his vision, temperament and ambition have been moulded and sculpted by a succession of individuals who have deeply influenced his development. The comprehensive influence of his parents is, of course, paramount, as with us all. When his mother Maria finally allowed him to attend the local school at the age of eight, he seemed unable to adapt to his new routine. He was a bored and inattentive pupil who became a disruption in his class and he was drawn to other delinquent boys who gravitated towards the local youth gangs that were a feature of the Baskov Lane community. In addition, Volodya was short in stature, which resulted in him being regularly bullied by the larger, older boys, though he was also always confident.

At the age of twelve young Volodya met the first person who, apart from his parents, was to have a decisive influence on his life. Anatoly Rakhlin ran a martial arts club called the Sambo Club. Sambo is a mixture of hand-to-hand combat techniques that were developed in the Red Army in which judo is the primary mode of self-defence and the discipline was just what the pugnacious yet diminutive boy was in need of. It held his attention like nothing else had and the ethos of judo provided him with a set of values that he added to his mother's religion and his father's political views. Under the influence of this new father figure, Volodya developed an attitude and belief that served him well throughout his teenage years and into his adult professional life.

Anatoly Rakhlin was immediately drawn to the young Putin, as he got to know this waif-like youngster with his obvious intelligence, his tenacious single-mindedness and his passion for judo. What particularly impressed Rakhlin was Volodya's mature self-control, demonstrated by the manner in which he could flip from an aggressive belligerent forcefulness during a bout to courteous amicability as soon as the contest was over. Rakhlin noticed a strange kind of emotional control and aloofness unusual in one so young.

For the next few years, under the watchful eye of his mentor, Volodya perfected his judo skills and deepened his understanding of the composure and poise of its philosophy. His performance at school improved considerably and then at the age of fifteen Volodya was introduced to the work of his next great guide and influence: the writer Vadim Kozhevnikov, a man whom he never met but whose book, *Shield and Sword: The Amazing Career of a Soviet Agent in the Nazi Secret Service* and the subsequent television series, was to have a life-long impact on Volodya. *Shield and Sword* is the story of the super-spy Major Aleksandr Belov – a kind of Russian James Bond – who penetrated the Nazi High Command during the Great Patriotic War, providing the Red Army with key information about German military strategy that saves Mother Russia from almost certain defeat. It is a middle-brow work of fanatical patriotism and it made Volodya want to become a spy. Fuelled by his grandiosity and a sense of supreme confidence, distilled and nurtured by his adoring mother, the inspired young teenager now understood where his future lay. As he later recalled: 'What amazed me most of all was how one man's effort could achieve what whole armies could not. One spy could decide the fate of thousands of people.'

By the age of sixteen his mind was made up: he made his way to the Leningrad KGB headquarters and offered his services to the Russian security services. A kind and understanding officer at the KGB headquarters informed him that the organisation didn't just accept volunteers who wandered in off the street and explained that applicants applied through the formal channels when they had either completed a spell of military service or graduated from university. The determined teenager pressed his case and asked what degree he should study for. The indulgent KGB officer was quite clear: a law degree would be best. With this instruction firmly embedded in his mind Volodya worked hard at school and two years later he began his law studies

In 1970 Vladimir Putin entered the Leningrad State University and graduated in 1975. At university he met his next great mentor and influence, law professor Anatoly Sobchak. But before this important collaboration in Putin's future political advancement took place, he began his career in the KGB.

By 1975 the KGB was a vast bureaucratic organisation which had oversight of Soviet society and intelligence policy at home and abroad. Its reach included counterintelligence, economic security, military intelligence, customs and border control and it was also responsible for the security of the country's leadership and nuclear military sites. After his initial training Putin joined the Secretariat of the Directorate, a kind of personal department or HR division of the KGB. This was a far cry from the heroics of his hero Aleksandr Belov, as he sat at his desk filing innocuous personal documents all day and then returning to his mum and dad in the evening, but a year later Putin was transferred to the Second Directorate, which was concerned with counter-intelligence. There Putin worked in a division that maintained social order and political control inside the Soviet Union. Later, rumours circulated that Putin was part of the team involved in silencing such dissidents as the writer Alexander Solzhenitsyn and the scientist Andrei Sakharov and became familiar with – and used the network of – psychiatric hospitals that incarcerated the leading critics of USSR, whose political opposition was classified as irrational, mental derangement. After a period in this Second Directorate Putin was transferred to the KGB's First Directorate, which gathered intelligence internationally.

Initially Putin was not sent abroad and colleagues informed him that the KGB required their officers to be married before they were sent away, fearing that erotic dalliances could leave their agents open to blackmail, and so in April 1983 he asked his then girlfriend, Aeroflot air-hostess Lyudmila Shkrebneva, to marry him. The couple were married in late July and spent their honeymoon touring Ukraine by car.

Before long Putin was promoted to Major and sent to the elite school for foreign intelligence, known as the 'Red Banner Institute'. Once his training was complete he hoped to be sent to the capitalist West but as he waited for his first foreign appointment he was involved in a brawl with a group of hooligans on the Leningrad metro. This lapse in judgement tarnished his reputation and instead of being posted to the West he was sent to East Germany, to the provincial backwater of Dresden. He arrived in August 1985 and immediately began his work as a liaison officer with the East German Security Service, 'the Stasi'. A few months later Lyudmila and their baby daughter joined him.

Apart from this liaison work, Putin's other main responsibility was to recruit agents who had access to Western Europe, agents who would do the work that he had always hoped to do. The targets for infiltration were the numerous American and NATO military bases in West Germany, as KGB leaders were obsessed with the danger that NATO represented to the Soviet Union, despite the fact that a charismatic new leader, Mikhail Gorbachev, was attempting to use his policies of perestroika and glasnost to improve the country's relations with the West.

While Gorbachev preached a de-escalation of Cold War tensions, Major Putin and his KGB team still prepared for the worst and continued to gather information about economic, political and military developments in NATO countries. Putin's operational boss now became the Stasi General Horst Bohm, the head of the Dresden security services, who had an extremely high regard for his Russian deputy and who shared Putin's anxiety about NATO's growing strength and the unexpected, worrying change of policy of the new Soviet Government. The two men became friends and General Bohm was pleased when Putin was promoted to Colonel in 1987. Together these two hardliners watched with mounting concern as the liberal reformers who now occupied the Kremlin continued to deconstruct the power and control that the Soviet Union had maintained over its East European satellites during the previous forty years.

Then, in August 1989, Hungary opened its borders with Austria and East Germans could now use this route to escape to the West. A few months later the German Democratic Republic agreed that citizens could leave for the West in sealed trains that passed through Dresden en route to Austria. Crowds of Dresdeners now filled the local railway station, hoping to force their way onto the trains, but heavily armed East German security forces blocked their way to the station. A few weeks after, on 9 November, the DDR government famously – and almost accidentally – gave permission for East Berliners to cross into West Berlin and within a few days the infamous Berlin Wall had been breached. The crowds in Dresden became bolder and on 5 December a furious group of people stormed the Dresden Stasi headquarters and demonstrators entered the KGB offices, where Putin was serving as the duty officer. The guards on the gate, at the sight of the belligerent crowd, quickly retreated back into the building and in their place Putin confronted the mob, saying: 'Don't try to force your way into this property. My comrades are armed and they are authorised to use their weapons in an emergency.' The crowd faltered and remained where they were. Putin then rang the local Red Army tank unit to request reinforcement, who said that he mustn't do anything without direct orders from Moscow. A little while later he was told that 'Moscow is now silent', words that would forever haunt him.

This was one of the defining events of Vladimir Putin's life. This sense of betrayal and the collapse of Russian power in Eastern Europe had a profound impact on Putin who described it – and the subsequent disintegration of the Soviet Union – address as 'the greatest geopolitical catastrophe of the twentieth century' in his 2005 annual State of the Nation.

Harold F. Searles concept of the 'afflicted mother' has already been touched on and Maria Putin was a prime example. She had faced the devastation of losing two children, she had lived through the horrors of the Siege of Leningrad and she had had to endure the harshness and depravation of the post-war Stalinist Soviet State. In addition she was married to a wounded veteran and a strict party member who showed her very little sympathy or tenderness. No wonder she turned to her miraculous only child for some reparative redemption to compensate for this glut of misfortune.

Many of my clients, particularly if they are only children and feel a compelling responsibility for their afflicted mother, are psychologically disposed to constellate a life that is entirely designed to comfort and appease their mother's tortured pain. This providential central task of their lives, if amplified by the fertilising impact of the maternal idealisation, will then be inflated by Kohut's concept of 'grandiosity' and can be bloated into an altogether grander ambition.

As Vladimir Putin's adulthood matured and developed, it can be argued that his responsibility for his mother became magnified into a conviction that he had the strength and capacity to save 'Mother Russia'. This developing hyperbolic self-confidence eventually expanded into a further conviction that he alone had the power to save the 'Holy Motherland' as the Communist experiment collapsed, a messianic role that began to emerge for the first time as he sat impotently in the Dresden headquarters of the KGB. Perhaps at this critical juncture his conflation of his 'afflicted mother' with his 'afflicted motherland' eventually clarified his life's mission. He would join the ranks of Peter the Great, Catherine the Great and particularly Czar Alexander who – having witnessed the near-extinction of Russia at the hand of Napoleon – had steered Mother Russia to her greatest victory as he led the European alliance that defeated the French Emperor and his Grand Armée. That first hint of what his destiny might become began to take shape as the Soviet Union started to implode.

From his Dresden perch Putin now watched the collapse of Soviet power and influence in Eastern Europe. Many of his friends in the Stasi lost their jobs and were immediately ostracised as they had worked for the hated DDR security services. His friend Stasi General Horst Bohm committed suicide and Bohm's deputy Horst Jehmlich blamed Putin personally for the Soviet betrayal. He and his colleagues now had the miserable job of burning all the KGB files in the Dresden office. With this demeaning job complete and German reunification imminent, Putin was recalled to Moscow, convinced that his beloved Motherland had been betrayed by its new leadership. During much of 1990 he wasn't even paid and as the family returned home he discovered that no accommodation was available for them despite the fact he was a KGB colonel. Once again the Putins and their two children had no alternative but to share his parents' cramped apartment.

A few months later the situation improved when he was offered a position at his old university as 'Rector of International Affairs', just at the time when his former law professor Anatoly Sobchak was becoming one of Leningrad's leading political figures. It was Anatoly Sobchak who would elevate his old pupil to a whole new level of political activity, not as an unseen KGB officer working diligently behind the scenes, but as a decisive figure in the recalibration of his country's future as its Communist Party began to fragment, and with it the whole edifice of the Soviet State.

After being elected to the Leningrad City Council, Anatoly Sobchak became a prominent member of the Congress of People's Deputies in Moscow and then Chairman of the City Council in his home city. On becoming Chairman, he asked an old KGB contact if he could recommend somebody with KGB experience whom he could trust as an adviser and who would know how to deal with the security services and his contact suggested Vladimir Putin. The two men were reunited and Sobchak was only too pleased to appoint him immediately. Sobchak decided to stand in the forthcoming mayoral elections. He received 66 per cent of the vote, in an election that also decided the city's name, a revision to its old Russian name of St Petersburg. Sobchak immediately promoted Putin to Director of the City's Foreign Relations department.

That summer of 1991, Putin and Lyudmila took their two daughters to a Baltic coast resort close to Kaliningrad for an extended holiday and while they were away, a cabal of hard-liners, including the KGB Director Vladimir Kryuchkov, launched a coup against Gorbachev. Boris Yeltsin famously opposed the coup and was joined by Anatoly Sobchak in organising the necessary resistance against the plotters, whose putsch collapsed within a week. A greatly diminished Mikhail Gorbachev returned to Moscow and very quickly the Soviet Union as a political entity began to unravel.

The KGB also began to fracture, with many of its officers joining Yeltsin's democrats and Colonel Putin, barely having a say in the matter, found himself working for the charismatic mayor, who was now one of the country's leading politicians. Once the coup had collapsed, Putin was clear that his future lay with Sobchak.

After the collapse of the attempted coup Sobchak was regarded by many as the most important politician in Russia and the newspaper *Kommersant* described Putin as 'a man as close to Sobchak as Prince Mershikov was to Peter the Great'. Putin now started to host leading political visitors from the West, including the US Secretary of State James Barker and the British Prime Minister John Major, but as far as Putin was concerned the most exciting visitor was the great veteran diplomat Henry Kissinger, who showered Putin with compliments. Sobchak could see how Putin charmed these foreign dignitaries, so he promoted him to deputy mayor and gave him the key job of attracting foreign investors to invest in their city.

Given this opportunity to tend to the wounds of the

afflicted Motherland, Putin immediately had success in persuading Western brands to build factories in the city. Household brands such as Heineken, Pepsi, Coca-Cola, Ford and Wrigley all opened manufacturing units in St Petersburg, as Putin began to establish his city as Russia's 'window onto the West', following Peter the Great's strategy. Putin was now known throughout Russia as a significant state entrepreneur and as a highly effective operator who was driven not by his own ambition but by his zealous loyalty to his boss, Anatoly Sobchak.

One man who was becoming only too aware of this powerful and effective St Petersburg double act was President Yeltsin, who saw that the charismatic Sobchak and his 'enforcer' were a very definite threat to his future authority. Sobchak was up for re-election in 1996 and although his pre-eminence in St Petersburg seemed unassailable, Yeltsin and his group of supportive oligarchs thought otherwise. Surreptitiously they began to promote their own candidate for the role of Mayor of St Petersburg.

Using all sorts of underhand methods, and supported by considerable Kremlin financial resources, the President's candidate narrowly won the mayoral election. Most unexpectedly both Sobchak and Putin had lost their jobs, but at that moment Putin's fourth and most significant mentor came to his rescue. In the summer of 1996, Boris Yeltsin had just won his second presidential election and soon after he instructed his chief of staff Anatoly Chubris to invite Putin to Moscow. Within six weeks Putin had a new job, inaugurating his epic Moscow career. At Yeltsin's command Putin became deputy to Pavel Borodin, who presided over the highly influential presidential property management directorate. However in March 1997 Putin was again, on Yeltsin's instruction, transferred to a new job and he became the Head of the Main Control Directorate, making him a de facto deputy chief-of-staff in the presidential administration, one step nearer to Boris Yeltsin himself who was watching Putin carefully and liking what he saw. Yeltsin then quickly promoted him once more to the first deputy director of the presidential administration.

But this job didn't last long. Yeltsin was getting reports that the FSB (Russia's equivalent to the KGB) was developing a dossier on the president himself, accusing him and his family of charges of corruption. He decided he needed much more control over the security services and to install his own man at the head of the FSB. And who better than Vladimir Putin, a KGB veteran, whose loyalty to the president was beyond question? To his amazement Putin became, on 25 July 1998, director of the FSB.

Yeltsin invited Putin to his dacha to discuss his new job. The President wanted to make the FSB less political and to rationalise its huge bureaucracy and he suggested promoting Putin to the rank of General, but Putin refused, saying he wished to become the first civilian head of the FSB. Putin's promotion caused consternation among the FSB top brass and many KGB veterans who now ran the FSB resented being ruled by a little-known KGB nobody who had never risen above a series of insignificant provincial posts. How could such a parvenu hold such an important position? But Putin proved them all wrong. He comprehensively reorganised the FSB, pruning its unwieldy size and bureaucracy, cutting the numbers working at the Moscow headquarters from 6,000 to 4,000 and abolishing a number of moribund and time-serving departments.

Putin remained as the FSB director for only eight hectic months and Yeltsin became more and more certain that Putin's highly effective competence and indisputable loyalty were exactly the asset he needed to find a way to retire gracefully in the summer of 2000 in a country renowned for the manner in which it disposed of its leaders.

At this point in time a restless and highly critical Duma, led by ex-Prime Minister Primakov (whom Yeltsin had sacked) and the Mayor of Moscow, Yuri Luzhkov, were talking of impeaching Yeltsin for corruption. The Duma's next parliamentary elections were due in the autumn of 1999 and Yeltsin felt certain that the loyal Vladimir Putin might be just the man to help him avoid an ignominious downfall.

On the 5 August 1999, Putin was invited to the presidential dacha for a secret meeting and Yeltsin offered him the job of prime minister, making it clear that Putin's first task would be to form a new political party which could defeat the Primakov/Luzhkov alliance in the forthcoming Duma elections. In his memoirs *Midnight Diaries* (2000), Yeltsin recorded Putin's response: 'I don't like elections. I really don't. I don't know how to run them and I don't like them.'

Despite this rather infantile rant Yeltsin said he understood and reassured Putin that he would be helped by a team of political strategists who knew how to manage an election: what he wanted was for his new prime minister to display confidence, authority and a military bearing he knew the country longed for. And, of course, he wanted a prime minister to provide effective opposition to those Duma politicians who were after his blood.

Putin accepted the challenge and appointed his own political strategist, Gleb Pavlovsky, to run the election campaign. This infamous character immediately suggested launching 'The Unity Party' into which the oligarchs, frightened by the possibility of a Duma impeachment, poured the necessary funds with oligarch Boris Berezovsky's television channels mercilessly attacking Primakov and Luzhkov. But more significant than the oligarchs' support was the extraordinary success of the new prime minister himself.

Soon after Putin became prime minister there were a series of lethal bombings in apartment blocks in Moscow and in several provincial cities. These were immediately blamed on Chechen separatist terrorists, leading to a wave of hysteria among the Russian public who had recently witnessed a failed Russian Army invasion of Chechnya and now the Chechens appeared to be using terrorist tactics within Russia itself. Although rumours circulated that these bombings were a series of grotesque false-flag operations run by the FSB, such allegations found little leverage within Russia and the public hysteria gave Putin the opportunity to send the army back into Chechnya, but this time using brutal levels of extreme violence. Gleb Pavlovsky had the new prime minister fly into the combat zone in a two-seater military jet to inspire and support the young Russian soldiers. He handed out medals, gave inspirational speeches and met the village elders who still supported Russia, as their villages were liberated by the army. All this was carefully choreographed and Putin's heroic leadership was televised across the country and his domestic popularity soared. Needless to say, Primakov, Luzhkov and their allies were trounced in the parliamentary elections.

Five days after the vote, a relieved Yeltsin, so full of gratitude for his prime minister's successes, met Putin at his private Moscow residence. In *Midnight Diaries* Yeltsin remembers the conversation they had: 'I told my Prime Minister "I want to step down this year Vladimir Vladimirovich. Yes this year. That's very important. The new century must begin with a new political era, the era of Putin. Do you understand?"'

The recently written new Russian constitution stated that should the president resign, the prime minster would become acting president and that ninety days later, an election to vote for a new president would take place. After initial reluctance Putin agreed. The two men began making historic plans and Yeltsin was reassured that a smooth transition, protecting him and his family, now seemed possible. On New Year's Eve in 1999, in the dying hours of the old millennium, Yeltsin announced his immediate resignation on television and Vladimir Putin gave his first presidential address of the new millennium the very next morning. As Yeltsin left the Kremlin for the last time, he turned to Putin and said: 'Take care of Russia'.

Putin's first three or four years as president suggested to Russians – and to expectant international politicians, business executives, military chiefs and media commentators – that the new Russian leader offered the world a tremendous opportunity. As the then British prime minister Tony Blair said: 'The leadership of President Putin offers not just hope to Russia but also hope for the wider world.'

Following his landslide victory in the 2000 presidential election Putin enjoyed some immediate good fortune. The international oil price rose substantially and with oil being the country's largest export this gave the Russian economy a significant boost, providing Putin with the perfect opportunity to achieve his primary goal: to increase the prosperity of ordinary, average Russian citizens after they had had to endure the country's economic collapse during the previous decade. Salaries and wages rose markedly, pensions increased and investment in the country's infrastructure was significantly boosted. The Russian population enjoyed a level of affluence never experienced before as Western brands filled the shops and supermarkets.

At the same time as this growth in the national economy took place, Putin decided to strengthen the country's ties with Western democracies. He invited the Secretary General of NATO, George Robertson, to Moscow for talks and after the success of this meeting, he invited Tony Blair to St Petersburg to consolidate these improvements in East–West relations. Having appointed a cadre of economic modernisers and reformers, Putin began to cultivate relations with international leaders and business organisations who increasingly began to invest in Russia.

After his meeting with Putin in Moscow, Tony Blair persuaded his friend George Bush to end his opposition to Russia joining the G7 and very soon the G7 became the G8 and Russia became a fully paid-up member of this key international group of the world's richest nations. Discussions were even under way to consider the possibility of Russia becoming a NATO member, but sadly this tremendously promising outlook for Russia's integration into the key Western economic and military partnerships was short-lived.

The first signs of a very different, far less benevolent Vladimir Putin became evident in October 2003 when Mikhail Khodorkovsky – the richest and most effective of the oligarchs who owned the country's largest oil company – was arrested. In the summer of 2003, in a televised discussion between the President and the leading oligarchs, Khodorkovsky had had the temerity to criticise the Russian government for high levels of corruption that he said were ruining the economy. This was too much for Putin. Khodorkovsky was arrested and, having been charged with trumped-up allegations of fraud, was convicted and then sent to prison where he remained for eleven years. Meanwhile the government appropriated the oil company Yukos.

With depressing regularity Putin began to sack his coterie of liberal advisors and replace them with old cronies from the KGB and FSB and he altered the country's constitution which gave him the opportunity to rule for his entire life. In the 2004 presidential election all sorts of democratic rules and norms were ignored and abused, handing Putin a manipulated landslide victory. Non-governmental organisations were now suspended and media and TV companies were taken over by the government. Finally Putin closed down *Novaya Gazeta*, the last independent newspaper in Russia. Other political opponents were tracked down by FSB assassins at his command. Boris Nemtsov was shot on Red Square in 2015 and in 2018 Sergei and Yulia Skripal were poisoned in Salisbury in England. Alexei Navalny was also poisoned by government agents in 2020 and, having survived this murder attempt, was placed in a Siberian prison camp where he died at the hands of his FSB minders. A dictatorship reminiscent of the Stalinist autocracy now appeared to have returned to twenty-first-century Russia. When Putin launched his February 2022 invasion of Ukraine, the Western democracies finally took action, launching draconian economic sanctions against Russia while sending billions of dollars of armaments and economic aid to beleaguered Ukraine.

Bogged down in a brutal war of his own making, Putin is personally responsible for the horrendous death toll that has surpassed the 1 million mark and he seems completely unconcerned by the terrible loss of lives and misery that his war has caused. As a result he is branded a war criminal, accused of crimes against humanity and Russia has become a pariah state, reliant on other pariah states, such as Iran and North Korea, for military help. Why has Putin's time in office, which started so promisingly, gone so tragically wrong?

Carl Jung was a great admirer of the Greek philosopher Heraclitus and was particularly drawn to his concept of 'enantiodromia', a tendency in all systems and in all human experience whereby the more extreme a position that the system or person adopts, the greater the tendency is for the system or individual to experience a complete swing to the opposite extreme. Jung noticed how this propensity occurred regularly in the lives of his patients, particularly when aspects of their Shadow began to emerge, that could turn an empathetic, humane and benevolent individual into a narcissistic malevolent bully.

While Putin was in the KGB, and during his loyal service to Anatoly Sobchak and Boris Yeltsin and in the early years of his presidency, he displayed a set of personality characteristics that everyone around him was impressed by. His slightly introverted, modest personal charm; his mild manner when talking or putting forward his views; his considerable capacity for loyalty to those he served and towards those who in turn served him; his love and patriotism for his motherland; his diligence and industrious work ethic; his sobriety and his intellectual and intuitive intelligence: these were clearly apparent to all those who met him. Twenty years later British prime minister Boris Johnson said of Putin: 'Now we see him for what he is – a blood-stained aggressor who believes in imperial conquest.' Those contrasting descriptions of Putin are both true and describe the sheer range of polarities that mark Putin's character and the enantiodromic transformation of his personality during his presidency, during which he has become a vengeful, inhumane dictator.

In the last hundred years, due to this enantiodromic shift to the Shadow, three other men moved from a position of charisma and magnetic charm that engendered devotion among their national populations to a level of bestial inhumanity that reached genocidal proportions. Without doubt Putin's historic reputation will place him on that dubious podium with Hitler, Stalin and Mao Zedong, megalomaniac dictators who, with the compliance of their national populations, merged the dark effluence of their own aggressive personal Shadows with the Shadows of their respective citizens. In doing so they released a vicious barbarity rarely matched in human history, exacerbated by the technological sophistication of the weapons and ordinance available to them. As a species, humanity is now faced with a shift from the hoped-for disappearance of the Shadow of nuclear war to a situation where this dreadful Shadow has now become a potential reality.

As we have seen, Maria Putin's intense idealisation of her child embedded within his psyche a grandiosity that, as his career prospered, conferred upon him a sense of rigid dogmatic certainty. This biased, prejudiced view of the world became an inflexible, indisputable truth, allowing Putin the certain belief that his course of action could be ethically justified by the required end, even if it meant the death of millions. This sense of hubristic overconfidence was sharpened further by his obsessive love of his 'motherland' and the certainty of his perceived historic role in her defence fuelled by the discipline and experience of his KGB career as well as by the impact of the Russian people's collective paranoia, a consequence of their repeated historic trauma and a national methylated gene pool. All those factors give him a sense of his own providential position as his country's saviour, a messianic vision that had its earliest origins in his childhood when he sensed that he was his mother's redeeming saviour. Indeed all dictators tend to share this mixture of indisputable certainty, paranoia and a sense of messianic mission that justifies any means in the defence of their nation and the preservation of their autocratic rule.

The subsequent consequences of the lethal derangement of such dogmatic certainty were conveyed by the scientist and broadcaster Jacob Bronowski while filming his epic BBC series *The Ascent of Man* (1973). He waded into an infamous pond at Auschwitz, where many of his own family members had died, into which the ashes from the nearby gas ovens had been deposited and said:

> This is the concentration camp and crematorium of Auschwitz. This is where people were turned into numbers. Into this pond were flushed the ashes of some four million people. That was not done by gas. It was done by arrogance. It was done by dogma. It was done by ignorance. When people believe that they have absolute knowledge, with no test in reality, this is how they behave. This is what men do when they aspire to the knowledge of gods.

The more certainty – the more sure an individual, a culture, a nation is of itself and of its infallible sense of virtue – the greater the Shadow will be and the more capable it will become of committing these kinds of atrocities. As individuals, and as citizens of countries and cultures, we must acknowledge and take responsibility for our Shadow. We must also retain sufficient humility to question that itch for certainty that human beings are attracted by.

When countries conflate their national Shadows with messianic leaders whose own personal Shadows and methylated genes fuel their paranoid aspirations, all semblance of compassion, humanity and rationality is stalled and the worst of human nature will once again reappear, in yet another eruption of our collective Shadow. Vladimir Putin is the latest manifestation of such a leader.

Anima and Animus
(Angela Merkel)

T hroughout his life Carl Jung painted pictures and sculpted carvings, which he regarded as a means of exploring the depths of his psyche. This creative expression of his inner nature provided him with a crucial connection to the complexities of his unconscious.

At the age of eighty-three, towards the end of his life, he carved two stone reliefs on the wall of his Tower at Bollingen, where he was spending more and more time in a state of solitary reflection on the inner myths that had guided his life. The first of these was an image of the Russian bear with his immense paw touching a globe, which represented the Soviet Union's threat to our planet now that the Communist state was armed with nuclear weapons. The second was of an archetypal woman figure, a representation of what Jung called the anima, who is grasping the udder of a mare which she is milking, predicting the age of Aquarius when the feminine principle will be dominant, an era that falls under the constellation of Pegasus, the horse.

Although Jung was interested in astrology, he never took such ideas literally: rather he regarded our dreams, our iconography, our art, our religion and other systems of belief as templates that transmit information and messages from our individual psyches and the wider collective unconscious, and can give us some idea of the future destiny of our species and its evolutionary fate. In light of these beliefs it's safe to assume that Jung is saying, via these last two carvings, that the animus, with its dominating patriarchy, needs to be replaced by the female principle of the Aquarian age before some final chauvinistic lunge activates some terminal catastrophe.

Jung's concept of the animus and the anima were not bounded by the binary state of gender, but rather straddled both genders. In other words, Jung saw the psyche in its ideal, balanced essence as androgynous. The individual, mature personality would find a synthesis of both the male and female principle, a blend and balance of both the anima and animus and the animus-driven male – if he reached his full psychological maturity – would develop the finer qualities of his anima. The anima-disposed female would find her full maturity, having embraced the finer qualities of her animus. For Jung the full blossoming of individuation could only be achieved in this conflation of the best aspects of the male and female principles.

For Jung this synthesis of the animus and anima was not only an essential element of individual psychological development: Jung also believed that the collective unconscious of humanity would have to achieve this balance between the male and female principles if our species was to evolve safely. Observing at first hand, in the last years of his life, the catastrophes of the first half of the twentieth century, this vital synthesis seemed a distant hope as the dominating male principle appeared rampantly hyperactive.

However after his death in 1961 the transit of the second

half of the twentieth century did suggest that his prediction might come true, as some significant elements of the feminine principle began to emerge in the wider collective consciousness. As has been noted before, the conciliatory influence of the United Nations, the European Union and the World Bank considerably reduced global political tensions, restricting military conflict to local disputes; the Communist system of government in Russia and Eastern Europe collapsed; the fierceness of Chinese communism was eased after the death of Chairman Mao and in the Western democracies social and economic policy contained greater magnanimity. Around the world empathy and the nurturing, regenerative aspects of the feminine principle seemed to be more evident

Today, however, it appears we have only reached a liminal transitional phase of this evolutionary blending of the animus and anima as the male principle seems to be determined to recover its dominance, as exemplified in the Ukrainian–Russian War, the Russian totalitarian government, the two terms of the Trump presidency in America (with its strident climate change denial and attacks on women's rights), the shift to the right in many European governments and the reignition of the Middle East conflict. These all suggest that the worse aspects of the male principle are making a bid to reassert themselves.

One of the earliest germinating shoots of the re-emergence of the animus-anima synthesis occurred in the opening weeks of the twenty-first century in Germany, when Angela Merkel became the first female leader of the Christian Democratic Union. Within five years she had become Chancellor of Germany, a position she held for sixteen years, ushering in a new kind of politician who exhibited so many anima qualities, including a predisposition towards nurture and reconciliation and also a huge amount of empathy, so much so that the German people came to call her, affectionately, 'Mutti' or 'Mummy'. She appeared free of the usual political rhetoric and less overtly confrontational and came across as a unique politician who seemed to blend both male and feminine elements of the animus and anima.

Both the animus and anima have qualities that exist on spectrums which range from human flaws, failings and shortcomings to impressive personal strengths, virtues and talents, a range of human qualities that were on full display when Donald Trump met Angela Merkel during the property tycoon's first presidential administration. So often during these meetings Trump exuded all his arrogance, discourtesy and disingenuous rhetoric while Merkel matched his bluster with forbearance, patience and quiet but resolute firmness.

In March 2017 and then again in May 2018 Merkel visited the White House. In her first meeting with the new American President, she was shocked by the manner in which he almost immediately launched an aggressive tirade on the principal institutions of the Western Alliance. As soon as the meeting started he announced, in a belligerent tone: 'Angela, you owe me one trillion dollars', a wildly inaccurate jibe to emphasise Trump's reluctance to go on supporting NATO. What became known as the new president's 'insult diplomacy' seemed to be primarily aimed at the leaders of his allies in Europe, Canada and Japan and Trump never spoke to Vladimir Putin in this manner, as he appeared to admire his autocratic style and seemed to tacitly agree with the Russian dictator that democracy was an irritating inconvenience. In his second meeting with Angela Merkel, which only lasted fifteen minutes, Trump declared that 'the EU is worse than China, except smaller'. He then threatened to impose swinging tariffs on European steel and aluminium and launched a vehement attack on German car imports, concentrating his wrath on Mercedes, BMW and Porsche.

Yet perhaps Trump's most insidious, delusional misjudgement was reserved for the mountain of incontrovertible scientific research which confirmed the devastating inevitability of global warming. Time and time again Trump insisted that the global warming conspiracy was merely one of the worst examples of 'fake news' designed to undermine the American coal and steel industries and because nothing should stall his clarion call 'to make America great again' he would take the US out of the 2015 Paris Agreement on climate change.

Angela Merkel's response to Trump's diatribes came in May 2019 when, on a trip to America, she didn't waste her time returning to the White House but rather travelled to Harvard to give the university's annual commencement address, a speech delivered over many years by significant world figures, including Nelson Mandela. In an almost explicit criticism of President Trump she said:

> We have to think and act globally not nationally, together instead of alone. Take nothing for granted. Our individual freedoms are not guaranteed. Democracy, peace, prosperity

aren't either . . . Protectionism and trade conflicts endanger free world trade and the foundations of our prosperity. Climate change and the resulting rises in temperature are caused by humans. Going it alone we will not succeed. Don't build walls. Break down walls. Lies should not be called truth, nor truth lies.

More than any words that came before or after, this speech exemplified the fact that the leadership of the Western democracies had shifted from the American Presidency and now seemed to reside in the safe and reassuring pair of hands provided by an unassuming sixty-five-year-old woman who had been bought up in communist East Germany and who had been voted into power in four successive elections by an adoring German public. Angela Merkel, probably the most powerful woman who has ever lived, provided a completely new type of leadership, a most effective synthesis of the best animus and anima qualities.

In fact, Donald Trump finally came to admire Merkel's diplomatic skills. Time and again his insults, bombast and bullying would be met by her silence, evasion, understatement and dry wit. The more he ratcheted up his self-congratulatory hyperbole, the more she resisted him with her self-controlled sobriety. It was as if 'Mutti' knew exactly how to deal with this naughty little boy. He once asked a newly-arrived German ambassador to Washington: 'Are you as intelligent as your boss?' And after disrupting a NATO conference with his 'insult diplomacy', the naughty little boy was heard to say to a member of the press: 'Isn't she great? . . . Love this woman.'

Merkel's fellow European leaders, all exasperated by Trump, watched in awe as she dealt with the bully from the White House using diplomatic skills that were honed throughout her childhood as the daughter of a Lutheran pastor. When Horst Kasner married Merkel's mother he bluntly informed her that his relationship with God and Jesus would automatically take precedence over their marriage and that he would go to extreme lengths to preach his Christian beliefs where they were most needed. So deeply was this ideal embedded in Kasner that soon after Merkel's birth on 17 July 1954, he moved his family from the relative freedom of Hamburg in West Germany to East Germany, where the communist rule of the German Democratic Republic had formally banned the worship of God. Reluctantly the authorities realised that their national insistence on atheism would never quite snuff out the Christian spirit in the very home of Martin Luther and so, on a tiny salary, Horst Kasner was allowed to go about his business, provided in every other way he complied and upheld the communist orthodoxy.

As he had done with his wife, Kasner made it clear to his daughter that his Christian faith and his work in his parish was far more important than being a father. As a result of this austere, aloof style of parenting, Angela continued to seek his approval, which became the prime driving force for her quiet ambition throughout his life. Her decision not to have children, for instance, was a decision that was influenced by her father.

Initially all her ambition was directed at becoming an academic, a research chemist of exceptional brilliance and diligence. With little parental encouragement, Angela's aspirations were supported by two points of inspiration: she was obsessed with Marie Curie who, like her, was bought up in a homeland which was divided and occupied by Russia. Having left Poland, Marie Curie graduated in Paris where, despite the chauvinism and misogyny of French scientific circles, she became the only person ever to win the Nobel Prize in two different disciplines. Of Curie's discovery of radium, Merkel wrote: 'She made this discovery because she was confident that she had a good idea . . . if you believe in an idea, even if you are alone, if you pursue this idea and suffer through the highs and lows you will ultimately reach your goal, if the idea is right.'

The other feature of Merkel's life which underpinned her drive and determination was her Christian faith. 'For me religion belongs to the private sphere. It allows me to be forgiving to myself and of others and prevents me drowning in my responsibilities. If I were an atheist it would be more difficult to carry such a heavy burden.' In a speech she gave in 2014, she said 'The most difficult thing and the important thing is love. If you read the Bible and the Book of John, it doesn't refer to love as a sentimental word but rather to actual deeds. This love is unconditional and fearless. It is "serving".' This view would infuse her political creed where word or political rhetoric were far less important than actions. In another speech as Chancellor during a Protestant church convention she stressed that self-knowledge and self-confidence were crucial in the experience of both offering and accepting love. In her words: 'You are only able to love in the first place if you love yourself, if you believe in yourself, if you know yourself.'

This self-acceptance, this self-love and self-awareness resulted in her modest and restrained ego and the fact she avoided blatant attention-seeking political rhetoric. Unlike most other male political leaders she never tried to dominate or score points and was only interested in finding a way of patiently moving towards her political goals, which were formulated through the lens of her Christian ethics.

Her other guiding principle was her deep desire to begin to change the gender imbalance of German, European and world politics. In the same way that Merkel was inspired by the example of Marie Curie, she would in turn encourage female politicians throughout the world with her example. Throughout her tenure as Chancellor she had on her desk a framed portrait of Catherine the Great and her closest colleagues were a trio of exceptionally talented women: Beate Baumann was her chief of staff, Eva Christiansen was her media advisor and her closest cabinet colleague remained Defence Minister Ursula von der Leyen, who would eventually become President of the European Commission. With Merkel at their centre, this coterie of gifted women – who were not only close colleagues but also inseparable friends – were devoted to the task of transforming Germany and the European Union. Merkel insisted that they always spoke candidly and gave a clear account of their own views even if they disagreed with their boss. As Eva Christiansen said: 'There are no flatterers on her staff. We can criticise her.' Needless to say feminist issues were always at the top of the agenda in this inner cabinet.

As has already been emphasised, Merkel was highly suspicious of political rhetoric and although her speeches were often disparaged for being dull and flat, she felt that the ability to excite a crowd was a hazardous talent, bearing in mind Hitler's explosive rabble-rousing speeches were still a vivid memory for many older Germans. For Merkel words were an asset to be used judiciously. She even disliked her admired friend Barack Obama's moments of puffed-up rhetorical dazzle. She insisted on always being true to herself: softly spoken, reserved, demure, almost diffident in her restrained delivery and her view was that successful political discussion should be depersonalised, as anything egotistical would corrupt and distort the debate. Honesty, candidness and a kind of abnegation of the ego should direct political discourse in a well-mannered, courteous exchange of views, which would provide the best chance of effective political solutions being achieved.

One of her strongest beliefs was that Germany still needed to atone for the monstrous depravity of the Holocaust, for which her nation should be eternally judged. After meeting a group of Holocaust survivors in Israel in 2008 Merkel delivered one of her greatest speeches:

I bow before you victims. I bow before the survivors and before those who helped them survive. The Shoah fills us Germans with shame . . . The break with civilisation that was the Shoah left wounds that have not healed to this day. It seemed to make relations between Israel and Germany impossible . . . It has taken more than forty years before Germany as a united whole acknowledged and embraced its historical responsibility and the state of Israel. Here of all places, I want to explicitly stress that this responsibility is part of my nation's raison d'être.'

The audience of the Knesset members and Holocaust survivors rose to their feet in applause. Yet the greatest act of national atonement came in August 2015, when Merkel declared that Germany would not turn away refugees in defiance of European Union policy. 'If Europe fails on the question of refugees, then it won't be the Europe we wished for.' Such an unabashed, powerful, compassionate moral choice was made by no other world leader.

The ethical consequence of her insistence that Germany's whole existence was predicated on its continual need to atone for the Holocaust resulted in the country welcoming one million refugees from Syria, Libya, Iraq and Afghanistan. Whatever the political consequences might be, Merkel had to follow the imperative of this clear moral decision, imposed on her by the iniquities of the previous German generation. This admirable ethical policy – shedding all aspects of normal political expediency – did not end her government as some commentators predicted and in 2017, she was returned to power by the German electorate for an unprecedented fourth term.

Under her guidance, German economic prosperity soared and throughout the world, Merkel had become Europe's most widely admired leader who in all but name led the EU throughout much of her sixteen years as Chancellor. I feel sure that if this style of government could be widely duplicated throughout the world, we would very soon pass beyond our current crises.

In Carl Jung's 1927 collection of essays *Aspects of the Feminine* he wrote: 'Women's psychology is founded on the principle of "Eros", the great binder and loosener, whereas from ancient times the ruling principle ascribed to the male is "Logos". The Concept of "Eros" could be expressed in modern times as psychic relatedness and that of "Logos" as objective interest.'

If we agree with this assertion then we can probably say that, at its best, the feminine principle is a way of being that resonates with the qualities of empathy, compassion, emotional intelligence and relatedness. It exudes the capacity for intimacy, love and devotion, the soulful, the intuitive and has a preference for ethical wisdom over technological intelligence.

On the other hand the male principle is goal-orientated, productive, pro-active, competitive and intellectual, with an emphasis on rational pragmatism, which is empirically analytic and directs its ambition toward technological advance. It is by and large ego-driven and attention-seeking, always looking for an advantageous edge in the competitive male environment it invariably finds itself in. When pushed it will flair up into the aggressive and belligerent postures that mark its nature.

For the last 2,500 years, humanity's evolution has been driven by the male principle with its competitive urge. It has produced not only an extraordinary technological proficiency, but also a dark Shadow to this intellectual brilliance which has shown itself to have a terrible capacity for inhumane brutality. In the last one hundred years alone we have seen our technological creativity bring us close to the edge of extinction, a threat that exists just as much today To survive the Shadow cast by our male-driven technological achievements, our evolutionary process needs consciously to adapt to the environmental reality we now face: an enantiodromia shift that must now allow the feminine principle to rein in and take priority over testosterone-driven male ego-directed ambition. To put it simply: our ethical wisdom must temper and direct our technological intelligence. If it doesn't, this obsolete, atavistic male drive will eventually destroy us all.

Angela Merkel was perhaps the first global leader who appeared to understand the need for the feminine ethical principle to now take precedence over the competitive male principle. It is indeed an irony that through her policies of national atonement for the Holocaust and her humane decision to welcome one million refugees to make their home in Germany, the nation that only eighty years ago was led by Hitler and Himmler became the moral compass of Europe.

Conclusion

T oward the end of his thousand-page colossus *The Better Angels of our Nature: Why Violence Has Declined*
(2011), Steven Pinker refers to one of the most tenacious
survivors in all human history. Tsutomu Yamaguchi, who
lived in the Japanese city of Nagasaki, was a young engineer
who worked for Mitsubishi Industries and from time to time
made the journey to his company's shipyards in Hiroshima,
a five-hour journey to the north. At the beginning of August
1945, he was coming to the end of a prolonged visit to Hiroshima and was making his way to the train station via one of
the Mitsubishi offices when he noticed a large plane, high in
the sky, drop two small parachutes. Moments later the whole
city was engulfed by what he described as 'a great flash in the
sky'. The Enola Gay's horrendous payload killed somewhere
between 90,000 and 140,000 of Hiroshima's residents, but
Yamaguchi survived, suffering ruptured eardrums and
burns over the top half of his body. Somehow he crawled to a
nearby air-raid shelter where he rested for twenty-four hours
before returning home the following day. Two days later the
Americans dropped a second atomic bomb that they named
'Fat Man' on Nagasaki. Yamaguchi survived this second
devastation and lived on until 2010 when he died at the age
of ninety-three.

Steven Pinker is interested in Tsutomu Yamaguchi because of his view that almost all violence is committed by men, quoting the Japanese survivor's statement: 'The only people who should be allowed to govern countries with nuclear weapons are mothers, those who are still breast-feeding their babies.'

After quoting Yamaguchi, Steven Pinker goes on to say: 'From the time that they are boys, males play more violently than females, fantasise more about violence, consume more violent entertainment, commit the lion's share of violent crimes, take more delight in punishment and revenge, take more foolish risks in aggressive attacks, vote for more war-like policies and leaders and plan and carry out almost all the wars and genocides.'

This rendition reminds me of my own childhood in the 1950s. From the age of six to twelve I was the proud owner of a huge arsenal of plastic weapons that ranged from swords, shields, helmets, cowboy six-shooters, machine guns, bazookas, grenades and science-fiction ray guns. Every epoch of weaponry was represented in this armoury and I recruited my younger brother into our army of two, which was just as well as we needed to be constantly vigilant, protecting our community from the murderous Germans who lurked around every corner. Our knowledge of our country's victorious war over these fiendish Germans was forever being increased by our insatiable appetite for our weekly comic *War Picture Library.* We just couldn't understand our peculiar younger sister who didn't share our passion for military readiness, preferring her doll's house, and all her boring friends seemed – like her – completely disinterested in our war games and weapon systems.

Pinker's book maintains that we are living in the most peaceful period of human history and that violence, both civil and military, are in sharp decline. This most optimistic of texts was published in 2011 when we basked in the post-Cold-War confidence that international conflict was now an anachronism as the leading nations of the world came together to meet the perils of global warming and overpopulation. A pragmatic Vladimir Putin ruled in a friendly Russia, which provided Europe with cheap gas, while an equally friendly China offered us an immense array of inexpensive consumer durables. Thank goodness we no longer needed to spend quite so much on costly military assets and could now enjoy what became known as 'peace dividend'.

Yet Pinker's analysis seems far less plausible as we consider the global state of affairs in mid-2025. The Russian–Ukrainian war, which at the time of writing has been raging for over three years, has a death toll of over a million, and the ghastly war in Gaza displays levels of brutality that seem almost beyond comprehension. Similarly civil wars have decimated populations in Syria, Iraq, Yemen, Sudan and Libya. It appears that Putin has his sights on Moldova, the Baltic States and beyond, whilst China's stated government policy includes the invasion of Taiwan. The global-warming denier, currently resident in the White House, has stated his strong desire to colonise Greenland and turn Canada into the 51st US State and rampant nationalism – and even imperial acquisition – are back in fashion. Finally the current global military crises push our ecological troubles even further down the priority list as our polluted planet sends us warning after warning of its parlous deterioration.

And yet I still think that there is a case for Pinker's continued optimism. I have noticed how my clients all share a similar dynamic as they attempt to reduce the hold that their neuroses have on their lives, loosening the detrimental impact that these complexes have on their general wellbeing and state of mind. I watch as they make significant strides forward in their patterns of experience that serve them well and then – just when things are going swimmingly – suddenly they revert back to old worn-out neurotic habits that impair their further progress. It's as if they all adopt a 'two steps-forward, one step-back' model of behaviour which results in an interrupted forward momentum; it's as though this one step back has the benefit of reminding them of their neurotic inclinations, which gives them a little more insight into the anatomy of their complex and provides us with fresh insight into how they might avoid this reactive toxicity in the future.

Perhaps as a species, this two-steps forward followed by one-step back is how civilisation progresses. As the horrors of the two world wars, followed by the tensions of the Cold War, began to dissipate, it appeared we might have overcome the prime neurosis of our species, but now paranoid, narcissistic recourse to brutal state violence, driven by the male principle, has reappeared, as Vladimir Putin, in terms of psychological maturity, takes us all one step back. But perhaps if the horrors of Ukraine and Gaza can somehow be resolved, this dreadful one step backwards can encourage a further two steps forward. But what would be the necessary conditions that would staunch this current one-step backwards and ignite the next two steps forward?

I think the answer lies in the title of Steven Pinker's book which he borrowed from Abraham Lincoln's speech when he took the 'oath of office' after his first presidential election victory. On 4 March 1861, Lincoln's first inaugural address ended with a plea to his fellow Americans to avoid a civil war by not breaking 'our bonds of affection', by showing magnanimity and understanding by engaging 'the better angels of our nature'.

Using this phrase Lincoln was referring to our compassion and empathy, our self-control and rational moral sense and our capacity for tolerance and kindness: he was pleading for a more enlightened and restrained response to the political division and discord that his country faced.

As Tsutomu Yamaguchi and Steven Pinker both suggest, it is the female principle that can generate this spirit of reconciliation and empathy that Lincoln called for. In a section of his book entitled 'Feminisation', Pinker gives a comprehensive, persuasive set of arguments whereby the qualities and virtues of the feminine principle, if developed and adopted by our culture, will result in a considerable reduction in both the individual's and humanity's recourse to violence. The two best examples we have so far of this spirit of humane peaceful reconciliation that the feminine principle can achieve have been Nelson Mandela's South Africa and Angela Merkel's period as Chancellor in Germany.

Perhaps this has reached a stage of evolutionary necessity. If, as a species, we don't give up our atavistic itch for nationalistic, competitive aggrandisement and the male-driven brutal violence it generates, if we don't find a way to lay to one side this anachronistic, collective narcissism that drives men like Putin, humanity as a global community will be overwhelmed by ecological disaster which will bring an end to our species.

But I am optimistic that we still have enough time to make this evolutionary adjustment to avoid the end of the human Anthropocene. We need a vision of our species' capacity for individuation, whereby it can reach a stage of collective maturity which dispenses with the senseless slaughter of national state violence. Once this is achieved and these potentially fatal distractions have been laid to rest we can focus our full global attention on finding a cooperative, internationally embraced strategy to halt our current ecological descent towards some extinction event.

Psychoanalysis, during the last 125 years, has developed a viable programme to help us reach a considerable degree of individual maturity. Perhaps this model can be extrapolated and recalibrated to secure a gradual path which allows our species to reach full collective maturity. This I believe, as Yamaguchi and Pinker suggest, can only be achieved by harnessing the regenerative power of the feminine principle.

Acknowledgements

Without the support and encouragement of my wonderful editor, Rosalind Porter, this book would never have been written and without the vigilance of her sharp editorial eye the final text would have been far less elegant. The patient contribution of Fiona Todd over several years in preparing the text has also been invaluable. I owe a debt of gratitude to both these friends and colleagues. And, as ever, a big thank you to all my clients from whom I have learnt so much. It has been a pleasure and a privilege working with you.